The Concept of Enterprise Architecture from Theory to Practice

Even though the field of enterprise architecture (EA) has matured, many organisations still struggle with its development and implementation, particularly those organisations involved in continuous transformational cycles and subjected to different environmental trends. This book is intended to assist organisations in getting a grip on the factors influencing EA implementation and gaining a deeper understanding of why things happen the way they do in the practice of EA. It is a comprehensive and definitive resource that is useful to both business professionals and academics.

The book presents an approach for the development, implementation, and institutionalisation of EA that is independent of any method or other architecture frameworks. It can be applied directly using a realistic selection of organisational variables. The approach has two distinctive features that support EA, even in complex environments:

- From both technical and non-technical perspectives, it identifies influencing factors and how they manifest in the practice of EA in an organisation.
- It offers linear and practical mechanisms for developing and implementing EA to fortify the practice of the concept in an organisation.

This approach represents a significant contribution to EA.

Starting with descriptions for EA, the book offers deepened models and frameworks for the development and implementation of EA at the domain level. It also covers factors upon which a model is built for the institutionalisation of the concept. Additionally, the book discusses the implications of EA for sponsors, architects, and other stakeholders responsible for EA development, implementation, and institutionalisation.

Tiko Iyamu holds a PhD in information systems from the University of Cape Town, South Africa. Currently, he is a professor at the Faculty of Informatics and Design at Cape Peninsula University of Technology, South Africa, have previously served as a professor at the Tshwane University of Technology, South Africa, and the Namibia University of Science and Technology, Namibia. He has also spent time as a visiting professor at the Flensburg University of Applied Sciences, Germany. His areas of focus are enterprise architecture, health informatics, big data analytics, mobile computing, and IT strategy. He has authored eight books including *Applying Theories for Information Systems Research, Enterprise Architecture for Strategic Management of Modern IT Solutions*, and *Advancing Big Data Analytics for Healthcare Service Delivery*, edited five books and more than 170 peer-reviewed research articles in a wide range of journals, conference proceedings, and book chapters. Iyamu is an associate editor of the journal *Education and Information Technologies (EAIT)*, *The African Journal of Information Systems (AJIS)*, and a former associate editor of *International Journal of Actor-Network Theory and Technological Innovation (IJANTTI)*. He has received several awards in research and excellence in the supervision of postgraduates.

The Concept of Enterprise Architecture from Theory to Practice

Tiko Iyamu

CRC Press
Taylor & Francis Group
Boca Raton London New York

CRC Press is an imprint of the
Taylor & Francis Group, an **informa** business

AN AUERBACH BOOK

Designed cover image: r.nagy, Shutterstock contributor

First edition published 2024
by CRC Press
2385 Executive Center Drive, Suite 320, Boca Raton, FL 33431

and by CRC Press
4 Park Square, Milton Park, Abingdon, Oxon, OX14 4RN

CRC Press is an imprint of Taylor & Francis Group, LLC

© 2024 Tiko Iyamu

ISBN: 978-1-032-48807-3 (hbk)
ISBN: 978-1-032-48072-5 (pbk)
ISBN: 978-1-003-39087-9 (ebk)

DOI: 10.1201/9781003390879

Typeset in Adobe Garamond
by Apex CoVantage, LLC

Contents

Preface

Organisations are progressively intertwined in an increasingly competitive front. Fundamentally, the survival, sustainability, and profitability of organisations anywhere in the world have little choice but to make good use of information technology (IT) solutions, evident from academic studies and business annual reports in the last two decades. This heightens the challenges in selecting or developing and implementing IT solutions to support and enable organisations' goals and objectives. Thus, as detailed in this book, many organisations employ enterprise architecture (EA) to healthily bridge the gap between business and IT units, model business logics and functions, manage increasingly overwhelming information flow, and govern the deployment of rapidly growing IT solutions. However, many challenges from technical and non-technical perspectives, some hysterically, confront the implementation of EA. Hence, it is difficult to find organisations that have successfully implemented and institutionalised the concept.

As with most IT solutions, the implementation of EA involves people, processes, and technology. Technical and non-technical factors significantly influence the success or failure of EA practice in organisations. It is thus important to determine and consider the influencing factors, and this is particularly critical for organisations operating in unstable and complex environments where EA can be used to address the challenges and complexities.

In this book, EA is divided into four domains: enterprise business architecture (EBA), enterprise information architecture (EIA), enterprise application architecture (EAA), and enterprise technical architecture (ETA). The book offers a more pragmatic method for developing and implementing domain architectures towards achieving distinctive deliverables and addressing the challenges that have hampered the practice of EA in organisations for many years.

The book is underpinned by an understanding that business artefacts and IT solutions are social constructs which exist through human relationships and interactions within structures. A social construct is a philosophical concept that exists in subjectivism and not in objective reality. In this context, the construct results from human interaction and exists because humans agree that it exists. Thus, the success or failure of EA as a construct relies on human relationships and interactions in its development, implementation, and institutionalisation. Understandably, the success of EA can only be established in its practice and institutionalisation over a period. This is primarily because EA is iterative and institutionalisation is a process whereby a practice is assimilated, sanctioned, and legitimised into the norm. It will therefore not be disassociated, dismantled, or redesigned easily once institutionalised in an organisation. This creates a stable practice of the concept and makes the roles of the architects even more critical in the deployment of EA in organisations.

Explicitly, the book covers the effectiveness of change in the context of corresponding with the requirements, objectives, and goals of an organisation using EA, and explains why the concept has to be institutionalised. Change involves adaptations in practices, skills, and often beliefs about what is important and valuable, such as requirements of both technical and business aspects. It requires interactions and connectedness between the IT and business units to ensure uniformity; enforce conformance to standards, policies, and principles; and align skills, business processes, and technology solutions. In addition, change is intended to enable power sharing across different components and structures of an organisation to fortify ownership and accountability in EA practice. These are very significant for service improvement, increased productivity, and positive enhancement of interaction among actors within an organisation.

Comprehensively, the book explains how EA is a holistic approach that focuses on essential aspects of an organisation, from strategic planning to the operationalisation of business and IT solutions. This is to consistently effect significant change within an environment that deploys EA. Therefore, the EA approach is employed primarily to facilitate change from the current to a future state to ensure stability, flexibility and value addition, as informed by business requirements and organisational vision. The approach, therefore, allows an organisation to proceed at its pace while competing and progressing at the same time. It presents models and frameworks reflecting the consistent approach that adaptive enterprises could employ to build, maintain, and apply EA in their computing environments.

The book examines the concept of EA from theory to practice, and through models and frameworks, it provides guides on how to develop, implement, and institutionalise the concept in an organisation. In the quest to offer a fresh perspective, the book makes use of the actor–network theory, which focuses on shifting the negotiation of actors within networks from sociotechnical standpoints to viewing the practice of EBA in both private and public organisations. The book is designed to serve enterprise architects, IT managers, business managers, business analysts, chief information officers (CIOs), chief executive officers (CEOs), and others who show interest in the development, implementation, and institutionalisation of EA. Also, it will be of significance to academics, postgraduate students, and researchers.

The book consists of 13 chapters organised into four main parts: introduction, development, implementation, and institutionalisation. The first part comprises Chapters 1–3, which provide an introduction, highlight the distinction between information systems (IS) and IT, and give an overview of the EA concept, respectively. Chapters 4–7 form the second part of the book, detailing the development of the EA domains: EBA, EIA, EAA, and ETA. The third part of the book is about implementation, offering implementation approaches from four different but related dimensions, covered in Chapters 8–11, including practical experience using a case study. Finally, Chapter 12 and Chapter 13 in the fourth part of the book focus on the post-implementation and institutionalisation of EA and the need for skilled personnel to perform the tasks, respectively.

Acknowledgements

This is to humbly thank the leadership of the Department of Information Technology (IT), Cape Peninsula University of Technology for their continuous support. To the current and past members of the Research Forum in the IT department, I am thankful.

To my valued friends, Kenneth Ayere, Olayele Adelakun, Patrick Nwankwo, Hlomani Chauke, Zwelakhe Sithole, Tony Uwagbafor, Jerry Igwilo, Osaro Odemwingie, and Osagie Omoregbee: thank you for your advice and support over many years; it has contributed immensely to my learning and experiences in my journey.

To my siblings and cousins, I am privileged to be one of you. I am grateful for your consistent love, interest, and support in what I enjoyably, do. I will always feel a deep sense of gratitude to my family for your understanding, love, and care. To my treasured parents, thank you for the foundation and relentless guidance.

To my children, to whom this book is dedicated, I am proud and privileged to be your father.

Chapter 1

Introduction

1.1 Introduction

Despite the impressive technological advances in tools and methodologies, and the organisational insights provided by many years of academic and business research, the underperformance of information systems (IS) and information technology (IT) remains critical. In the past until today, organisations experience difficulties in many areas of their operations. The challenges are summarised as: managing existing IS/IT solutions, implementing new IS/IT solutions, maintaining compatibility of new IS/IT solutions with existing ones, changing from one IS/IT solution to another, governing the increasing volatile information flow, and changing from one business process to another. Significantly, and at one point or another, the challenges impact the performance of organisations and somehow hinder competitiveness, sustainability, and profitability. Some organisations realise that some of the challenges carry detrimental effects. Therefore, these challenges need to be addressed. Thus, many organisations employed approaches such as enterprise architecture (EA).

Also, the demand for better services by stakeholders and the general society is increasing at a rapid rate across the world. This in turn drives the deployment of IS/IT solutions to enable and support events, processes, and activities for the improvement and betterment of services to leverage sustainability and maintain competitive advantage. Many organisations, including government administrations, employ EA as an engineering approach and method to guide the enablement, facilitation, and support of IS/IT solutions to improve service delivery (Venkatesan & Sridhar, 2019; Zachman, 1996).

The concept of EA is not new; it has been evolving for more than three decades (Gampfer et al., 2018; Zachman, 1987), and it began to gain noticeable momentum in the late 1990s. Since then, the concept has significantly grown in interest among scholars and practitioners. The evolution of the concept reflects and can be viewed from three main angles: in scholarly work from both teaching and research perspectives (Ahlemann et al., 2021; Beese et al., 2022), increasing interest and deployment in public and private institutions (Olsen, 2017), and in the many frameworks that have emerged, such as The Open Group Architecture Framework (TOGAF), Gartner, Forrester, and the Federal Enterprise Architecture Framework (FEAF) (Iyamu, 2022). Kurnia et al. (2021a) describe the concept as a collection of artefacts that define the integration of processes and activities to improve business and IT alignment in an organisation. Thus, EA primarily helps to provide a big picture for an organisation, which covers information, business, and IT strategies.

Despite the increasing interest and effort shown across industries, many organisations continue to struggle and endure challenges in the development, implementation, and practice of EA. Some EA challenges remain in discourse and debate in various quarters of organisations and academic studies, including IS research. Despite these efforts, many of the challenges and complexities persist. Perhaps, the approaches employed are the same or minimal in difference. Thus, a fresh perspective that entails applying Structuration Theory (ST) as a lens is employed, to examine and gain a deeper understanding of EA, as presented in this chapter.

The concept of EA is the holistic classification of the processes and activities of an enterprise into domains, and it provides fundamental governance to manage and bridge the gap between strategic planning and implementation efforts iteratively. EA provides a mechanism that enables and supports communication about the essential elements and functioning of an organisation. EA being an iterative of technology solutions, business logics, and information flow conducted by humans through processes is evolutionary in nature. Thus, the theoretical extent of the concept and institutionalisation of the practice requires deeper understanding.

Contextually, three things that are of fundamental importance to this chapter and the entire book need to be clarified. First, the IT solution often referred to, comprises of software, database, hardware, and network elements. Where IS is referred to, it is not misconstrued or a contradiction. Second, the term 'enterprise' is used to refer to a defined geographical location of incorporated business units, with a system of culture, process, and technology components which are seen as one legal entity. Finally, 'organisation' refers to a public or private institution or enterprise.

The chapter is organised into seven main sections. First is the introduction followed by a discussion of EA and its domains. Next, the significance and challenges of EA are covered. The contributions of the book are presented, and finally, the chapter is summarised.

1.2 Enterprise Architecture

EA engineers the different units or divisions of an organisation towards a common goal and governs the information and IT solutions required within a competitive journey (Niemi & Pekkola, 2017). Also, EA supports the re-engineering, optimisation, governance, and decision-making processes of transformation in an organisation (Anthony Jnr et al., 2021). EA is therefore an approach with the capability to support the integration and management of an enterprise in its operations. Ajer et al. (2021) argue that EA is an approach that seeks to coordinate, integrate, and align the multiplicity of business and IT initiatives in organisations. Specifically, Anthony Jnr et al. (2021) claim that EA aims to align business with IT solutions from the standpoint of the stakeholders.

The notion behind EA is the idea of a holistic approach (Georgiadis & Poels, 2021), which means horizontal (across an organisation) and vertical (within units of an organisation) enterprise-wide. According to Ahlemann et al. (2021), EA began its evolution as a discipline in the late 1980s after Zachman had applied information architecture concepts from a constructional engineering perspective. Subsequently, EA is applied to define a collection of artefacts from the various aspects of an organisation, from an integrated business and IT perspective (Kurnia et al., 2021b).

EA is a process-oriented approach and not an event or project. This seems to have been understood by many of the promoters in many organisations. It therefore requires continued business and technical requirements to be translated in accordance with organisational goals and objectives. This is to respond to change through technology selection and application. EA continually facilitates other activities, such as the concept of reuse, systems' role definitions, and the modelling of optimal information flows. EA as a process guides organisational learning and constantly enables the learning of new things and the subsequent sharing of that learning. Through learning, opportunities are created, which can be used for competitiveness. Thus, the direction and vision of an organisation are critically important, primarily to determine the management and allocation of resources and infrastructure. This is done iteratively, and it becomes the norm in the organisation that deploys it.

EA is strategically positioned to facilitate processes, activities, and procedures within the computing environment of any organisation that adopts the approach. This includes the domains of EA, and it begins with project initiation and ends at the implementation stages. It can be and is used to promote the facilitation of frameworks to manage and share information meant to ensure that the business processes and activities are supported by technology infrastructures and applications. Furthermore, the frameworks are intended to guide data and information flow for organisational use.

The EA approach facilitates change, which affects not only business processes, clients, and partners, but also affects information and technology infrastructures supporting business applications. It is a challenging task to manage change by any means, including the adoption of the EA approach. The elements which make EA a change agent are discussed in the section that follows. On the basis that change is the focal factor for EA deployment, the elements are also used as a measurement criterion for the success and failure of EA in organisations.

Typically, EA is not a mastery of a single innovation, but ongoing learning, adaptiveness, and development of collaborative work cultures. Change in culture, increasing productivity, and enabling improved performance is always a high ambition of many organisations. EA helps in achieving the challenges of rapid change in organisations. Even at the demanding level, the EA approach is intended to guide in four major ways: (i) allowing concerned stakeholders a shared view of how the business processes are connected and interfaced; (ii) guiding how information flows within an organisation and between organisations; (iii) guiding how applications support and enable events and activities; and (iv) guiding what and how technologies are deployed in the context of the organisation.

The organisations' strategies are the means while the domains of EA are the ends in an attempt to achieve the vision of the organisation that deploys it. Change elements of EA affect both technical and business components of an organisation. This is a key factor in bridging the gap between business and IT through the domains of EA. Also, the change elements in EA have a strong influence on the development and implementation of a technology strategy and the amalgamation of both the IT and business units towards one vision.

1.3 Enterprise Architecture Domains

EA comprises domains, which include non-technical and technical components of an organisation that deploys it. As depicted in Figure 1.1, the domains of EA are four, traditionally: enterprise business architecture (EBA), enterprise information architecture (EIA), enterprise application architecture (EAA), and enterprise technical architecture (ETA). Each domain has its distinct roles and responsibilities. However, the domains are interconnected and interdependent of each other.

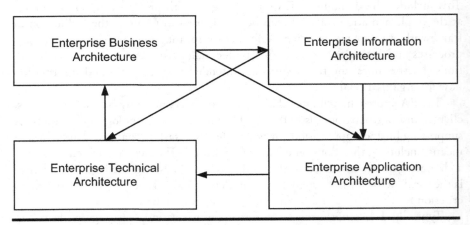

Figure 1.1   Enterprise Architecture Concept (Iyamu, 2015).

Also, the dependency happens iteratively through its deployment (development and implementation) lifecycle.

EBA provides a multi-phased design and value chain based on the common understanding of an organisation. According to Whittle and Myrick (2016), EBA defines the enterprise value streams and the relationships between events. EIA focuses on the rules and procedures used to manage and control information flow in an organisation. It categorises terms of information classes such as function, information, and resources for an organisation (Fahim et al., 2021). EAA provides a guide for the selection, implementation, and post-implementation of applications (Katuu, 2018). According to Batmetan (2022), EAA defines what an application does to manage processes, logics, and data, and provides information for executing business functions. ETA provides governance for the implementation of IT solutions and managing the interconnectivity and interdependence of hardware components (Kochanthara et al., 2021). Ismagilova et al. (2022) explain how ETA enables and supports the integrated design of technologies.

In the iterative process, first, it is the *business architecture* that fortifies the *business strategy*, through its support of the processes, events, and activities of the organisation. The integration which propels the effective management of tools (Gonzalez-Lopez & Bustos, 2019) is enabled by application and technology solutions. Iteratively, EA is used to manage and govern information systems and technologies (IS/IT) within an environment. This is to achieve increases in effectiveness, efficiency, and the reduction of risk via a new set of governance and operating models. This includes the rationalisation, consolidation, and integration of existing and future solutions to drive and achieve organisational goals and objectives for sustainability and competitive advantage.

The iteration process encompasses the current and future states over time and space. The results from both the current and future states are the outcomes of human and technological actions and interactions, which are produced and reproduced within space and over time. From a structuration perspective, Giddens (1984) describes such a process of reproduction as a duality of structure. In the reproduction of actions, both humans and technology act within heterogeneous networks in the organisation to develop, implement, and manage the architectures of the enterprise. It is difficult or near impossible to separate the human and technology aspects in the EA process, as neither operates in a vacuum.

1.4 The Significance of Enterprise Architecture

The significance of EA is founded on its primary aim and strengths, which are to bridge the gap between business and IT, and to enforce change from the current to the desired state. In the context of this book, 'change', as enacted by strategy, refers to a new way of working in an enterprise. In applying this new paradigm in organisations, it is argued in this book that we can take a different view and approach to improve the chances of success by adopting EA as an agent of change. EA helps us to consistently address the activities in the enterprise and many related concerns, such as the information and technology that support and enable business processes and activities. On this basis, it is critical for the process to continue.

In practice, many managers find themselves struggling and challenged with problems such as integration, consolidation, configuration, development, technology planning, software management, hardware, and processes. These problems have been widely shared among employees, managers, and organisations at large. The problem remains significant as they determine the success or failure of an IT environment within organisations. Thus, EA has been identified and acknowledged by many organisations, including private companies, government agencies and academic institutions, as an approach to enable, support and enhance both operational and strategic activities. As shown in Figure 1.2, EA in organisations is about three main components, namely: planning, deployment, and operation. The three components constitute the theory and practice of the discipline. Each of these components consists of several elements as highlighted in the description column of the figure.

Conceptualisation is necessary to better understand the phenomena in the context of practice. Figure 1.2 conceptualises the usefulness of EA to an organisation in addressing its challenges, as well as achieving its needs. Conceptualisation helps to bring meaning about EA to many stakeholders in an organisation. Based on its objectives, including governance, EA is fundamental to strategic planning, systems

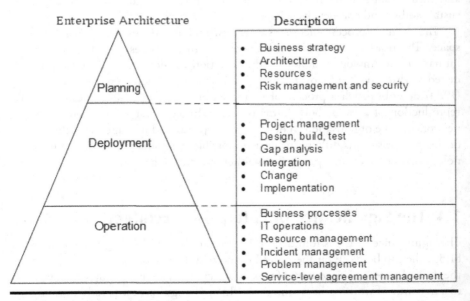

Figure 1.2   EA Conceptual Framework.

design, software and hardware deployment, and the production of multiple systems with different functionalities, but from the same basic architecture. On that basis, the development and implementation of EA are therefore critical steps in the strategic and operational governance and management of processes and activities, leading to organisational sustainability and competitive advantage in organisations.

The development, implementation, and practice of EA require a well-defined scope, mainly to guide in achieving its goals and objectives. The scope of EA is therefore the union of the enterprise, the business engineering, and the developments that are applied to it (EA). This includes the technical domains that support the processes and activities of IS/IT in an organisation. Thus, the scope of EA should be defined through pragmatism, a need to design and redesign, and continuous improvement in the functioning of an organisation. This is done through EA's domains, which are EBA, EIA, EAA, and ETA in the categories of planning, deployment, and operation, as shown in Figure 1.2.

1.5 Challenges of Enterprise Architecture

Significantly, the relevance of EA to an organisation has gained the attention of both public and private institutions across the world (Ahmad et al., 2022). Academics, too, have increasingly fostered their interest through their trade of research and teaching. Fernández-Cejas et al. (2022) claim that the EA objective is achieved through the creation of complementary perspectives from multiple viewpoints over the business events, IT solutions, and enabling communication between stakeholders. To the list of coverage and potential benefits, Rahmanian et al. (2022) add that business service is a crucial section of EA. Potentially, EA can be employed as a tool for managing, planning, and aligning organisations' business processes, information flow, application, and technology deployment (Georgiadis & Poels, 2021; Anthony Jnr et al., 2021; Niemi & Pekkola, 2017). Also, EA can be used to identify constraints in businesses and IT projects (Ajer et al., 2021).

Although EA remains popular in practice, many of its initiatives are continually confronted with substantial challenges (Löhe & Legner, 2014), some of which are demonstrated by low or slow implementation and institutionalisation (Kurnia et al., 2021a), scarcity of experts (Al-Kharusi et al., 2021), and limited understanding of the concepts (Robl & Bork, 2022; Ylinen & Pekkola, 2020). The challenges manifest in their limitations. Three of its main and most prevalent limitations from where other factors manifest in many organisations are identified and tabulated in Table 1.1.

Despite the increasing interest in EA in the last three decades, the benefits and value claimed in the literature are not supported empirically (Sukur & Lind, 2022; Niemi & Pekkola, 2016). Although the scholarly interest and focus are on the upside, research on EA principles is limited (Haki & Legner, 2021), which contributes to the challenges of the concept in practice. Thus, the concept continues

Table 1.1 EA Challenges

Limitation	Implication	Root Cause
Scope: EA is often scoped according to the knowledge of the architects rather than in alignment with the business goals, objectives, and foci.	Some EA projects are vague and are therefore, difficult to implement. Also, the scope is not defined by the organisation's vision.	The challenges of EA include ambiguity of the concept, difficult terminology, and complexity of the frameworks (Olsen, 2017).
Pragmatism: EA is often theorised due to a lack of understanding of the significance of business and IT strategies including the interpretation of the challenges.	This leads to building a 'white elephant', an EA that is not understood by many of the stakeholders and therefore, can hardly be implemented. Thus, EA hardly solves real issues or challenges of an organisation.	Primarily, this is because of the abstract nature of the ways that it is presented by both academics and professional bodies. Also, many IT personnel know little or nothing about business vision, goals, objectives, and strategies.
Buy-in: In many organisations, management and other stakeholders find it difficult to buy in and support the concept.	Interactions between the IT and business units often become misconstrued based on different understandings and interpretations.	Justification for EA value is difficult. This is primarily because many benefits of EA are intangible and value is achieved indirectly (Shanks et al., 2018).
Complexity: The approach can be highly complex, which therefore requires extensive training at the level of specialisation. However, it is difficult to find and retain experts in the field of EA.	Limited experts can be prohibitive to projects in that it can result in overspending resources. Also, it can create conflict between stakeholders based on different understandings and interests.	IT and the business personnel have no good working relationship; availability, performance, scalability, and interoperability of applications and systems are not getting better with changing times and space.

to face challenges as many EA practitioners struggle to extract return on investment (Kaisler & Armour, 2017). In addition to the growing challenges, Gong and Janssen (2019) suggest that the integration of EA capability into the organisation is a fundamental problem that carries many risks and affects decision-making processes in many organisations.

Empirical evidence from Ahmad et al. (2022) shows that the EA adoption rate remains slow on the uptake. This is attributable to its complexity, a multifaceted construct which is reflected in several research streams from both theoretical and empirical perspectives (Beese et al., 2022). Another problem identified by Niemi and Pekkola (2017) is that an explicit view of why, how, when, and by whom EA artefacts are used towards achieving their value and fulfilling their promises is not defined. According to Rahmanian et al. (2022), one of the challenges is that many leading-edge frameworks describe EA at the levels of abstraction and cannot provide an accurate syntactic and semantic description. Gong et al. (2020) explain how EA helps to comprehend stakeholders' views at different levels of abstraction in an organisation. Also, studies on EA adoption have often ignored the challenges of institutionalisation of the concept (Dang & Pekkola, 2020; Hylving & Bygstad, 2019).

While a long list of benefits presented and discussed in the literature continues, how and why EA leads to the benefits remain fragmented in practice (Ahlemann et al., 2021). This means there is less clarity or practical guidance on *how* to achieve and actualise the benefits of EA (Tamm et al., 2022). This book presents frameworks, models, and templates that guide EA deployment and practice, from development and implementation to institutionalisation of the concept. In some quarters, EA is regarded as an approach employed by the IT unit (Syynimaa, 2018). EA does not focus only on technology (Tamm et al., 2022); it is holistic in coverage across an organisation. This lack of clarity in some organisations creates confusion and adds to the challenges of where the value should come from. Owing to the challenges, many organisations are increasingly conscious of the deployment and practice of EA as a solution for managing business process-oriented activities and IT solutions holistically (Niemi & Pekkola, 2020).

As a result of these challenges, applications and systems development, integration, and implementation take longer than expected in many organisations, thereby making IT a cost centre. During the period of applications and systems deployment, requirements often change, and sometimes, they change so rapidly in the business units. Technology solutions are required for the change which continually happens in organisations. Change is often critical for gaining a competitive advantage; hence, it deserves and requires the utmost attention.

Based on the challenges, which have persisted for many years, the book sets out to answer the following questions. Does EA as an approach work in practice? How is EA developed and implemented? What are the factors that influence its institutionalisation in an organisation? These are some of the fundamental questions that this book sets out to examine from the standpoints of theorising the concept to its practice.

1.6 Contribution

The book examines EA in more detail, from a theoretical concept to practice. In each of the chapters, the book explores and presents outcomes through in-depth analysis, using sociotechnical theories. The outcomes should be viewed from two different perspectives, namely: (i) to provoke further academic research; and (ii) to encourage organisations in their interest in considering EA. In the past three decades, the gap between IT and business units has evidently increased in many organisations.

Although previous studies have identified numerous challenges in EA practice, only a few of them are empirical (Kurnia et al., 2021a). Also, none of these studies provide a specific solution, such as a step-by-step approach to how to develop EA, which this book presents in Chapters 4–7. Beyond development, implementation approaches, which include the use of the Zachman Framework are covered. Additionally, the factors influencing the institutionalisation of EA which is another area of the concept that is rarely covered or researched, are examined.

This book contributes to the advancement of EA by providing a pragmatic, step-by-step approach using models and frameworks that organisations can employ for the development, implementation, and institutionalisation of the concept. Each of the chapters demonstrates how varying degrees of actors' interactions and relationships can imbibe differentiation or disassociation in the development, implementation, or institutionalisation of EA in an organisation. From the perspectives of these domains, it conceptualises and explains the complications and bridges the gap between theoretical models and EA practice.

1.7 Summary

In this chapter, the concept of enterprise architecture (EA) is introduced. EA as an iterative process is depicted and discussed. The significance and challenges of EA are highlighted. In addition, the chapter presents some relevant fundamental questions the book intends to answer, from a success or failure perspective. This includes the areas of its scope, definitions, development, implementation, and value addition. This chapter serves as an introduction to this book, as it considers and recognises the perspectives of both practitioners and academics including students, to whom the concept might be new, or who might be unfamiliar with the subject. It also discusses the concept of EA from the perspectives of organisations. The chapter also briefly explains the effects of change and the nature of processes from the context of EA.

The book is intended to guide information technology (IT) and business managers on how to harmonise, balance, and leverage their IT solutions with business artefacts and requirements, and improve efficiency and effectiveness, to attain high competitiveness and requirements with IT solutions.

References

Ahlemann, F., Legner, C., & Lux, J. (2021). A resource-based perspective of value generation through enterprise architecture management. *Information & Management*, 58(1), 103266.

Ahmad, N. A., Drus, S. M., & Kasim, H. (2022). Factors of organizational adoption of enterprise architecture in Malaysian public sector: A multi-group analysis. *Journal of Systems and Information Technology, 24*(4), 331–360.

Ajer, A. K. S., Hustad, E., & Vassilakopoulou, P. (2021). Enterprise architecture operationalization and institutional pluralism: The case of the Norwegian Hospital sector. *Information Systems Journal, 31*(4), 610–645.

Al-Kharusi, H., Miskon, S., & Bahari, M. (2021). Enterprise architects and stakeholders alignment framework in enterprise architecture development. *Information Systems and e-Business Management, 19*, 137–181.

Anthony Jnr, B., Abbas Petersen, S., Helfert, M., Ahlers, D., & Krogstie, J. (2021). Modeling pervasive platforms and digital services for smart urban transformation using an enterprise architecture framework. *Information Technology & People, 34*(4), 1285–1312.

Batmetan, J. R. (2022). Model enterprise architecture for information technology services in universities. *International Journal of Information Technology and Education, 1*(4), 18–34.

Beese, J., Aier, S., Haki, K., & Winter, R. (2022). The impact of enterprise architecture management on information systems architecture complexity. *European Journal of Information Systems*, 1–21.

Dang, D., & Pekkola, S. (2020). Institutional perspectives on the process of enterprise architecture adoption. *Information Systems Frontiers, 22*(6), 1433–1445.

Fahim, P. B., An, R., Rezaei, J., Pang, Y., Montreuil, B., & Tavasszy, L. (2021). An information architecture to enable track-and-trace capability in Physical Internet ports. *Computers in Industry, 129*, 103443.

Fernández-Cejas, M., Pérez-González, C. J., Roda-García, J. L., & Colebrook, M. (2022). CURIE: Towards an ontology and enterprise architecture of a CRM conceptual model. *Business & Information Systems Engineering*, 1–29.

Gampfer, F., Jürgens, A., Müller, M., & Buchkremer, R. (2018). Past, current and future trends in enterprise architecture—A view beyond the horizon. *Computers in Industry, 100*, 70–84.

Georgiadis, G., & Poels, G. (2021). Enterprise architecture management as a solution for addressing general data protection regulation requirements in a big data context: A systematic mapping study. *Information Systems and e-Business Management, 19*(1), 313–362.

Giddens, A. (1984). *The constitution of society: Outline of the theory of structuration*. John Polity Press.

Gong, Y., & Janssen, M. (2019). The value of and myths about enterprise architecture. *International Journal of Information Management, 46*, 1–9.

Gong, Y., Yang, J., & Shi, X. (2020). Towards a comprehensive understanding of digital transformation in government: Analysis of flexibility and enterprise architecture. *Government Information Quarterly, 37*(3), 101487.

Gonzalez-Lopez, F., & Bustos, G. (2019). Integration of business process architectures within enterprise architecture approaches: A literature review. *Engineering Management Journal, 31*(2), 127–140.

Haki, K., & Legner, C. (2021). The mechanics of enterprise architecture principles. *Journal of the Association for Information Systems, 22*(5), 1334–1375.

Hylving, L., & Bygstad, B. (2019). Nuanced responses to Enterprise architecture management: Loyalty, voice, and exit. *Journal of Management Information Systems, 36*(1), 14–36.

Ismagilova, E., Hughes, L., Rana, N. P., & Dwivedi, Y. K. (2022). Security, privacy and risks within smart cities: Literature review and development of a smart city interaction framework. *Information Systems Frontiers, 24*(2), 393–414.

Iyamu, T. (2015). *Information technology enterprise architecture: From concept to practice* (2nd ed.). Heidelberg Press. ISBN: 8-3-659-61206-0

Iyamu, T. (2022). *Enterprise architecture for strategic management of modern IT solutions* (1st ed.). Auerbach Publications.

Kaisler, S., & Armour, F. (2017, January 4–7). 15 years of enterprise architecting at HICSS: Revisiting the critical problems. In *Proceedings of the 50th Hawaii international conference on system sciences*. Hilton Waikoloa Village.

Katuu, S. (2018, December 10–13). The utility of enterprise architecture to records and archives specialists. In *2018 IEEE international conference on big data (big data)* (pp. 2702–2710). IEEE.

Kochanthara, S., Rood, N., Saberi, A. K., Cleophas, L., Dajsuren, Y., & van den Brand, M. (2021). A functional safety assessment method for cooperative automotive architecture. *Journal of Systems and Software, 179*, 110991.

Kurnia, S., Kotusev, S., Shanks, G., Dilnutt, R., & Milton, S. (2021b). Stakeholder engagement in enterprise architecture practice: What inhibitors are there? *Information and Software Technology, 134*, 106536.

Kurnia, S., Kotusev, S., Shanks, G., Dilnutt, R., Taylor, P., & Milton, S. K. (2021a). Enterprise architecture practice under a magnifying glass: Linking artefacts, activities, benefits, and blockers. *Communications of the Association for Information Systems, 49*(1), 668–698.

Löhe, J., & Legner, C. (2014). Overcoming implementation challenges in enterprise architecture management: A design theory for architecture-driven IT Management (ADRIMA). *Information Systems and e-Business Management, 12*(1), 101–137.

Niemi, E. I., & Pekkola, S. (2016). Enterprise architecture benefit realization: Review of the models and a case study of a public organization. *ACM SIGMIS Database: The Database for Advances in Information Systems, 47*(3), 55–80.

Niemi, E. I., & Pekkola, S. (2017). Using enterprise architecture artefacts in an organisation. *Enterprise Information Systems, 11*(3), 313–338.

Niemi, E. I., & Pekkola, S. (2020). The benefits of enterprise architecture in organizational transformation. *Business & Information Systems Engineering, 62*(6), 585–597.

Olsen, D. H. (2017). Enterprise architecture management challenges in the Norwegian health sector. *Procedia Computer Science, 121*, 637–645.

Rahmanian, M., Nassiri, R., Mohsenzadeh, M., & Ravanmehr, R. (2022). Test case generation for enterprise business services based on enterprise architecture design. *The Journal of Supercomputing, 1*–31.

Robl, M., & Bork, D. (2022). Enterprise architecture management education in Academia: An international comparative analysis. *Complex Systems Informatics and Modeling Quarterly, 31*, 29–50.

Shanks, G., Gloet, M., Someh, I. A., Frampton, K., & Tamm, T. (2018). Achieving benefits with enterprise architecture. *The Journal of Strategic Information Systems, 27*(2), 139–156.

Sukur, A., & Lind, M. L. (2022). Enterprise architecture to achieve information technology flexibility and enterprise agility. *International Journal of Information Systems and Social Change (IJISSC), 13*(2), 1–20.

Syynimaa, N. (2018, March 21–24). Enterprise architecture: To business or not to business? That is the question! In *International conference on enterprise information systems.* SCITEPRESS Science And Technology Publications.

Tamm, T., Seddon, P. B., & Shanks, G. (2022). How enterprise architecture leads to organisational benefits. *International Journal of Information Management, 67,* 102554.

Venkatesan, D., & Sridhar, S. (2019). A rationale for the choice of enterprise architecture method and software technology in a software-driven enterprise. *International Journal of Business Information Systems, 32*(3), 272–311.

Whittle, R., & Myrick, C. B. (2016). *Enterprise business architecture: The formal link between strategy and results.* CRC Press.

Ylinen, M., & Pekkola, S. (2020, June 15–17). Jack-of-all-trades torn apart: Skills and competencies of an enterprise architect. In *Proceedings of the 28th European conference on information systems (ECIS).* Association for Information Systems.

Zachman, J. A. (1987). A framework for information systems. *IBM Systems Journal, 26*(3), 276–283.

Zachman, J. A. (1996). Enterprise architecture: The view beyond 2000. In *The proceedings of 7th international users group conference for warehouse repository architecture development.* Technology Transfer Institute.

Chapter 2

Information Systems and Information Technology

2.1 Introduction

As introduced in Chapter 1, the concept of enterprise architecture (EA) covers the broad spectrum of the business and computing units of an organisation, or enterprise. The deployment of EA seems more complex from the computing perspective because of the wide-ranging nature of the environment. Simplistically, the complexity is underpinned by a convolution of the heterogeneity of the computing solutions. Thus, it is essential to discuss what makes up the complexity or how the challenges manifest, to enable or constrain its own deployment, use, and management.

As the misunderstanding and confusion lingered on, Iyamu and Kekwaletswe (2010) conducted an empirical study using four different organisations focusing on business goals, culture, transformative, and technological settings in their computing environment, to understand the confusion between the information systems (IS) and information technology (IT) disciplines. The differences and similarities between IS and IT solutions are increasingly challenging for non-computing specialists. This becomes more challenging for the sponsors of computing projects or those enabled by services of the IS and IT solutions. However, the distinctions are not easily distinguished or transparently separated. Thus, some non-computing specialists struggle to assign roles, responsibilities, and tasks to the disciplines. The lack of distinction manifests and creates challenges in areas such as: (i) designing systems; (ii) defining technology deployment; (iii) understanding the system and technology requirements; and (iv) developing and implementing EA domains to support organisational goals and objectives.

DOI: 10.1201/9781003390879-2

Evidently, the two disciplines are not the same, that their solutions are inter-related, and that they have distinct sets of learnings and career paths. The confusion contributes to why the concepts are either loosely or interchangeably used. Consequently, the confusion manifests in many ways to disrupt or influence activities of career path development and the allocation of roles, responsibilities, and tasks including the development of EA. Although IS and IT focus on computer-based solutions, there is a distinct boundary between the concepts or fields. This chapter highlights some of the distinctions between IS and IT.

To develop or implement EA, it is fundamental to understand the distinction between IS and IT. Plausibly, the distinction provides an unambiguous connection between IS and IT requirements in deploying and practising EA in an organisation. Also, it helps to provide better explanation and clarification of organisational needs and benefits to stakeholders.

The chapter is organised into four main sections. It starts with an introduction. This is followed by a discussion of computing as an environment that comprises two distinct fields, IS and IT. Thereafter, it discusses the two disciplines with focus on the distinction. In the section that follows, the implications of the distinction between IS and IT are explored. The inter-relation between IS and IT is discussed. Finally, the contribution of the chapter is highlighted.

2.2 Computing Environment

Computing is the process of using computer technology or system to provide solutions. It encompasses the design and development of software, network, and hardware systems for a wide range of purposes, including tasks such as storing, processing, and managing information. For the computing tasks to be effective and efficiently used require architecting. Architecture is the design of logical and physical inter-relations and defines the interconnectivity of the computing components. The architecture is used as a framework to provide a set of governance (standards, principles, and policies) (Iyamu, 2022), which guide the development of computing solutions across an enterprise (Lo et al., 2022). This means that the computing architecture outlines the technology and system functionalities, compatibilities, and design.

Computing comprises two main components, IS and IT (Tallon et al., 2019). Systems can be found in technology, and technology exists in systems. This creates confusion for many of the specialists, users, and actors whose works or activities are interconnected with the solutions of IS or IT. Simplistically, Abebe et al. (2020) state that the technology element in information systems is referred to as IT. Dwivedi et al. (2019) explain how the acceptance and use of IS and IT solutions have been a concern for research and practice. Also, each of the components provides tools, approaches, and means to facilitate activities and events such as storing and manipulating data (Liu et al., 2022), system development (Baham & Hirschheim, 2022), and transporting data or information (Lo et al., 2022).

In this chapter and book, computing is defined as a structured environment which encompasses software, hardware, and networking, including processes and interfaces, to enable and support the goals and objectives of an individual, group, or organisation. Computing has long been a significant element in the strategy and operation of many organisations that deploy it. During the last two decades, it has become increasingly important for many more organisations worldwide and across sectors, including government administrations. With this increasing role, investment in computing solutions (systems and technologies), assets, and support have become a significant element in organisations that they support and enable. This has led to several works, dating back two decades, such as Niederman et al. (2016), Papp and Fox (2002), Hackney et al. (2000), Kling (2000), and Ciborra (1996).

More organisations depend on computing strategies which entail architecture design to support and enable their business processes, activities, and services. Strategies of many organisations involve both external and internal factors, including employees of the computing environment and the entire organisation that deploys it (Dehgani & Navimipour, 2019). The reliance requires a clear distinction between the two concepts, to an exponential degree.

Both IS and IT are embedded in providing computer-based solutions (Lowry et al., 2017). Thus, many people find it difficult to differentiate between the two fields of discipline. Hence, a rhetorical question commonly arises, whether IS and IT are the same. The question is often handled with a frivolous attitude for various reasons. Also, the question lags in literature, and the confusion, therefore, peddles on. Intriguingly, in many quarters, some of the questions that are often asked include the following. Which of the fields, IS or IT, is better? What is the difference between the fields of IS and IT? What are the similarities between the concepts of IS and IT? The questions rage on in both business and academic domains.

2.3 Information Systems and Information Technology

IS and IT are separate concepts within the computing environment. The terms IS and IT have often been loosely and interchangeably used, even by professionals. This could be attributed to either the extent of knowledge of the subjects or based on the practical unconsciousness of individuals. Practical consciousness consists of the things an actor knows tacitly about and how to 'go on' in the contexts of social life without being able to give them direct discursive expression. Giddens (1984, p. 375) defines practical unconsciousness as "What actors know (believe) about social conditions, including especially the conditions of their own action, but cannot express discursively; no bar of repression, however, protects practical consciousness as is the case with the unconscious".

Many individuals in the computing environment often refer to themselves as IT specialists when the personnel are trained or specialises in IS functions. Also, many organisations refer to and classify their computing environments as the IT unit, department, or division. The issues underlying these differences and lack of distinction between IS and IT have over the years engaged many within and outside the computing field, particularly students and professionals. There have been attempts to distinguish between the two concepts through academic definitions and experiences drawn from practice. Additionally, explanations have been obtained from many years of academic documentations.

The increasing dependence on IS and IT has come a long way. IS is a method of delivering information in accordance with organisational needs (Daniels, 1994). In Daniels' view, IT is the technological apparatus that conveys information. Daniels argues that technology is not a requirement for an information system, but a translator of symbols into a usable form. Kendall (1992) advances the view that an information system exists only to serve the business systems of which it is a component. According to Hicks (1993), information system is a formalised computer-based system that can collect, store, process and report on data manipulation and usage from various sources to provide the information necessary for managerial decision-making.

Through IS, an organisation executes its business plans and attempts to realise its business goals. Lederer and Gardiner (1992, p. 1) refer to this as "a portfolio of computer-based applications", while Ward and Peppard (2002) define IS as the means by which people and organisations utilising technology gather, process, store, use, and disseminate information. It is thus concerned with the purposeful utilisation of IT. In the same line of understanding, IT refers specifically to technology, essentially hardware, software, and telecommunication networks, which are tangible (e.g., servers, personal computers, routers, and network cables) and intangible (software of all kinds). IT facilitates the acquisition, processing, storing, delivering, and sharing of information and other digital content (Ward & Peppard, 2002).

The distinction between the two concepts is extended to strategy, because it inevitably affects the understanding and consequently leads to how the strategy is defined, developed, and executed in the organisations. The strategy is either embedded or governed by EA. Boar (1993) defines strategy as the process by which corporate objectives for the future are identified in response to perceived opportunities and threats, and by understanding company strengths and weaknesses, activities are selected and resources allocated to meet those objectives. Strategy hence provides direction, concentration of effort, consistency of purpose, and flexibility. Strategic planning defines objectives and assesses both the internal and external situations, which include the process of alignment (Gable, 2020). This introduces the required concepts, controls, and new techniques, establishes good relationships, and identifies tasks and responsibilities, thus defining the planning of resource requirements. The exemplary illustration of IS and IT alignment by Galliers (2020) vitally exposes the need for differentiation between the disciplines.

The recent emergence of technology as a key resource makes it necessary to have a strategy for its proper deployment within the organisation. Walsham and Waema (1994) argue that IT needs a strategy to achieve its aims and objectives. No doubt, 'IS or IT strategy' is a significant factor in driving towards a specific direction. Interestingly, Teubner and Stockhinger (2020) did not separate the concepts. Instead, they emphasise that the 'IS/IT' strategy is of central importance for organisations. Galliers (2020) argues that the two aspects of IS/IT strategy should be aligned. Before such alignment takes place, the distinction is explicitly essential. Otherwise, the confusion, overlapping, and duplication hide in the midst and manifest into a prohibitive exercise.

IS or IT or both strategies determine and establish the technological direction within the computing environment of an organisation that deploys them. Also, the business objectives and goals are deterministic factors for developing IS and IT strategies (Wirtz & Lovelock, 2021). Thus, the business vision is a starting point for developing an IT strategy. The vision acts as the framework upon which the IT strategic intent is developed and implemented. The development and implementation of either IS or IT strategy do not necessarily follow the same process or involve the same people.

The development of IS or IT strategy is conducted by collecting data or requirements from both current (as-is) and predicted internal and external environments. Thus, IS or IT strategy planning should clearly define objectives and assess both internal and external situations. IT strategy development planning (Wirtz & Lovelock, 2021) includes the process of introducing the required disciplines, controls, and new techniques, establishing good relationships and identifying tasks and responsibilities. Circumstantially, Li et al. (2012) inquire whether the strength of IT controls the management of IS.

The implementation of IS or IT artefacts is the execution of technological change within the organisation that deploys them. Different actors within the organisation are likely to have different views on how to implement as well as how to use the technologies. Gottschalk (1999) argues that the term 'implementation' could have a variety of meanings to different people, and therefore suggests that management must first define the term implementation and subsequently the implementers must understand the definition. In the process of definition, boundaries are established and components are identified, which helps differentiate between IS and IT.

The following observations were identified from the existing literature.

i. There is a general acceptance that a difference exists between IS and IT within the computing environment (Abouzahra & Ghasemaghaei, 2022; Smith et al., 2007). This has implications for architecting the solutions of the disciplines.

ii. There is less emphasis on the definition of IT strategy in the field of computing (Williams et al., 2022).

iii. There is no clear definition of IT strategy, and most literature and discussion have focused on strategic information systems planning (SISP) (Rainer & Prince, 2021; Orlikowski & Robey, 1991).

From these observations, as well as other works such as Mithas and Rust (2016), Monteiro and Hanseth (1996), Atkinson (2000), and Lee and Whitley 2002), it would seem that no agreement exists about the definition of IT strategy. This could be attributed to the challenging pose by the overlapping nature of IS and IT, which manifests from a lack of clear distinctions between the disciplines.

2.4 The Inter-Relation between IS and IT

There are three basic components common to both the development and implementation of IS or IT and their solutions. The components are technology, process, and people. The components are key to how IS or IT are developed, implemented, managed, or used in an environment. Fundamentally, the components are critical to the success or failure of the computing environment's support and enablement of the business processes and activities towards competitiveness. This section describes these components.

Habitually, IS and IT are considered synonymous by many people. In practice, IS and IT are two separate concepts in the computing environment. IS focuses on the management of information systems, which include business applications and processes, to support an organisation's goals and objectives. IT is concerned with the exploration of hardware and software, including networks. IT offers various solutions to enhance development through enablement and support to create, process, store, secure, and exchange electronic data and information. Figure 2.1 illustrates the inter-relationships between IS and IT, including the architecture components that align both disciplines and their solutions in a computing environment.

There is a satisfactory account of the definition of IS, which translates to its strategy, as explained in the introductory section of this chapter. In similar disposition, IT strategy is defined as follows.

> IT strategy is the technical design which serves as the road map over a period of time for the implementation of information technology and information systems by people using a formal process.

This definition is intended to guide an understanding of the distinction that exists between IS and IT, as well as to examine the impact the concepts have on each other. Also, it provides knowledge awareness to the professionals in the computing environments of organisations.

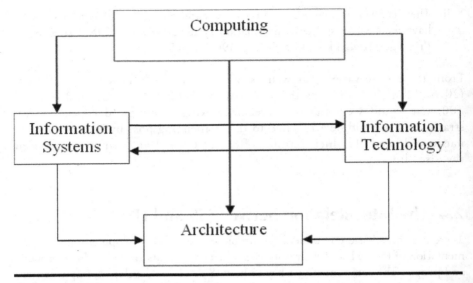

Figure 2.1 Components of Computing.

IT is a term that is broadly and widely used in most organisations. It has long dominated its related component, IS. However, there are vital attributes:

i. It recognises that IT strategy can neither be formulated nor implemented in isolation from IS.
ii. It recognises the inseparable relationship between the social construction of IT and IS in the technological environment. A social construct results from human interaction, which means that it does exist because humans agree that it does.
iii. It acknowledges the role of human involvement in the interpretation of the concepts, thereby making meaning of the artefacts and the implication of the associated meanings.

The distinction between IS and IT by itself cannot influence the outcome of computing. The main aspect of the influence lies in what people make of the distinction. Also, how the people involved internalise the distinction is what matters the most. Additionally, the internalisation shapes and justifies the means, through design, development, and execution of the subject.

Primarily, seven areas of practice within the computing environment are considered the most significant, as shown in Figure 2.2. The areas are hardware engineering, software development, business systems development, networking, architecture, and systems analysis and design. Figure 2.2 categorises these areas of practice into IS and IT disciplines.

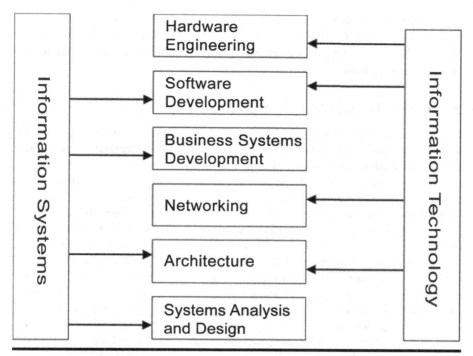

Figure 2.2   Distinction between IS and IT.

2.4.1 The Information Systems Component

The concept of IS refers to the management of information, technology, processes, and people. The component consists of systems through which an individual or organisation carries out its activities, processes, and logic (Lowry et al., 2017). The systems are consciously and unconsciously used by the end-user (those who act on behalf of the business). This also means that those who develop (software developer, programmer), analyse, and design the systems are usually in the information systems unit or domain.

2.4.2 The Information Technology Component

The IT component of the computing environment consists of artefacts such as hardware and software. The hardware is all physical or tangible artefacts of technology, which includes servers, disks, and networks, and other connecting cables (Tallon et al., 2019). The hardware is sometimes referred to as technology infrastructure. Distinct from IS software, IT software is tools that enable IS software. Some examples are operating systems, software development tools (such as COBOL, Visual Basic, and C computer languages), and antivirus software.

In isolation, neither IS nor IT components can alone achieve the goals and objectives of the organisation that deploys them. Both components depend on each other to determine and provide technological solutions based on an individual's needs and an organisation's goals and objectives.

2.4.3 The Architecture Component

EA is a constructive structure of integration that logically connects IS and IT solutions capabilities required to enable and support an enterprise's processes and activities towards sustainability and competitiveness. This includes data governance, networks, and communications. Also, integrating computing solutions is intended to ensure data security and recovery, which makes architecture even more momentous. Integration enables the coexistence of technologies, including those that are heterogeneous (Qadri et al., 2020). Another implication is the lack of comprehensiveness in using computing solutions to enable and support business goals and objectives.

Architecture is involved in IS as well as in IT. Iyamu (2022) explains how EA is used as a tool for integrating information systems and technologies within an environment. It is the strategic design and implementation of systems and technologies, including processes and governance. All systems and technologies are architected. The primary goals of the component are to identify, formulate, ratify, and approve systems and technical architectures, including policies and standards within which systems and technologies are deployed and managed in the organisation.

2.5 Implications of the Challenges between IS and IT

How the terms, IS and IT are continuously loosely used can potentially change the way computing environments are structured. It also leads to a certain understanding which subsequently begins to shape the categorisation and deployment of IS and IT solutions. Primarily, the chapter provides four fundamental insights that can be viewed from a challenging perspective and guide future preparedness. First, it manifests during task allocation. Second, it demonstrates how certain factors of IS and IT solutions influence and rely on each other to support and enable services, processes, and activities in practice within an organisation. Third, it shows how human understanding, action, and organisational structure (roles) can affect the technological strategic direction within the computing environment. Fourth, it visualises how the confusion that enmesh IS and IT distinctiveness influences career pursuits.

2.5.1 The Implication for Task Allocation

The activities of IS and IT are carried out within structures that exist in the computing environment of an organisation. Parts of these structures were created by the allocation of tasks to individuals and teams to enable and support technologies, systems, and business processes. Thus, a lack of distinction between IS and IT can negatively impact the allocation of tasks in the computing environment. Karimi-Alaghehband and Rivard (2019) emphasise how architecture, instead, is used to deliver IT capability. Another implication is that a lack of understanding of the distinctiveness of the field can be detrimental to early-career personnel. For example, a lack of understanding of the distinction between the IS and IT affects some candidates' chances (or opportunities) if they are not able to distinguish and put computing solutions into categories during job interviews. In some cases, candidates' curriculum vitae and qualifications suggest something different from their responses or pursuits.

What is increasingly ironic but important is how the loose use of the terms reflect in strategic documents in which IS and IT are differentiated. EA divides IS and IT solutions into application and technical domains, as seen and explained in subsequent chapters of this book. In some organisations, people are appointed to positions and assigned tasks based on seniority level in the computing environment. This is regardless of whether the appointment or tasks are of an IS or IT nature or area of specialisation. This does not help the situation, particularly for younger employees or early-career specialists. More importantly, the approach affects the quality of work produced in the areas where appointments are made, or tasks are assigned based on the level of seniority instead of the area of specialisation.

2.5.2 The Confusion in Practice

The terms IS and IT are loosely and interchangeably used by many people, including early-career specialists (Iyamu & Kekwaletswe, 2010). How both concepts are used during conversations, including in formal settings, sometimes creates confusion for the practice. For example, when a manager describes "IS strategy as a plan or approach around technologies for the future direction and how it aligns with and supports the business process . . . it is driven by the business". It clearly shows that many professionals do not understand the difference, or, the boundaries between IS and IT, in their various computing environments. The lack of a clear distinction between IS and IT does not only affect the structure and tasks allocations, it also affects practice. Specialists and managers make the issue more problematic instead of being the custodians by clarifying the distinction between the two concepts at a given opportunity.

Continually, some employees think it is too academic to try to distinguish between IS and IT. At this point, the architect provides technical leadership and guidance. In turn, architects are seen as not pragmatic enough. Thus, in many organisations, employees are more comfortable with the use of the term IT, regardless of the functions being described, whether they are IS- or IT-related. In such circumstances, employees in the computing environment of the organisation consider themselves IT personnel. The human resources (HR) department in the organisation follows suit. The prevalence and domineering nature of the use of the term IT makes it a preferred choice of study in the computing environment. As a result, many aspiring candidates prefer to study IT rather than IS where some of them would have been more successful.

What is frivolously more interesting is that many employees in some organisations, particularly those which do not have a clear understanding of the differences between IS and IT, are aware of the utmost importance of computing to the organisation. Hence, it is vital to impress on the employees an understanding of how IS and IT solutions are distinguished, communicated, and interpreted. This is important and of interest to both the academic and business domains, for two main reasons: it manifests in the quality of work produced in practice, and it guides strategic direction, development, use, and management of computing solutions.

2.5.3 The Impact on Structure

The roles and responsibilities determine the task and activities and reflect on employees' responses to structures within the computing environment. Consequently, this affects the development and implementation of computing strategy, support for processes, and management of systems and technologies in an organisation. These actions and responses also reflect on how the design, development, and implementation of computing activities are interpreted, how the various tasks involved are allocated, and how these tasks are sanctioned and carried out. This can manifest in the quality of work, which potentially can somehow induces compromise. For example, during software development, a senior software developer is tasked with the responsibility of selecting infrastructure for a project, based on their level of seniority in the organisation, resulting in manipulation of structures to accommodate certain individuals.

From a technical perspective, misguided appointments within a structure creates an opportunity for subordinates to take advantage of their manager's lack of full understanding of their functions, thus making them produce work of less quality often not scrutinised, and unconsciously engineering fragility into the existing structure. In a conversation, an employee once admitted: "My manager does not have networking and security background and experience; as such, he relies on me for most of his decisions . . . of course, I do sometimes take advantage of his feeble knowledge of tasks under his auspices".

2.5.4 The Influence on Career Pursuit

In practice, there are hardly any vacancies that describe IS jobs. Vacancies in the computing environment are referred to as IT positions. However, the distinctions can be identified through the specification and requirements, on the one hand, and on the other hand, by reading through the curriculum vitae of the candidates. Many employment agencies are consistently faced with the challenge of differentiating between IS and IT candidates in sourcing candidates for their clients. It proves to be even more difficult for them as they are not specialists in the computing field. It is increasingly a problem as recruiters must differentiate and categorise between the IS and IT focus when sourcing candidates.

It is prevalent to have the architecture team in the IT department in the structure of the organisation. This makes the employees, particularly the less experienced ones, think that architecture (or EA) is an IT issue or only related to IT solutions. Those who aspire to be IT architects thought it would be easier to achieve their goal if they sought positions in the IT department (Iyamu & Kekwaletswe, 2010). This explains and helps to gain a deeper understanding as to why many practitioners including academia find it difficult to communicate with their audiences and ought, therefore, to use the term 'IS/IT' instead.

2.6 Summary

IS (information systems) and IT (information technology) are two common terms in the computing environment. This chapter firmly confirms that both terminologies have, for many years, been loosely used by many people, including those in practice. Significantly, the chapter highlights the implications which lack of distinction between IS and IT have on structure, career, and practice from both academic and business perspectives. Additionally, the chapter draws attention to how applying IS and IT solutions can be negatively affected by not understanding the distinction between IS and IT in practice. It thus contributes to developing IS and IT strategies, which can be of benefit to managers and specialists in the computing environment. This is intended to be of value in defining roles, responsibilities and strengthening the relationship between the two disciplines.

The other contribution of this chapter is its aim to be of significance to decision-makers and professionals, including managers and employees of the organisation within the computing environment. It is expected that its key contribution will arise from the understanding of the distinction. Through this, a better understanding of the impact on employees and structures will be gained.

References

Abebe, R., Barocas, S., Kleinberg, J., Levy, K., Raghavan, M., & Robinson, D. G. (2020, January 27–30). Roles for computing in social change. In *Proceedings of the conference on fairness, accountability, and transparency* (pp. 252–260). ACM Press.

Abouzahra, M., & Ghasemaghaei, M. (2022). Effective use of information technologies by seniors: The case of wearable device use. *European Journal of Information Systems*, *31*(2), 241–255.

Atkinson, C. (2000). The 'Soft information systems and technologies methodology' (SISTeM): An actor network contingency approach to integrated development. *European Journal of Information Systems, 9*(2), 104–123.

Baham, C., & Hirschheim, R. (2022). Issues, challenges, and a proposed theoretical core of agile software development research. *Information Systems Journal, 32*(1), 103–129.

Boar, B. H. (1993). *The art of strategic planning for information technology*. John Wiley & Sons, Inc.

Ciborra, C. U. (1996, December 16–18). Improvisation and information technology in organizations. In *Proceedings of the international conference on information systems* (pp. 369–80). Association for Information Systems.

Daniels, C. N. (1994). *Information technology: The management challenge*. Addison-Wesley Publishing Ltd.

Dehgani, R., & Navimipour, N. J. (2019). The impact of information technology and communication systems on the agility of supply chain management systems. *Kybernetes, 48*(10), 2217–2236.

Dwivedi, Y. K., Rana, N. P., Jeyaraj, A., Clement, M., & Williams, M. D. (2019). Re-examining the unified theory of acceptance and use of technology (UTAUT): Towards a revised theoretical model. *Information Systems Frontiers, 21*(3), 719–734.

Gable, G. G. (2020). Information systems research strategy. *The Journal of Strategic Information Systems, 29*(2), 101620.

Galliers, R. D. (2020). On confronting some of the common myths of information: Systems strategy discourse. In *Strategic information management* (pp. 56–70). Routledge.

Giddens, A. (1984). *The constitution of society*. Polity Press.

Gottschalk, P. (1999). Implementation predictors of formal information technology strategy. *Information & Management, 36*(2), 77–91.

Hackney, R., Burn, J., & Dhillon, G. (2000). Challenging assumptions for strategic information systems planning: Theoretical perspectives. *Communications of the Association for Information Systems, 3*(9), 2–23.

Hicks, J. (1993). *Management information systems: A user perspective*. West Publishing Company.

Iyamu, T. (2022). *Enterprise architecture for strategic management of modern IT solutions*. Routledge, CRC Press.

Iyamu, T., & Kekwaletswe, R. M. (2010, April 16–18). Importance of the distinction between information systems and information technology. In *2010 2nd IEEE international conference on information management and engineering* (pp. 342–348). IEEE.

Karimi-Alaghehband, F., & Rivard, S. (2019). Information technology outsourcing and architecture dynamic capabilities as enablers of organizational agility. *Journal of Information Technology, 34*(2), 129–159.

Kendall, P. (1992). *Introduction to systems analysis and design: A structured approach* (2nd ed.). Wm. C Brown Publishers.

Kling, R. (2000). Learning about information technologies and social change: The contribution of social informatics. *The Information Society, 16*(3), 217–232.

Lederer, A. L., & Gardiner, V. (1992). The process of strategic information planning. *Journal of Strategic Information Systems, 1*(2), 76–83.

Lee, H., & Whitley, E. A. (2002). Time and information technology: Temporal impacts on individuals, organizations, and society. *The Information Society, 18*(4), 235–240.

Li, C., Peters, G. F., Richardson, V. J., & Watson, M. W. (2012). The consequences of information technology control weaknesses on management information systems: The case of Sarbanes-Oxley internal control reports. *Management Information Systems (MIS) Quarterly, 36*(1), 179–203.

Liu, D., Zhang, Y., Jia, D., Zhang, Q., Zhao, X., & Rong, H. (2022). Toward secure distributed data storage with error locating in blockchain enabled edge computing. *Computer Standards & Interfaces, 79*, 103560.

Lo, S. K., Lu, Q., Zhu, L., Paik, H. Y., Xu, X., & Wang, C. (2022). Architectural patterns for the design of federated learning systems. *Journal of Systems and Software, 191*, 111357.

Lowry, P. B., Dinev, T., & Willison, R. (2017). Why security and privacy research lies at the centre of the information systems (IS) artefact: Proposing a bold research agenda. *European Journal of Information Systems, 26*(6), 546–563.

Mithas, S., & Rust, R. T. (2016). How information technology strategy and investments influence firm performance. *MIS Quarterly, 40*(1), 223–246.

Monteiro, E., & Hanseth, O. (1996). Social shaping of information infrastructure: On being specific about the technology. In W. J. Orlikowski, G. Walsham, M. R. Jones, & J. I. DeGross (Eds.), *Information technology and changes in organizational work* (pp. 325–343). Chapman and Hall.

Niederman, F., Ferratt, T. W., & Trauth, E. M. (2016). On the co-evolution of information technology and information systems personnel. *ACM SIGMIS Database: The Database for Advances in Information Systems, 47*(1), 29–50.

Orlikowski, W., & Robey, D. (1991). Information technology and the structuring of organizations. *Information Systems Research, 2*(2), 143–169.

Papp, R., & Fox, D. (2002, August 9–11). Information strategy development: The strategic alignment imperative. In *Proceedings of the 8th Americas conference on information systems (AMCIS)*. Association of Information Systems.

Qadri, Y. A., Nauman, A., Zikria, Y. B., Vasilakos, A. V., & Kim, S. W. (2020). The future of healthcare internet of things: A survey of emerging technologies. *IEEE Communications Surveys & Tutorials, 22*(2), 1121–1167.

Rainer, R. K., & Prince, B. (2021). *Introduction to information systems*. John Wiley & Sons.

Smith, H. A., Mckeen, J. D., & Singh, S. (2007). Developing information technology strategy for business value. *Journal of Information Technology Management, 18*(1), 49–58.

Tallon, P. P., Queiroz, M., Coltman, T., & Sharma, R. (2019). Information technology and the search for organizational agility: A systematic review with future research possibilities. *The Journal of Strategic Information Systems, 28*(2), 218–237.

Teubner, R. A., & Stockhinger, J. (2020). Literature review: Understanding information systems strategy in the digital age. *The Journal of Strategic Information Systems, 29*(4), 101642.

Walsham, G., & Waema, T. (1994). Information systems strategy and implementation: A case study of a building society. *ACM Transactions on Information Systems, 12*(2), 159–173.

Ward, J., & Peppard, J. (2002). *Strategic planning for information systems* (3rd ed.). John Wiley & Sons.

Williams, J. A., Torres, H. G., & Carte, T. (2022). A review of IS strategy literature: Current trends and future opportunities. *Journal of Computer Information Systems, 62*(1), 1–11.

Wirtz, J., & Lovelock, C. (2021). *Services marketing: People, technology, strategy*. World Scientific.

Chapter 3

The Concept of Enterprise Architecture

3.1 Introduction

Enterprise Architecture (EA) is an approach intended to improve the management of business functions and governance of information systems and information technology (IS/IT) solutions of complex enterprises (Zachman, 1987). EA comprises domains; traditionally, they are enterprise business architecture (EBA), enterprise information architecture (EIA), enterprise application architecture (EAA), and enterprise technical architecture (ETA) (Iyamu, 2022b). As depicted in Figure 3.1, the domains are interrelated and interdependent. Each of the domains of EA has distinctive types of deliverables, analysis methods, processes, and participants in development, implementation, and practice. The domains define processes and activities between IT and business units of an organisation into common goals and objectives. Through the common goals, the domains make an ongoing representation of existing and plans to support and enable ever-changing business and IT strategies. This includes the consequential business processes, information flow, application requirements, and technology selections and deployment.

EA has been defined differently in many studies and by various practitioners, but they all focus on common goals and objectives. EA is a paradigm whose premises are to address challenges that come with change, particularly in both the computing and business environments of an organisation that deploys it. Thus, EA is viewed as a change agent because it facilitates change in ways that adequately consider new emerging paradigms and requirements that affect an organisation's goals and objectives (Masuda et al., 2021). Also, EA focuses on change at both operational and strategic levels (Georgiadis & Poels, 2021; Iyamu, 2015). Hence,

DOI: 10.1201/9781003390879-3

EA is considered a blueprint that is developed, implemented, maintained, and used to explain and guide how IS/IT, information management, and business processes can be used efficiently to accomplish the goals and objectives of an organisation.

EA is a collection of artefacts that describe the aspects of an organisation, from business processes to IT solutions (Kotusev et al., 2023). From a comprehensive perspective, EA encompasses business and IS/IT artefacts from operational to strategic viewpoints (Masuda et al., 2021). EA provides guides in the form of models, blueprints, and roadmaps towards specific directions for sustainability and competitive purposes (Iyamu, 2022a; Gampfer et al., 2018). Beese et al. (2022) suggest that in practice, many organisations employ EA, standardise IS/IT solutions, and harmonise their efforts to avoid unnecessary redundancies and inconsistencies. Additionally, EA supports the re-engineering, optimisation, governance, and decision-making processes of transformation in an organisation (Anthony Jnr et al., 2021).

On the one hand, organisations' activities, which include service delivery practices, organisational structures, and requirements keep changing and manifesting themselves in different ways. On the other hand, IS/IT solutions also keep evolving rapidly. Historically and evidently, nothing except change is permanent in organisations, and by implication, the changing activities and events affect services and competitiveness. As a result, there has been significant emphasis on how organisations manage business transformation and IS/IT solutions' advancements. For EA to fulfil its objective and fill the gap between the goals of the stakeholders and what can be delivered in practice (Belfadel et al., 2022), it must be flexible, adaptive to change, and govern with principles. According to Haki and Legner (2021), in practice, EA principles should guide the design and evolution toward predefined values and outcomes.

Based on these premises, EA is intended to enable an organisation to achieve its goals and objectives by bridging the gap between strategic planning and implementation efforts through a strategy process that is holistic in coverage and enterprise-wide in its scope. The effort is executed through the domains. Roelens et al. (2019) suggest that the EBA provides a common understanding of the formulation of the organisational goals and objectives through its multi-faced blueprint approach. The EIA puts information into containers of chains and classes that support the interoperability of actors' activities and enable users (Fahim et al., 2021; Venkatesan & Sridhar, 2019). Through EAA, applications that can be used for business objectives, processes and events are defined, subsystems are integrated, and coexistence is managed (Dwipriyoko et al., 2019; Laumann & Tambo, 2018). The ETA enables governance and procedures that provide health governance as well as detect deficiencies in IT solutions crucial for business enhancement (Iyamu, 2022b).

Relying on the potential, some organisations have deployed EA and many more have shown interest in the concept. Interest has grown significantly in the last two decades, with a focus on its main objectives, which are strategy, transformative process (change), and bridging the gap between business and IT units. EA focuses on bridging the communication gap between business and IT units to improve alignment in an organisation (Kotusev et al., 2023). According to Anthony Jnr et al. (2021), EA frameworks are aimed at providing structure to manage changes and instil transformation. Griffo et al. (2021) emphasise why it is essential to bridge the gap between units and the EA domains, towards stronger alignment. Through the domains, strategic intentions are fortified, events and activities are transformed, and gaps between business and IT units are narrowed. From different angles, Chapters 4–9 demonstrate how these objectives can be achieved in organisations.

In large organisations where EA is mostly adopted, strategy is a critical step in the growth and development of initiatives, which are directed at a competitive advantage. According to Mack and Frey (2002), the primary reason for creating an overall IT architecture is to build the new as well as manage the transition from the old to desire state. Change to business goals seems to have significant consequences across the domains of the enterprise (Iyamu, 2022a; Radeke, 2010). This includes transforming requirements and procedures within the organisational structure and business processes for competitiveness, using IT solutions (software and hardware) (Kaidalova et al., 2018). This is because of slow response time as some organisations struggle to adapt to technological and business changes that continue to happen at a rapid rate in their environments (Löhe & Legner, 2014; Jonkers et al., 2006).

In view of this stated focus, the objectives of this chapter are four-fold, to discuss the concept of EA and highlight some of the critical factors which, in this book, are how it can be: (i) employed as a strategy; (ii) deployed and practised through governance; (iii) used to facilitate change; and (iv) used to enable the bridging of gaps between business and IT units in an organisation. Although these initiatives have been discussed in the literature, this introduces them to a practice approach, as presented in Chapters 4–8 of this book. This chapter is organised in sections in the following order: after the introduction of the chapter, EA is discussed in the form of a literature review. Next, the objectives of the chapter relating to EA as strategic, transformative, and bridging of gaps are covered, respectively. The chapter concludes with a summary.

3.2 The Concept of Enterprise Architecture

In many organisations, EA is intended to provide the required flexibility in enabling strategic intent, transforming the organisation, or bridging the gap between business and IT units in the fast-paced and rapidly growing IT and business environments (Kitsios & Kamariotou, 2018; Kappelman, 2002; Cook, 1996). Thus, EA defines the scope, scale, and nature of required change to holistically transform an organisation (Gong et al., 2020; Niemi & Pekkola, 2020) Also, it helps to identify the resources that must become involved and provides a platform which is intended to consistently address activities, such as the IT solutions that enable and support governance and the process of business initiatives in an organisation (Riwanto & Andry, 2019; Armour et al., 2007).

Thus, EA is an approach that solidifies the bridging of the gaps that exist between business and IT units in an organisation (Kotusev et al., 2023). From a different angle, Tamm et al. (2022) describe EA as an important capability for managing IS/IT solutions. Additionally, EA supports the analysis of information flow, design of business-oriented processes, and enablement of IT solutions (Fernández-Cejas et al., 2022). EA is a framework that allows experts and leaders to govern the different aspects of an organisation to integrate business functions efficiently and effectively with IT solutions, from both operational and strategic perspectives (Sukur & Lind, 2022; Foorthuis et al., 2016). Thus, EA can be used as a strategic tool for addressing heterogeneous business activities and diverse IT solutions.

Because of the offering, EA is increasingly relied upon as a valuable instrument for operationalising and implementing events and activities. According to Constantinides et al. (2018), EA enables value-creating interactions between business and IT stakeholders in dynamically transforming an organisation. Thus, EA is increasingly embraced by many organisations in both the private and public sectors, to improve the value of business and IT solutions' return on investment (Dang & Pekkola, 2020). This includes relating design and processes of business and selection and deployment of IT solutions, which are enforced through policies, standards, and strategies. This could be attributed to the fact that policies and standards of EA are heterogeneous in that they influence each other across the domains (Iyamu, 2022a; Nardello et al., 2020; Fischer et al., 2010). As shown in Figure 3.1, the domains of EA are interdependent and have influence on each other during the processes of development, implementation, and practice.

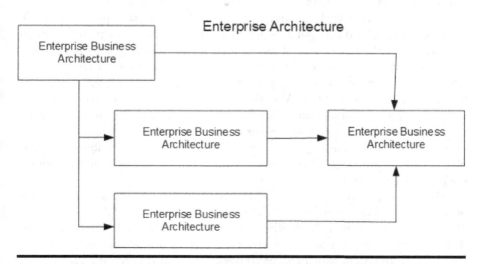

Figure 3.1   Relationship of EA Domains (Iyamu & Mphahlele, 2014).

EA is therefore inevitably viewed as a fundamental approach to strategic planning, systems design, software and hardware deployment, and multiple IT solutions production, which uphold different functionalities but are formed upon the same basic architectures (Iyamu, 2022a; Belfadel et al., 2022; Youngs et al., 1999). As a result, despite disparities in requirements from both the business and IT units, EA ensures uniformity, reuse, and manageability of change from the current state to the realisation of the strategic intent, and thereafter. Many of the processes and activities which occur in the computing environment of organisations are categorised into domains of EBA, EIA, ETA, and EAA. This includes selection, deployment, maintenance, management, and use of information systems and technologies and the services provided by the business units within the organisation.

In some organisations, EA serves as a tool for identifying, managing, and reusing processes and patterns through existing and planned architectures (Kochanthara et al., 2021; Mengmeng et al., 2019). This is not always as smooth as it is claimed because perspectives and contexts make the difference. According to Spewak (1992), from the development to implementation stages of EA, there are various challenges from both technical and non-technical perspectives. From corroborative viewpoint, Iyamu and Dewald (2012) suggest that the computing environment is structured as a hierarchical complex system within which heterogeneous activities take place and are managed by individuals and groups of employees to bring about change.

3.3 The Practice of Enterprise Architecture in Organisations

The scope of EA is the union of an organisation, the business re-engineering and development that is applied to it, and the technical domains that support and enable it. Thus, EA is defined through a pragmatic need: the need to design and redesign and to improve the functioning of the organisation continuously. In organisations, EA is applied in different contexts to enact governance, enable strategy, facilitate the transformation process, and aid the bridging of the gap that might exist between business and IT units. Also, through its domains, EA helps in the design, documentation, and implementation of process-oriented activities in an organisation. In addition, Ajer et al. (2021) argue that EA is a systematic way of designing, planning, and implementing processes and technology changes to address the complexity of an organisation. These views are often echoed in many quarters within the professional terrain.

Thus, the deployment and practice of EA are influenced by various factors, some of which are well documented in the literature (Kotusev et al., 2023; Tamm et al., 2022; Shaanika & Iyamu, 2018; Simon et al., 2013; Zachman, 1996). Specifically, this chapter focuses on factors considered critical to the deployment and practice of EA in an organisation, which are the strategic nature of EA (Iyamu, 2022a), governance (Ahmad et al., 2022), transformation purposes (Anthony Jnr et al., 2021;

Niemi & Pekkola, 2020), and bridging the gaps between business and IT units of an organisation (Dale & Scheepers, 2020; Zachman, 1997). These factors are considered critical based on their inter-relationship, interdependence, and nearly inseparable nature in the deployment and practice of EA in organisations.

3.4 Practising Enterprise Architecture through Governance

Each domain is guided by associated architecture governance, which comprises policies, principles, and standards (Ismagilova et al., 2022; Gong et al., 2020). Two fundamental activities happen in the existence of governance for EA purposes. First, the policies, principles, and standards are defined, developed, and implemented based on the requirements of both business and IT units of the organisation. Second, through governance, various initiatives and deliverables are developed, implemented, managed, and practised. The policies, principles, and standards depend upon and are driven by each other as depicted in Figure 3.2. The policies of the domains of the EA are intended to guide the organisations in their directions towards achieving competitive advantage over time. They are formulated based on the vision, strategy, and requirements of the organisation. The policies lead to the development of guiding principles. This means that principles are formulated based on existing policies and thereafter guide the development of standards. These are the boundaries within which business and technical requirements are articulated, planned and implemented (Batmetan, 2022). The principles reflect the collective will of the organisation.

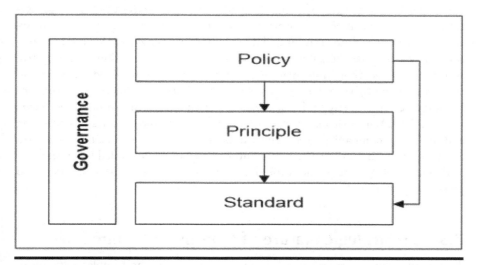

Figure 3.2 EA Domains Governance.

The purpose of the principles is to enable an organisation to take an incremental and iterative approach to transition into formal modelling, while allowing it to influence decision-making immediately and consistently. This increases the efficient and effective execution of tasks. The standards guide and provide detail about technology products and the way they are configured to deliver a reusable building block of IT solutions. Thus, principles and standards are used as evaluation criteria to direct decision-making more discretely and comprehensively in an environment (Fischer et al., 2010). However, the implementation is sometimes complex. Primarily, this is because the execution of the governance is often based on individuals' and groups' understanding. Therefore, meanings are associated with the main artefacts: organisational requirements, IT solutions, and business needs. Hence, it is highly significant to have a common understanding of these artefacts, which are often based on the goals and objectives of the organisation.

Technical requirements are as critical as the business requirements in the engineering and management of change, through EA governance. Technical requirements are defined, developed, and implemented in both the technical and application domains of EA (Spijkman et al., 2021). However, the drivers are derived from information and business architectures. Thus, many organisations are determined to establish and understand the current state of their environments, and to identify deficiencies, if any, through gap analysis. Particularly, senior executives are always keen to understand how EA could be applied to reasonably articulate their future business environments and strategies. Thereafter, they use the gap analysis method to assess the impact of change and associated risks on their businesses. To achieve this, the roles and responsibilities of the stakeholders become critically important.

Additionally, through domains, EA provides governance to many activities, such as data usage, deployment of IT solutions (software and infrastructure), and general management of computing activities and processes in an organisation. Consequently, based on governance, an organisation can have a better understanding, which leads to an informed decision (Masuda et al., 2018). For example, through governance, decisions can be improved in the selection of innovative concepts, such as digital information use, server consolidation, and virtualisation that are dictated by the requirements of the organisation. If practised, governance becomes a culture, a way of doing things in the environment. Through its change process, the EA approach attempts to find different and better ways of enhancing and increasing companies' productivity in competitive ways that can be enveloped as a culture (Iyamu, 2015). Therefore, innovation should be guided by governance as defined by EA. This includes the selection and deployment of technology and process engineering.

3.5 The Strategic Nature of Enterprise Architecture

The organisational requirements lead to the development and implementation of the EA architecture strategic process (ASP). The ASP, as shown in Figure 3.3, is a four-step approach, which comprises the current state, requirements, checklist, and the desired state. Purposely, the approach can be used to enforce the practice of EA in an organisation. The ASP is iterative, as depicted in the figure; it begins with the current state and reaches a desired state. In the final step of the first iteration, the desired state is analysed against the current state to detect and understand the gap and deficiency that could affect the process of achieving the organisational goals and objectives. For improved managerial responsibilities, EA further facilitates the assessment and process of value in the current business environment and the conception of strategic alternatives being considered at the time.

One of the intricate challenges in managing change is gaining an accurate view of the current state. Shanks et al. (2018) suggest that it becomes more obvious that EA is critical and significant in providing a more accurate view of the status quo. In addition to other benefits, this could lie in the potency as argued by Georgiadis and Poels (2021) that EA, from its strategic approach standpoint, facilitates business design, planning processes to ensure business continuity, compliance of IT solutions, and risk management. As shown in Figure 3.3, once the status quo is identified, an action plan follows and the organisation's requirements are gathered in a documented manner, and appropriately.

Employing the ASP in the practice of EA in an organisation entails three linear steps. First, the function of the ASP components is defined. The functions of each component of the ASP are tabulated in Table 5.1, which is complementary to

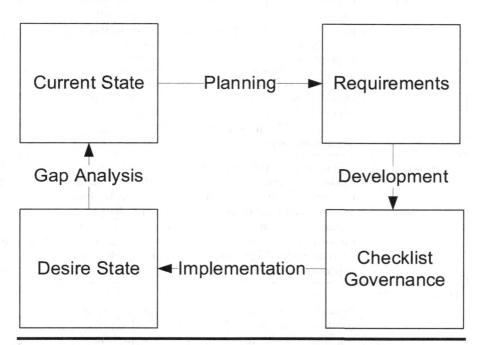

Figure 3.3 Architectural Strategic Process.

Figure 3.3. Second, each of the four components of the ASP is enabled by planning, development, implementation, and gap analysis, respectively. This means that each domain of EA applies the ASP approach. Third, each component of the ASP defines a unique set of standards and templates for its deliverables. By implication, there should be validations from one step (component) to another in achieving the aims of the ASP in an organisation. The ASP approach is iterative, reflective of a checklist and accompanied by an action plan. Through this process, an organisation can comfortably consolidate technologies and business solutions from a tactical to strategic intent. The possible actions are contained in functions as presented in Table 3.1. The actions and plans are different, depending on the domain.

The current state is reflective of the present (as-is) circumstances of artefacts, from the standpoint of both business and IT units (Gampfer et al., 2018). For each of the architecture areas, which consists of technical and non-technical factors, the current state is identified and documented. A standard format of documentation (template) is applied to enable consistency, uniformity, readability, and an

Table 3.1   Functions of Architectural Strategic Process

Change Process	Functionality
Current State	Inventory and documentation of existing business and technical artefacts. Processes and IT are put into perspectives and categories, through which specific change can be engineered. Also, this helps to understand roles, responsibilities, and the nature of available resources.
Requirements	Business and IT architectural requirements gathering. This includes components relationship, business, and IT alignments. It involves an understanding of functions and events, which require enabling and supporting organisational goals and objectives.
Governance	This consists of policies, principles, and standards, which guide the selection (built or buy), deployment, and use of IS/IT artefacts. It involves the formulation of business processes and information flow. It guides design, replacement strategy, and proof of concept of both business and technology activities in the organisations. It is used for technology compliance, which guides testing and implementation.
Desired State	The governance assists to reach the desired state. It is validated against the current state, and a gap analysis is conducted. The desired state is intended to help the organisation with sustainability and competitiveness.

understanding to a greater height by the general audience in an organisation. It serves as an input for the assessment of the current state during the architecture development, implementation, and practice. Thereafter, the domains of the EA are completed, as the foundation from which gaps are identified. The current state of inventory is continually updated in an iterative approach.

Based on the business and technology requirements, as well as environmental and industry trends, the EA defines end-of-life for each of the business and technological artefacts in an organisation (Rahmanian et al., 2022; Kitsios & Kamariotou, 2018; Hauder et al., 2013). Implications of the component are viewed and reflected upon in terms of the impact EA has or could potentially have on an organisation's events, processes, and activities. Within the architecture, the implications as foreseen on other related or depended-on components can also be examined. For example, the changing of a server could have an impact on the software and other IT solutions it hosts.

Planning is conducted in both the business and IT units within the domains of the EA in an organisation that deploys it. According to Georgiadis and Poels (2021), the planning phase ensures the sustainability of the support and the enabling of the IT solutions' processes and activities. Also, the planning constitutes and defines how methods, policies, and principles are formulated; how employees' skillsets are managed; how knowledge and business processes are used; how hardware, software, and networks are applied; and how applications, data, and interfaces are employed. The level of detail represented depends on the phase, maturity, scope, and requirements of the organisation.

The final phase of the process is a transition to the deployment of IT solutions. It consists of conducting gap analyses across the architecture areas to determine corrective measures, develop prioritised migration plans, and finally draw up implementation plans. These measures and plans indicate which projects can deliver the project or activity towards the desired state. Iteratively, the initiated projects are required to transition the organisation from its current state to the future state.

3.6 Transforming Organisation through Enterprise Architecture

In many organisations, transformation or transformative agenda is often influenced by both internal and external factors. Anthony Jnr et al. (2021) argue that EA provides a mechanism to support the planning, management, and improvement processes of transformation. Some of the internal factors are business and IT strategies, roles, and responsibilities, technical know-how, and financial budget. Technology innovations, industry trends, market competitiveness, and government policies are some of the external factors which influence processes and activities in many organisations. Based on the influencing factors, each domain provides a unique view of the enterprise, leading to its capabilities to make a difference. Also, transformation using EA happens at both business and IT levels through requirements modelling and scheming.

Primarily, the EBA provides the tools, models, and techniques, which participants employ to manage the impact and implication of change on business processes and the information of clients and partners (Correani et al., 2020). Similarly, the EIA supports and enables the management of change in information flow and exchange between applications as well as processes; the ETA facilitates technology innovation to manage the transformation of IT solutions; and the EAA enables the development and portfolio management of business and technical applications (Laumann & Tambo, 2018). Thus, the level of success or failure of EA could be measured by the effect of transformative outcomes as engineered by EA in an organisation. The measurement includes the pace of transformation or change and the difference it engineers in an organisation.

Additionally, in many organisations, transformation is engineered by processes, information flows, business functions, and technology innovations, as well as personnel movements from one unit to another (Iyamu, 2015). Often, transformation is inevitable, primarily because it aids renewal and enhances competitiveness. What is needed is how transformation could be managed to promote efficiency and reduce deficiency in an organisation (Gong et al., 2020; Kaidalova et al., 2018). The frequency of transformation is even more challenging to an organisation and its employees and general stakeholders. This is mainly because of the impact and implications it can potentially have on the current and future states of an organisation. Policy, principle, and standards guide transformation.

The business requirement is a key driver of transformation in an organisation. It becomes more intriguing when it is implemented through an EA iterative process. The requirements are often extracted from the organisation's strategies, which include operational goals and strategic intents being pursued at the time. Riwanto and Andry (2019) explain how requirements fundamentally foster strategies and enable alignments between business artefacts and IT solutions. The requirements focus mainly on the strategic objectives of the organisation, which are transformed into day-to-day operations. The requirements also include the drivers and trends of the organisation's vision and strategy. The drivers are influenced by factors such as quality, time, economics, and environmental trends. EA is deployed to achieve the flexibility needed to address change in the fast-paced and rapidly growing IT and business environments. This approach is followed with the intention of engineering and managing the organisational needs. This includes facilitating change through the adaptation of innovations of technology to develop a business process model in a uniform and flexible manner. This could materialise and be successful only if EA aligns with the business strategy and has the buy-in of the business executives.

The technical requirements are another quintessential driver of transformation in many organisations. Constantinides et al. (2018) suggest that technical requirements are a source of strategic opportunity and competitiveness. The requirements are usually based on business processes and activities, which are meant to support and enable a competitive advantage. The requirements drive the introduction, selection, and deployment of new technology by focusing on function activities, scalability, compatibility, and interoperability. Furthermore, the technical requirements focus on re-engineering the current state of IT solutions. It translates the business requirements into a common terminology, which enables a consistent semantic meaning across IS/IT in an organisation. These are the primary focus areas of the ETA and EAA domains. Through this approach, for example, technologies are certified as usable or obsolete from the perspectives of governance and manageability. As a result, a change in any technology often affects business events, processes, and activities.

3.7 Bridging the Gap through Enterprise Architecture Domains

The success or failure of EA heavily relies on alignment, bridging the gap between the business and IT units, and specialists, including the executive personnel in an organisation (Ajer et al., 2021; Mengmeng et al., 2019). One of the strengths of the EA approach is to foster and encourage cohesion between the business and IT units on a common organisational goal and purpose. The understanding typically concerns a change of processes, management, methods, design of IT solutions, and pattern and selection of business and technological artefacts. According to Chitsa and Iyamu (2020), EA helps to provide leverage and bridge the gap between the enabled and the enabler. EA is instrumental in facilitating a closer relationship, as well as bridging the gap between the business and IT units through the sharing of a common view and vision of what has to be done and how tasks should be allocated and executed. The relationship makes it possible for the domains to align with both the business and IT strategies of an organisation.

One of the main requirements or justification for deploying EA in many organisations is rationalisation, purportedly to bridge the gap that might exist between the business and IT units. This is the rationale that is often used as a selling point. The promoters habitually emphasise and prioritise the need to bridge gaps and strengthen how the business and IT units interact towards achieving organisational goals and objectives (Tamm et al., 2022; Roelens et al., 2019). This is accentuated during the process of developing, implementing, and practising EA, but is often affected by a rapid change of events. To achieve the required flexibility to handle the fast-paced IT, continuously bridging the gaps between the focal units, business and IT is inevitable. This is often expressed as a serious challenge in many organisations. As a result, there is an emphasis on business vision and requirements, and how they are extracted, documented, and achieved.

Bridging the gap between business and IT units does not happen in a vacuum; it involves the essential factors and can be carried out through different channels (domains). From the literature, the most critical factors that are required in

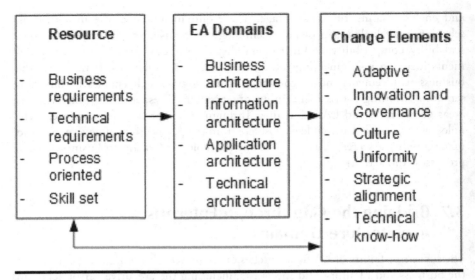

Figure 3.4 Bridging the gap through EA Domains.

engineering change that can bridge the business and IT units are business requirements, technical requirements, process orientation, and skillsets (Al-Kharusi et al.,
2021; Hinkelmann et al., 2016). Logically, the bridge event is through the domains
of EA. As shown in Figure 3.4 as an exemplar, the factors are mapped with the
domains and the elements necessary for bridging gaps, engineered by constant
interaction among the actors from both the business and IT units of an organisation. The mapping is carried out to make sense of the inter-relationship between
the factors and their interpretation, as well as how they can engineer interactions
through the EA domains in an organisation.

The domains are not independent of each other; they consist of business deeds
and IT solutions' activities of an organisation (Iyamu, 2015). Change to one domain
has an affect and influence on others. The domains experts collaborate and must
ensure that the contents of the domains corroborate with each other in their under-
takings and deliverables. This is illustrated with the linking arrows in Figure 3.4.
Typically, business pursuits of improvement or reactions depend upon how well the
closing of a gap is systematically engineered. The discussion that follows should be
read together with Figure 3.4 to get a full appreciation of how certain elements and
factors are used to interact with the domains to effect change in closing any existing
gaps between focal units in an organisation.

3.7.1 Enterprise Business Architecture

Based on an organisation's vision and strategy, business requirements are formulated. Roelens et al. (2019) viewed this as the realisation of a strategic fit within the

business architecture, which is an important challenge for organisations. The EBA approach is used to develop the principles, standards, and policies in guiding the development and implementation of a response plan for the organisational vision and strategy, which requires iterative interaction and execution of plans between business and IT units. It also ensures a uniformity of processes between the units, when possible, across an organisation. In addition, the EBA imbues close ties between business and IT units in two main ways.

First, the 'journey' of bridging the gap begins with the executive team and the managers of line of business and IT units through the development and use of strategic models intended to adapt to the changing needs of the organisation. Second, the gap between strategy development and tactical decision-making is a shortcoming of many strategic plans. Thus, EBA eliminates much of the guesswork for operational managers of both business and IT units by interpreting the impact of strategic plans at operational levels, from the perspectives of both business and IT units. This includes the prioritisation of plans, collectively. This is ensured by providing necessary guidance and concerns the organisation's information assets meant for knowledge workers, information processors, IT application developers, infrastructure managers, and executives. Correani et al. (2020) emphasise that through business architecture, organisations can create appropriate value.

3.7.2 Enterprise Information Architecture

The elements as shown in Figure 3.4 are intended to improve communication and corroboration of actions of business and IT units to effect change through their impact on the organisation's key factors. The EIA approach is used to define the availability and use of information for business requirements and other key business processes, as shown in Figure 3.4. The approach enables the underlying processes and skillsets for changing needs in organisations. Venkatesan and Sridhar (2019) suggest that the architecture provides tools and methods for the interrelationship between enterprise business processes, stakeholders, and information classes from both business and IT perspectives. Primarily, the EIA engineers bridge gaps between business and IT through two main techniques.

EIA is used to bridge gaps between business and IT units is by collaboratively defining the sources of information and ensuring the availability and use of the information by the key business processes, which are enabled and supported by the underlying application and technical architectures (Iyamu, 2015). Thereafter, identify the information flows that are intended for optimisation (increased velocity, density, and reach) to foster an inter-relationship and interaction between the business and IT units in the organisation. Consequently, the information entities that need to be defined and used consistently across the information value chain to increase the value of information across the organisations and the external transactions can be achieved.

3.7.3 Enterprise Technical Architecture

In deploying new technologies, which are usually based on functional and utility advantages, the ETA approach is used to facilitate an alignment between business and technical requirements. This fosters the relationship and interaction between the business and IT units. Also, it ensures compatibility and interoperability with strategic IT solutions. However, Ismagilova et al. (2022) provide a subtle warning that technical sophistication can also create gaps between the enabled and the enabler if not properly managed. These points are key to rapid response and continual changes in many organisations. Engaging with business helps ETA architects to provide configuration standards and guidelines on how standard products can be applied, supported, and managed within an environment. ETA is adopted to manage IT solutions through collaboration between business and IT units.

Through interactions, the business unit delivers requirements to provide the principles, standards, configurations, processes, and governance mechanisms which can be used to establish and maintain adaptive IT solutions and application reuse methods (Iyamu, 2015). Additionally, ETA drives the introduction of new technologies, based not only on functional and utility advantages, but also on compatibility and interoperability with existing architectures, to enhance business processes. Robustly, this is key to the rapid implementation of configuration standards for IT solutions, guidelines in applying standards to products, and principles to integrations (Fischer et al., 2010). It is suggested that this provides both a view of the recommended technology and a basis for assessing the impact of new and replacement technologies within the context of an organisation.

3.7.4 Enterprise Application Architecture

EAA defines how software applications and systems are designed and deployed, usually guided by requirement outcomes from the interaction between business and IT units. Essentially, this is to ensure that the applications and systems cooperate or coexist with each other on the same platform and environment to avoid business disruption. The EAA provides standards and guidelines that support the building, reuse, and buying of robust applications for business and technical productivity gains. The EAA reveals a separation between external and inbuilt services in an application (Kaidalova et al., 2018), which should help bridge some of the gaps between business and IT. These provide the opportunity to employ the EAA approach to manage the application through an oriented process, innovation, and adaptiveness. Other primary focus areas of the EAA are to define gaps, provide a framework, ensure technology fit, and enable the reuse of applications for business purposes.

From collaboration and corroboration in requirements between business and IT units, EAA defines the gap between the existing and desired systems' functions to satisfy EBA and EIA requirements. In addition, the architecture provides a framework for migration by taking into account not only functional requirements but also an investment strategy in IT solutions (Katuu, 2018). Resulting of interaction between business and IT units, the process ensures the 'technology fit' of existing and planned systems, which relate and interact with ETA and the entire technology infrastructure in an environment. EAA engineers' reuse is considered a key component for success in the drive to facilitate change. The change focuses on guiding developers towards systemic analysis, design, and development of business components and objects.

3.8 Implications of Deploying Enterprise Architecture

Consequently, three implications are associated with the deployment and practice of EA from this chapter's perspective. The implications are in the use of a template, which is practice-oriented; cultural effect on the actors in conducting their various tasks and in the deployment and practice of EA; and sourcing skillsets and appropriately assigning tasks to the personnel.

3.8.1 The Use of a Template

Each of the EA domains should have specific templates designed to help achieve both business and IT goals and objectives from the following perspectives: (i) review of the current state, mainly to detect deficiency; and (ii) identification of gaps and planning for the future, primarily to create opportunities. The review is expected to be a major process which could be carried out as frequently as in every quarter in an organisation. However, the frequency of such activity depends on the complexity of the environment.

Templates can also be used for reviewing and predicting events in each of the domains. The iterations of the review process make the areas covered to become more stable, uniform, and easily accessible. This is because the templates reduce guesswork and trial-and-error processes, including selecting information and technology artefacts and deploying them. This encourages and helps to bridge the relationship gap between architects and other employees in the IT unit, on the one hand, and between the IT and business units, on the other.

3.8.2 The Culture Effect

The rules, norms, and procedures together create a specific culture, which can be institutionalised over time in an organisation. Institutionalisation is the process whereby practice is assimilated into the norm. It is covered in Chapter 12 of this book. In an institutionalised state, it becomes difficult to disassociate, dismantle, or redesign a process or events. This affects the human actors while carrying out their responsibilities. Also, it often reflects in the use of technology artefacts, including support and management. For example, in some organisations, no software can be installed on the network server without written approval from the domain expert, who is often a member of the architecture team. This becomes the norm. It is intended to help change individual attitudes and approaches in carrying out tasks in a standardised manner within the computing environment of an organisation.

Culture is one of the key elements through which EA impacts change in many organisations. Within the scope of the organisational requirements, EA is developed, implemented, and practised. Certain factors of a personal nature need a particular organisational culture in which to thrive, or to feed on internal policies. Similarly, certain internal policies would only be possible within a particular organisational culture. EA provides a uniform process for the selection and deployment of technology infrastructures, as well as for the documentation of the current state of business processes, data, and infrastructures. In addition, EA is essential in maintaining consistency regarding future states of technology artefacts in organisations.

3.8.3 The Required Skillset

In terms of responsibilities and accountabilities, there are domain architects managed by senior architects, often titled architecture managers or team leaders in some organisations. EA is managed by the chief architect by the structure of many organisations.

However, a lack of skillsets poses a serious challenge, as well, especially in the area of business architecture. Many organisations that deploy or intend to deploy EA do not have enough skilled people to carry out the tasks as defined by the concept of EA. Some organisations fare better as they continue to build a resource base, as well as develop an employees' retention strategy. However, the cost of the retention of people with specialised skills could also be prohibitive. As a result, some organisations find it difficult to implement some changes due to a lack of technical know-how. This has impacts and influences on productivity and competitiveness, which EA is intended to promote.

3.9 Summary

Neither change nor the development, implementation, and practice of enterprise architecture (EA) are simple in any organisation. This is usually measured by the value the practice of EA brings to the organisation. This chapter demonstrates and provides more insights into how return on investment depends on how well business and technical requirements are articulated, and how people interpret the processes and the technologies they make use of, to support, and enable business activities for competitiveness. In addition to the objective of the chapter, it helps to gain a better understanding of how the requirements for developing and implementing EA are gathered in organisations, the impact of each architecture domain on the organisations' processes and activities, the differences which the development and implementation of EA bring into organisations, and how the differences which are engineered by EA are identified and incorporated into the organisational structure.

The other contribution of this chapter arises from implications for the decision-makers who are responsible for sponsoring EA, including the architects who design, develop, and implement the approach. This chapter comprehensively highlights that decision-makers need to understand the functions, dynamics, and causes of what, why, and how the practice of EA brings about value, through change, to both the business and information technology (IT) units of an organisation. Additionally, the chapter aims to be significant to decision-makers, professionals, and information systems researchers, including managers and employees in the computing environment of organisations. It is expected that the key contribution will arise from an understanding of the fundamental elements through which the EA approach can be better practised in an environment. Through this, a considerable benefit of the contribution of non-technical factors in the deployment of EA is gained.

References

Ahmad, N. A., Drus, S. M., & Kasim, H. (2022). Factors of organizational adoption of enterprise architecture in Malaysian public sector: A multi group analysis. *Journal of Systems and Information Technology, 24*(4), 331–360.

Ajer, A. K. S., Hustad, E., & Vassilakopoulou, P. (2021). Enterprise architecture operationalization and institutional pluralism: The case of the Norwegian Hospital sector. *Information Systems Journal, 31*(4), 610–645.

Al-Kharusi, H., Miskon, S., & Bahari, M. (2021). Enterprise architects and stakeholders alignment framework in enterprise architecture development. *Information Systems and e-Business Management, 19*(1), 137–181.

Armour, F., Kaisler, S., & Bitner, J. (2007, January 3–6). Enterprise architecture: Challenges and implementations. In *The proceedings of the 40th international conference on system sciences* (pp. 217–217). IEEE.

Anthony Jnr, B., Petersen, S. A., Helfert, M., Ahlers, D., & Krogstie, J. (2021). Modeling pervasive platforms and digital services for smart urban transformation using an enterprise architecture framework. *Information Technology & People, 34*(4), 1285–1312.

Batmetan, J. R. (2022). Model enterprise architecture for information technology services in universities. *International Journal of Information Technology and Education, 1*(4), 18–34.

Beese, J., Aier, S., Haki, K., & Winter, R. (2022). The impact of enterprise architecture management on information systems architecture complexity. *European Journal of Information Systems*, 1–21.

Belfadel, A., Amdouni, E., Laval, J., Cherifi, C. B., & Moalla, N. (2022). Towards software reuse through an enterprise architecture-based software capability profile. *Enterprise Information Systems*, *16*(1), 29–70.

Chitsa, F., & Iyamu, T. (2020). Towards enterprise technical architecture for the implementation of the South African NHIA. *Advances in Science, Technology and Engineering Systems Journal*, *5*(2), 724–728.

Constantinides, P., Henfridsson, O., & Parker, G. G. (2018). Introduction—platforms and infrastructures in the digital age. *Information Systems Research*, *29*(2), 381–400.

Cook, M. A. (1996). *Building enterprise information architectures: Reengineering information systems*. Prentice-Hall Inc.

Correani, A., De Massis, A., Frattini, F., Petruzzelli, A. M., & Natalicchio, A. (2020). Implementing a digital strategy: Learning from the experience of three digital transformation projects. *California Management Review*, *62*(4), 37–56.

Dale, M., & Scheepers, H. (2020). Enterprise architecture implementation as interpersonal connection: Building support and commitment. *Information Systems Journal*, *30*(1), 150–184.

Dang, D., & Pekkola, S. (2020). Institutional perspectives on the process of enterprise architecture adoption. *Information Systems Frontiers*, *22*(6), 1433–1445.

Dwipriyoko, E., Bon, A. T. B., & Sukono, F. (2019). Enterprise architecture planning as new generation cooperatives research methods. *Journal of Physics: Conference Series*, *1179*(1), 012094. IOP Publishing.

Fahim, P. B., An, R., Rezaei, J., Pang, Y., Montreuil, B., & Tavasszy, L. (2021). An information architecture to enable track-and-trace capability in Physical Internet ports. *Computers in Industry*, *129*, 103443.

Fernández-Cejas, M., Pérez-González, C. J., Roda-García, J. L., & Colebrook, M. (2022). CURIE: Towards an ontology and enterprise architecture of a CRM conceptual model. *Business & Information Systems Engineering*, 1–29.

Fischer, C., Winter, R., & Aier, S. (2010). What is an enterprise architecture principle? In *Computer and information science 2010* (pp. 193–205). Springer.

Foorthuis, R., Van Steenbergen, M., Brinkkemper, S., & Bruls, W. A. (2016). A theory building study of enterprise architecture practices and benefits. *Information Systems Frontiers*, *18*(3), 541–564.

Gampfer, F., Jürgens, A., Müller, M., & Buchkremer, R. (2018). Past, current and future trends in enterprise architecture—A view beyond the horizon. *Computers in Industry*, *100*, 70–84.

Georgiadis, G., & Poels, G. (2021). Enterprise architecture management as a solution for addressing general data protection regulation requirements in a big data context: A systematic mapping study. *Information Systems and e-Business Management*, *19*(1), 313–362.

Gong, Y., Yang, J., & Shi, X. (2020). Towards a comprehensive understanding of digital transformation in government: Analysis of flexibility and enterprise architecture. *Government Information Quarterly*, *37*(3), 101487.

Griffo, C., Almeida, J. P. A., Guizzardi, G., & Nardi, J. C. (2021). Service contract modeling in enterprise architecture: An ontology-based approach. *Information Systems*, *101*, 101454.

Haki, K., & Legner, C. (2021). The mechanics of enterprise architecture principles. *Journal of the Association for Information Systems*, *22*(5), 1334–1375.

Hauder, M., Schulz, C., Roth, S., & Matthes, F. (2013, June 5–8). Organizational factors influencing enterprise architecture management challenges. In *21st European conference on information systems (ECIS)*. Association for Information Systems Press.

Hinkelmann, K., Gerber, A., Karagiannis, D., Thoenssen, B., Van der Merwe, A., & Woitsch, R. (2016). A new paradigm for the continuous alignment of business and IT: Combining enterprise architecture modelling and enterprise ontology. *Computers in Industry*, *79*, 77–86.

Ismagilova, E., Hughes, L., Rana, N. P., & Dwivedi, Y. K. (2022). Security, privacy and risks within smart cities: Literature review and development of a smart city interaction framework. *Information Systems Frontiers*, *24*(2), 393–414.

Iyamu, T. (2015). *Information technology enterprise architecture: From concept to practice* (2nd ed.). Heidelberg Press. ISBN: 8-3-659-61206-0.

Iyamu, T. (2022a). *Enterprise architecture for strategic management of modern IT solutions*. Routledge, CRC Press.

Iyamu, T. (2022b). Creating a technical architecture framework for m-voting application. *African Journal of Science, Technology, Innovation and Development*, *14*(1), 86–93.

Iyamu, T., & Dewald, R. (2012). The use of structuration theory and actor network theory for analysis. *International Journal of Actor-Network Theory and Technological Innovation*, *9*(4), 217–228.

Iyamu, T., & Mphahlele, L. (2014). The impact of organisational structure on enterprise architecture deployment. *Journal of Systems and Information Technology*, *16*(1), 2–19.

Jonkers, H., Lankhorst, M. M., ter Doest, H. W., Arbab, F., Bosma, H., & Wieringa, R. J. (2006). Enterprise architecture: Management tool and blueprint for the organisation. *Information Systems Frontiers*, *8*(2), 63–68.

Kaidalova, J., Kurt, S., & Ulf, S. (2018). How digital transformation affects enterprise architecture management—a case study. *International Journal of Information Systems and Project Management*, *6*(3), 5–18.

Kappelman, L. A. (2002). We've only just begun to use IT wisely. *Management Information Systems (MIS) Quarterly*, *887*, 116–902.

Katuu, S. (2018, December 10–13). The utility of enterprise architecture to records and archives specialists. In *2018 IEEE international conference on big data (big data)* (pp. 2702–2710). IEEE.

Kitsios, F., & Kamariotou, M. (2018). Business strategy modelling based on enterprise architecture: A state of the art review. *Business Process Management Journal*, *25*(4), 606–624.

Kochanthara, S., Rood, N., Saberi, A. K., Cleophas, L., Dajsuren, Y., & van den Brand, M. (2021). A functional safety assessment method for cooperative automotive architecture. *Journal of Systems and Software*, *179*, 110991.

Kotusev, S., Kurnia, S., & Dilnutt, R. (2023). Enterprise architecture artifacts as boundary objects: An empirical analysis. *Information and Software Technology*, *155*, 107108.

Laumann, F., & Tambo, T. (2018). Enterprise architecture for a facilitated transformation from a linear to a circular economy. *Sustainability*, *10*(11), 3882.

Löhe, J., & Legner, C. (2014). Overcoming implementation challenges in enterprise architecture management: A design theory for architecture-driven IT Management (ADRIMA). *Information Systems and e-Business Management*, *12*(1), 101–137.

Mack, R., & Frey, N. (2002). *Six building blocks for creating real IT strategies*. Gartner Inc. Retrieved April 14, 2010, from http://gartner.com/technology/research.jsp

Masuda, Y., Shirasaka, S., Yamamoto, S., & Hardjono, T. (2018). Architecture board practices in adaptive enterprise architecture with digital platform: A case of global healthcare enterprise. *International Journal of Enterprise Information Systems (IJEIS)*, *14*(1), 1–20.

Masuda, Y., Zimmermann, A., Bass, M., Nakamura, O., Shirasaka, S., & Yamamoto, S. (2021). Adaptive enterprise architecture process for global companies in a digital IT era. *International Journal of Enterprise Information Systems (IJEIS)*, *17*(2), 21–43.

Mengmeng, Z., Honghui, C. H. E. N., & Junxian, L. I. U. (2019). Resource allocation approach to associate business-IT alignment to enterprise architecture design. *Journal of Systems Engineering and Electronics*, *30*(2), 343–351.

Nardello, M., Han, S., Møller, C., & Gøtze, J. (2020). Incorporating process and data heterogeneity in enterprise architecture: Extended AMA4EA in an international manufacturing company. *Computers in Industry*, *115*, 103178.

Niemi, E., & Pekkola, S. (2020). The benefits of enterprise architecture in organizational transformation. *Business & Information Systems Engineering*, *62*(6), 585–597.

Radeke, F. (2010, August 12–15). Awaiting explanation in the field of enterprise architecture management. In *The proceedings of Americas conference on information systems (AMCIS)*. Association for Information Systems Press.

Rahmanian, M., Nassiri, R., Mohsenzadeh, M., & Ravanmehr, R. (2022). Test case generation for enterprise business services based on enterprise architecture design. *The Journal of Supercomputing*, 1–31.

Riwanto, R. E., & Andry, J. F. (2019). Enterprise architectures enable of business strategy and IS/IT alignment in manufacturing using TOGAF ADM framework. *International Journal of Information Technology and Business*, *1*(2), 7–7.

Roelens, B., Steenacker, W., & Poels, G. (2019). Realizing strategic fit within the business architecture: The design of a process-goal alignment modeling and analysis technique. *Software & Systems Modeling*, *18*(1), 631–662.

Shaanika, I., & Iyamu, T. (2018). Developing the enterprise architecture for the Namibian government. *The Electronic Journal of Information Systems in Developing Countries*, *84*(3), e12028.

Shanks, G., Gloet, M., Someh, I. A., Frampton, K., & Tamm, T. (2018). Achieving benefits with enterprise architecture. *The Journal of Strategic Information Systems*, *27*(2), 139–156.

Simon, D., Fischbach, K., & Schoder, D. (2013). An exploration of enterprise architecture research. *Communications of the Association for Information Systems*, *32*(1), 1–72.

Spewak, S. H. (1992). *Enterprise architecture planning: Developing a blueprint for data, applications and technology*. John Wiley & Sons Inc.

Spijkman, T., Molenaar, S., Dalpiaz, F., & Brinkkemper, S. (2021). Alignment and granularity of requirements and architecture in agile development: A functional perspective. *Information and Software Technology*, *133*, 106535.

Sukur, A., & Lind, M. L. (2022). Enterprise architecture to achieve information technology flexibility and enterprise agility. *International Journal of Information Systems and Social Change (IJISSC)*, *13*(2), 1–20.

Tamm, T., Seddon, P. B., & Shanks, G. (2022). How enterprise architecture leads to organisational benefits. *International Journal of Information Management*, *67*, 102554.

Venkatesan, D., & Sridhar, S. (2019). A rationale for the choice of enterprise architecture method and software technology in a software driven enterprise. *International Journal of Business Information Systems*, *32*(3), 272–311.

Youngs, R., Redmond-Pyle, D., Spaas, P., & Kahan, E. (1999). A standard for architecture description. *IBM Systems Journal, 38*(1), 32–50.

Zachman, J. A. (1987). A framework for information systems. *IBM Systems Journal, 26*(3), 276–283.

Zachman, J. A. (1996). Enterprise architecture: The view beyond 2000. In *The proceedings of 7th international users group conference for warehouse repository architecture development*. Technology Transfer Institute.

Zachman, J. A. (1997). Enterprise architecture: The issue of the century. *Database Programming and Design, 10*(3), 44–53.

Chapter 4

The Deployment of Enterprise Business Architecture for Organisation Enhancement

4.1 Introduction

Organisations are continually faced with complex and unwieldy challenges in assessing and articulating the changes needed to implement business strategies at a more detailed (operational) level (Zachman, 1996). Within this premise, enterprise business architecture (EBA) is sought as a possible solution to addressing challenges in many organisations (Iyamu, 2022). The EBA is one of the domains of enterprise architecture (EA) (Proper & Lankhorst, 2015), and it focuses on business processes and structure in an organisation (Jayakrishnan et al., 2020). The concept of EBA has been highly debated and discussed particularly by information systems (IS) and information technology (IT) specialists, in business and academic domains, over the last two decades (Gonzalez-Lopez & Bustos, 2019; Versteeg & Bouwman, 2006).

The lingering debate and discourse about the usefulness and value of EBA could be ascribed to its potential benefits, which are considered to be critically important in the wake of the continuing prevalence of competitiveness (Amit & Zott, 2015). Fischer et al. (2015) suggest that business architecture is purposeful to accelerate

DOI: 10.1201/9781003390879-4

change through processes and modelling. Another face of the argument is that without EBA, there would be a lack of cohesion between processes and inconsistencies in operational patterns of organisations (Hoogervorst & Dietz, 2015).

Though much has been posited about the potential benefits of EBA for organisations, little has been seen and achieved in reality and practice, so the debate rages on. In the assessment of Rouhani and Kharazmi (2012), there is insufficient attention towards EBA in organisations. Iyamu and Shaanika (2022) reaffirmed that assessment ten years later. Within this context, organisations are continually faced with challenges, such as rapidly evolving technologies and business needs affecting the composition and meaning associated with the EBA (Andini, 2021). This could be attributed to many factors, such as the complexity of some enterprises (Whittle & Myrick, 2016), as well as a lack of understanding and feeble clarification of the concept (Iyamu, 2015).

The theorised natured of the EBA concept can be linked to some of the constraining challenges identified in both organisations and academic research in some quarters (Iyamu, 2022; Saint-Louis & Lapalme, 2018). Gromoff et al. (2012) suggest that it is important to connect the academic theoretical view of business architecture with the actual demands of business service delivery (practical view). Some of the challenges of business architecture in many organisations arise from an incomplete understanding of the concept in organisations (Anthony Jnr, 2021; Lapalme, 2012). The reason for such incomplete understanding is unclear; hence, it is necessary to underpin this chapter with an ontology stance through an interpretive approach.

Ontology is a branch of philosophy concerned with the study of what exists (Jurisica et al., 2004), which includes the existence of EBA in an organisation. What is known to exist about EBA is socially constructed. Hennink et al. (2011) summarise social construction through interpretivism, which is suggested to be concerned with the fact that reality is constructed subjectively by social actors, in a social context, through social interaction. Ontology focuses on the nature of social reality, which includes claims about what exists and several views of the object or subject (Byrne, 2017), such as the deployment and practice of EBA in an organisation. Thus, ontological meanings are employed to understand the definitions and how the concept of EBA is collectively interrelated to impose structure on a domain, as well as constrain interpretations of terms of its existence in organisations. According to Coghlan and Brydon-Miller (2014), ontology covers the meaning of what exists or can be used to establish the exact stance of what lies underneath the nature of reality.

It is therefore positioned that a fresh perspective and new approach are required for the organisational design and operations of EBA, based on its deployment challenges. Thus, the question is, how can the EBA be developed, implemented and practised to enhance the business of an organisation? The question was answered through its clarification of the key tenets and provides a practical guide on how to develop and implement the EBA, which could be used in addressing organisational needs and challenges. This chapter is intended to assist professionals in holistically viewing and gaining a better understanding of how EBA can be developed, implemented, and practised in an organisation.

The remainder of the chapter is structured into five main sections, beginning with an introductory section. A review of literature that focuses on EBA in organisations is presented in the second section. Next, is the section that covers two perspectives: clarification of EBA tenets and a fresh attempt to comprehend the concept of EBA. In the section that follows, a guide on how to deploy and practise EBA is presented and discussed. Finally, the contributions of the chapter to both business and academia, from theoretical and practical perspectives, are highlighted.

4.2 Enterprise Architecture in Organisations

For many years, the EBA has interestingly been ontologically constructed by actors' interpretive understanding. From some of those constructs, Ren and Glissmann (2012) suggest that business architecture provides a comprehensive approach which can be used to identify information assets that are relevant to an organisation's competitiveness, on one hand; on another hand, Holm et al. (2014) argue that business architecture enables a means of model transformations. According to McDavid (1999), it provides an architectural view of business and ways in which EBA can be used for organisational goals and objectives. However, the criticality lies in the premise that the EBA is aimed at representing organisational strategy, which includes services, principles, and business scenarios.

The business environment is characterised by increased competition, fluctuating margins, unstable markets, and compressed opportunities, enabled by EBA (Iyamu, 2015). According to Eid-Sabbagh et al. (2012), business architecture is a collection of business processes and their interdependencies. The architecture focuses on the dimensions of an organisation, which consists of business processes, service structures, and organisation of activities. Anthony Jnr. (2021) argued that business architecture entails high-level abstraction of services. Also, business architecture gives direction to organisational aspects, such as organisational structuring, business design, administrative workflow, and logical processes (Iyamu, 2022). Iacob et al. (2014) suggest that this happens at both current and desired states, which motivates architectural change within the environment.

For an organisation to continue to exploit opportunities and remain competitive, the function of information systems planning must be fully integrated with the business strategic planning process as defined by EBA. According to Kang et al. (2010), business architecture includes business strategies, performance metrics, business processes, and the relationships between strategies and processes. Business architecture models organisational processes and activities towards the implementation of its strategy (Ren & Glissmann, 2012). In addition to the potential benefits, Tamm et al. (2022) argue that the architecture provides business scenarios that are mapped to the services of the organisation. Even though Lapalme (2012) explains that the strength of business architecture is basically rooted in its composition, which embodies that one business process is composed of several other business events, processes, and activities, it still poses complexity.

The complexity of EBA has contributed to misunderstanding the concept in many quarters. Iyamu et al. (2016) explain that some of the interactions and confusions that happen with business architecture could be of conscious or unconscious nature, which manifests from their subjective interpretation of terms and functions. This could be attributed to why many organisations struggle with EBA acceptance and implementation barriers, which manifest from factors such as communication and buy-in (Lapalme, 2012). Based on some actors' limited knowledge, EBA decisions are made which thereafter affect processes and business structuring. This has an impact on the ability of organisations to formulate and assess the components, which are required in process modelling, analysis, and design of the EBA. Rouhani and Kharazmi (2012) argue that it is difficult to correctly express business architecture's abilities without understanding its correct viewpoints.

4.3 Components of Enterprise Business Architecture

The core components of EBA are divided into two main parts: definition and clarification of the tenets, and understanding of the tenets towards EBA deployment.

4.4 Definition and Clarification of Tenets

Development and implementation efforts begin with a definition of EBA and the classification of its components. This is to clarify, outline, and understand the components involved in the development and implementation of the EBA in the context of an organisation (Iyamu et al., 2016). According to Koushik and Joodi (2000), business architecture is more than a collection of technologies and products; the architecture consists of several architectural models which define the blueprint purposely to meet the current and future needs of diverse users. The relationship between the components is vital as it influences how the models are designed and classified (Kotusev et al., 2022). The primary tenets of the EBA include business, business architecture, and a transformative scheme. As shown in Figure 4.1, each of the tenets has its characteristics, which together form the EBA. The outputs of the EBA influence the organisational structure it constitutes, such as the business logic, events, processes, information flows, and designs.

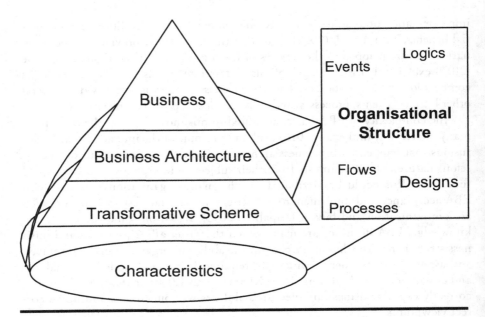

Figure 4.1   EBA Tenets.

Business: A *business* is a system, a collection of interacting units that works together to reproduce output, usually profit or public service. Ross et al. (2006) refer to business systems as a set of enterprise processes that define a stable set of capabilities needed to execute the operating model by an organisation. Change to one part of the system affects other parts and the output that the business produces. This could be attributed to the fact many businesses typically pursue improvement or respond to change without necessary reference to business schematics. The EBA allows for the translation of vision, strategy, requirements, and organisational processes through transformation processes and modelling.

Business architecture: Myrick et al. (2007) define the architecture of the business as an approach that is used to facilitate change from the current to the desired state. Iacob et al. (2014) argue that business models are elicited from both current and future business architecture within an organisation. In the context of this chapter, *business architecture* is therefore defined as the expression of the organisation's key business strategies and tactics, and their impact and interaction with business functions and processes that typically consist of the current and future state. Business architecture enacts the transformation of events, processes, and activities from one state to another in an enterprise (Andini, 2021).

Transformative scheme: The transformative scheme enables a transition to a new business model in the face of a major transformation in an organisation (Spieth

Table 4.1   The Key Tenets of Enterprise Business Architecture

Concept	Description
Connectivity	Ensures inter-relationship between technology and business units. It aligns and connects technology artefacts with business needs and information value networks across units of the organisation (Mengmeng et al., 2019).
Event	Facilitates the implementation of new business events and processes. It also provides technology options for business processes, modelling, and automation (Srinivas et al., 2021; Niu et al., 2013).
Functionality	Identifies business needs within perspectives and contexts. It provides a formal methodology for business requirements. Simon et al. (2014) explained how functional elements guide the analysis, planning, and change implementation by focusing on identifying and defining the essential business capacities and capabilities.
Operational	Translates business specifications into technical specifications. Identifies and analyses computational business events and activities (Correani et al., 2020; Engelsman et al., 2011), which provides a service delivery mechanism for advancing sustainability and competitiveness.
Measurement	Sets principles, guidelines, and standards to guide boundaries. Also, provides guidance and protection for approved product lists, and engineers criteria for direction and values, including performance, on an ongoing basis (Löhe & Legner, 2014).

et al., 2014). As shown in Table 4.1, the five main components of the transformative scheme are connectivity, event, functionality, operation, and measurement. Primarily, the components are used to link organisational events, processes, and activities, which include business models, information value networks, and alternative business scenarios. Also, through the transformative scheme, strategies are formulated and management is engineered (Iyamu, 2022), events are modelled, and functions and operations are organised (Jayakrishnan et al., 2020).

4.5 Understanding the Tenets towards EBA Deployment

The deployment of EBA requires an understanding of the tenets. Thus, the architecture of a business and the elements of the transformative scheme are discussed further in this section. This is to gain a more cohesive view of how the tenets interconnect with the business architecture in an organisation.

4.5.1 The Architecture of a Business

The architecture of business defines the events, functions, and operational activities which inform the ability and capability to have a clear view of the elements that constitute its formation. This includes objectives and organisational structure.

The objective of EBA is mainly to define the types of high-velocity information that passes between defined key processes and the integration requirements enabled by the underlying business applications and technical architectures. The architecture is used to explain the high-level structure and composition of business processes and logics in an organisation (Correani et al., 2020; Jonkers et al., 2012). However, in achieving its objectives, the EBA is neither developed nor implemented in isolation or a vacuum. It depends on the organisational (business) vision, needs, and requirements. A summary from Roelens et al. (2019) suggests that the business vision provides clarification on the future of the organisation by capturing the most important business strategies being pursued at the time. Spieth et al. (2014) argue that the business architecture addresses the strategic function of the business model, which is used to support management.

Business requirements are derived from the business strategies and they are expressed as functional statements (Shaanika & Iyamu, 2018). The requirements give direction and priority to the development of processes, patterns, and functions intended to address the organisational needs. Organisational structure or restructuring does not necessarily or by itself effect change in the business events, processes, and activities of an organisation. The change happens through the iterative process of the EBA (Iyamu, 2022). This makes the EBA critically important, as it continues to enforce change from competitiveness and sustainability perspectives (Andini, 2021).

EBA enables the organisation to effect business process change in a controlled manner, through a methodological approach. According to Myrick et al. (2007), architecture is a method of modelling frameworks to support business structure and its manageability. Within the EBA context, methodology defines priorities and articulates, initiates, anticipates, and controls the required change, from the current to the future state. From the same perspective, Holm et al. (2014) suggest that business architecture models are holistic and reflect the organisation's current and future states. Thus, I propose that the objectives of the EBA are primarily extracted from four main areas, as follows.

    i. Typically consists of the current-state and future-state models of business functions, events designs, process modelling, and information value chains (Anthony Jnr., 2021);

ii. Connects the business with the IT units, through interaction and re-engineering (Iyamu, 2015).
iii. Leads to the development of other domains of enterprise architecture, which include information, application, and technical architecture (Rouhani & Kharazmi, 2012).
iv. Defines business patterns, designs, and processes for advancing sustainable competitiveness (Roelens et al., 2019).

4.5.2 The Elements of the Transformative Scheme

The EBA characteristically adapts to changing business and technology requirements. Rouhani and Kharazmi (2012) suggest that business architecture can significantly influence an enterprise's strategy. Some of the premises of the EBA are that it is an agent of change and that it validates and extends the business strategy and vision, from holistic and realistic perspectives to operationalisation. The EBA, therefore, provides a knowledge base that catalogues and describes the work performed to realise an enterprise's mission, vision, goals, and objectives. Also, the architecture provides a starting point for achieving linkages between business, information, and technology domains (Beese et al., 2022). The EBA can therefore be used to model the impact of business visioning, based on the operations and strategy of the organisation.

Concerning the definition provided in this chapter, EBA can be described as a realistic and feasible approach to expose gaps in business processes and strategy, including IS and IT strategies, and the interaction in the relationship between business and technology (IS and IT) units. The interaction is enacted by models. According to Iacob et al. (2014), business models drive the needs and design of other architectures, such as the application, information, and technology domains. The transformative scheme enables business patterns and business architecture in general (Holm et al., 2014). In many ways, protuberant and prevalent among them are connectivity, event, function, operation, and management.

i. *Transformative scheme—Connectivity*: This element geographically identifies and connects business functions, logic, and processes towards the common objectives of an organisation. Nogueira et al. (2013) suggest that this represents a logistical view of the business functions involved in the value network models. Through the connectivity element, an organisational structure including geographical locations is virtualised as a function of the current and future enterprise value network (EVN). According to Jonkers et al. (2012), the business architecture defines the functions of EVN in an organisation, which Griffo et al. (2021) described as crucial to the ease of models and complexity of an enterprise.
ii. *Transformative scheme—Event*: The event is guided by how an organisation initiates and processes business logics and functions. Iacob et al. (2014)

overtly explained that business architecture change to an organisation is explicit through its modelling of business events over time. This includes how the change traverses the EVN. It thus designs business flows, documents the current means of handling events, and evaluates options for the improvement of functions and processes within the environment of the organisation that deploys it (Niu et al., 2013).

iii. *Transformative scheme—Function*: This element identifies the sub-processes performed by a business function (Simon et al., 2014). It defines the scope of the major organisational entities and captures the contribution of each business function that participates in the EVN of an organisation. Jonkers et al. (2012) argue that the business function engineers and shows the relationships that exist between events and EVN.

iv. *Transformative scheme—Operational*: The operational element shows the high-level interface requirements through which business events are processed. A business model addresses the operational aspects of an organisation, such as processes, linkages, or structures (Srinivas et al., 2021; Spieth et al., 2014). It is used to document information requirements of new business patterns and the evolving requirements as they change or evolve. Iacob et al. (2014) explain how the operational element is used to elicit requirements for the respective business units. It represents the business information and architectural requirements for integration and delivery of services, in supporting and enabling an organisation for competitiveness (Gonzalez-Lopez & Bustos, 2019).

v. *Transformative scheme—Measurement*: The primary aim is to address the values and detect the deficiencies that exist in the processes, functions, and events of an organisation. Myrick et al. (2007) think that through measurement, the structure is developed within which IS and IT solutions are built to support and enable the business goals and objectives of an enterprise. The measurement is therefore applied from two different perspectives: in managing the technical oversight and managing policy issues involved in business events, activities and operations (Löhe & Legner, 2014). This is done by executing projects to effect change. The projects ensure that both the organisational needs and architecture including operations and strategic intents are met through modelling. Measurement assists to exploit strengths in achieving desired goals, as well as to improve in the reduction of threats and weaknesses in an environment.

4.6 A Guide for Enterprise Business Architecture Deployment

For the deployment of EBA in an organisation, a guide is proposed. The guide consists of six components, primarily. In applying the components, a phase approach is employed, as depicted in Figure 4.2. The components are: (i) organisational needs,

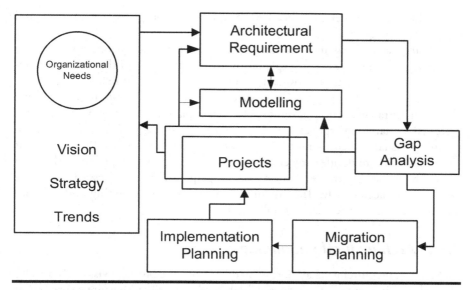

Figure 4.2   Business Architecture Deployment.

an interpretation of business vision; (ii) formulation of architectural requirements, an articulation of necessities; (iii) modelling of business processes and activities, patterning of actions; (iv) gap analysis, extraction of deficiencies and opportunities; (v) implementation, including migration from the current to the desired state, new resolute solution; and (vi) execution of projects to effect change, performance-oriented towards transformation. The components are primarily premised on the need to comprehend the scope and boundary, the articulation of the drivers through visioning, and the development of integration models, location models, business events, functions, and process decomposition models.

4.6.1 Organisational Needs

Organisational needs are propelled by many factors, internal and external. In the context of EBA, as shown in Figure 4.2, organisational needs are driven and guided by business vision, strategy, and environmental trends. Business visioning provides the process with a clear understanding of the organisation's direction and future. This can be challenging, as it is always difficult for an organisation to have a full and accurate view of the future. Srinivas et al. (2020) explain that in a changing competitive business landscape, many organisations are challenged by their traditional processes and static document-driven business architecture models or artefacts. As a result, the visioning phase is an exercise which is intended to create a forum for a strategic conversation through the organisational structures. This results in a unified view of objectives towards common goals that produce and reproduce actions.

What is also taken into consideration is the fact that an organisation may engage in different types of strategic business visioning. One of the goals of visioning is to manage a balance between long-term strategies (traditional strategic planning) and a tactical strategy to be pursued as a result of a short-term opportunity. Traditional strategic planning is more of a longer planning horizon, which is often preferred by large enterprises. An example of this strategy is digital innovation planning. Usually, such a long-term strategy takes between six and 18 months. It is always necessary to decide early enough on what opportunity to pursue in the short term, while assessing the impact on long-range plans, and if necessary, adjusting the strategies accordingly. The organisational needs from visioning and environmental trends drive the architectural requirements.

4.6.2 Architectural Requirements

Architectural requirements are formulated based on the business vision. The architectural requirements are considered high-level necessities that are expressed as functional statements within the context of an organisation. The requirements give direction and priority to EBA in an environment. Some of such requirements are: (i) rationalising core business processes across organisational units; (ii) defining organisational functional boundaries, roles, and responsibilities; (iii) streamlining and automating core business events and processes across functions; (iv) accommodating human resources planning processes; (v) exploring business research and development functions; (vi) defining, analysing, and segmenting performance and documentation of the customer base; and (vii) providing adequate and appropriate service delivery mechanisms.

For each architectural requirement (AR), there must be at least one business requirement (BR). The business requirements are used to create a structured representation of the events, processes, and activities of an organisation. The requirements encompass factors primarily intended to advance competitive advantage and sustainability. Also, the requirements can be used to shape the pursuits and direction of an organisation. This phase of EBA deployment enables specific needs and facilitates the contextualisation of both ARs and BRs. The ARs and BRs are identifiably numbered for differentiation and categorisation purposes. Table 4.2 shows a guide for an architectural requirement model.

4.6.3 Business Modelling

The business visioning and architectural requirements are drilled down into key processes, business events, and information flows, which drive new opportunities from the point of weakness to a position of strength. The factors are used to foster innovation, while modelling new business patterns to be followed by the

Table 4.2 Architectural Requirements

Architectural Requirements		Business Requirements	
AR1	Facilitates an organisation to implement its strategies over time, with minimal impact on ongoing service delivery	**BR1**	Enables the rationalisation of core business events and processes across an organisation
		BR2	Ensures that roles and responsibilities within an organisation are appropriately defined
		BR3	Enables effective transitioning of planning and coordination
AR2	Facilitates the provisioning of, and access to information and data by requirements, in a managed and controlled manner within an environment	**BR1**	Provides governance to ensure that appropriate information management policies are developed and institutionalised
		BR2	Provides governance and support and enables the security of information within and between organisations

enterprise. Innovation through modelling is accomplished by creating a series of models, which are systematic representations of engineering processes and activities in the context of an organisation. Modelling is used to identify the core drivers of organisational needs, from both technical and non-technical perspectives, including infrastructure, standards, policies, environmental trends, and administrative processes. The practice is aimed at enabling and supporting organisational needs that seek to improve and manage efficiency, effectiveness, and quality. The modelling of the functions and activities of a business consists of two main linking components: process modelling and business pattern, as depicted in Figure 4.3.

4.6.4 Process Modelling

Organisational process modelling is based on design, through which a business applies the enterprise value network (EVN), information value network (IVN), and business scenario (BS) models. Process modelling is thus aimed at the business functions, processes, and information flows to facilitate decision-making, perform impact analysis, identify innovation (such as digital innovation) opportunities, and create micro and macro views of the future state of an organisation.

As illustrated in Figure 4.3, process modelling evolves in EVN, IVN, and BS, which facilitate, support, and enable the development of business patterns process. The business patterns are used by the business event, function, location, and

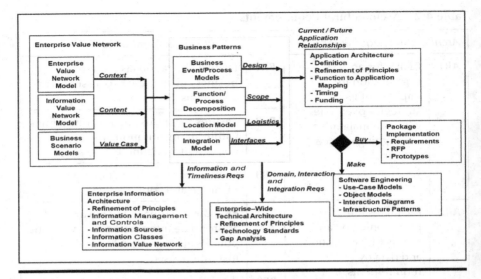

Figure 4.3 Enterprise Business Architecture Design Flow.

integration modelling to model parts of the business events and activities that are affected by a changing strategy. Primarily, this is why the application, technical, and information architectures depend on the processes and activities as modelled by the business patterns. The techniques that are used for modelling are aimed at providing business personnel and leaders with a holistic view of the enterprise. This is to stimulate an interactive dialogue among the stakeholders for evolving the overall processes and activities of the organisation, with a particular focus on EVN, IVN, and BS.

4.6.4.1 Enterprise Value Network

The enterprise value network (EVN) is a component of EBA that holds the context within which an enterprise's process and modelling are based. The component defines the critical functions required to deliver services (or products), at both internal and external sources. Also, it defines the interactions and relationships between elements and attributes, which in turn provide the functions of the business. Porter (2005) explains that the value chain has exploded into the EVN in many organisations. This is because of the available information and the emerging electronic approaches to businesses. Business environments resemble a web of fluid, ever-changing relationships, which are nodes on a network, rather than a fixed distribution channel.

The EVN fuses episodes through which the current business chain is dissected, a catalysis on the construction of a new approach is conducted, and an adaptive infrastructure is built. This includes business functions, organisation

Table 4.3 Enterprise Value Network

Analysis: Focus	Analysis: Artefacts	Key drivers	Interface
Overall business context	Alliance partners	Establish and examine a business scenario to understand the key alliance partners	The interface between business vision and requirements
Business 'ecosystem'	Key values and activities	Understand the functions and processes involved	Events, functions, and locations
High-level representation of the externalised	Value of the alliance	Understand and document the scenarios and values of the alliances	Business patterns and clients
Value of key activities and partners	Primary sources of value	Understand and document the source of sustainability and competitive advantage	IVN models

structure, roles, and technology. The approach is used to support and enable business value opportunities by eliciting responses from stakeholders, using questions such as: (i) within the context of the value chain, how is information a key component of value?; and (ii) how are opportunities or potential risks critical portions of the value chain in an environment? Based on the responses, analysis is conducted by following a specific stance that bears benefits for the organisation.

The first step in analysing the value network is to comprehend the business vision and requirements. The findings from the analysis become the primary input to the EVN definition, as shown in Table 4.3. Other inputs could include environmental trends and government legislation. This is the key goal in exploiting the business value network, which is often determined by four sets of scenarios: (i) processes and activities that support the organisation's goals; (ii) processes and activities performed by an organisation as its core competency; (iii) opportunities to increase value through partnerships with other organisations; and (iv) partnership, its value and how the relationship supports and enables the organisation to advance competitiveness. A value network model is created to appropriately depict both the vertical and horizontal linkages of business structure.

4.6.4.2 Information Value Network

There are three main steps involved in the IVN in an organisation. The first step is to define the area of focus, which includes the boundaries of operation. Thereafter, information is gathered about the artefacts defined within the scope. In the third step, an analysis is conducted to understand the challenges and create opportunities.

The IVN focuses on the content on which process modelling is built and carried out. It defines the sources of high-velocity information (HVI) and ensures its availability. Also, IVN defines how high-velocity information is used by different key business units and the processes employed. HVI consists of customers, suppliers, and partners information, which is shared within the IVN at both transaction and decision support levels. This is intended to maximise operational efficiency, precise strategic direction, and improved service delivery for sustainability and competitiveness.

Additionally, the IVN model focuses on two things: it describes the linkages within the value network and describes the value of the information product across the value network. Linkages exist horizontally across business units and vertically among suppliers, partners, and customers. Information is an artefact of business processes, and therefore supports the physical value chain. The value of information (infonomics) is determined by the competitive advantage gained through the use of information products.

The analysis from IVN is used to diagnose challenges or uncover opportunities in an organisation's events and processes. This is intended to leverage IS and IT solutions to create high-value and low-cost linkages with both internal and external parties across nodes and lines of business (LOB). Each of the nodes in the IVN is analysed, primarily to determine: (i) key information products that exist within vertical and horizontal linkages across an organisation's business structures; (ii) characteristics of the linkage, which include density, velocity, cost, and value; and (iii) opportunities that exist to leverage information products, through which costs can be minimised, valued and increase velocity. The approach that can be adopted by the IVN modelling is tabulated in Table 4.4.

Table 4.4 Information Value Network

Analysis: Focus	Analysis: Artefacts	Key Questions	EA Interface
i. Overall IVN logistics ii. Defines high-velocity information requirements iii. Defines key externalisation opportunities	i. Key IVN processes ii. Key IVN information flows iii. HVI requirements	i. What is key information? ii. What products can be leveraged to improve decision-making?	i. Business vision and requirements ii. Technical and information architectures iii. Information and technical architectures

4.6.4.3 Business Scenario

The business scenario component consists of a value case that is used for process modelling. It pulls the artefacts of the EVN and IVN models together into a series of alternative future states of business designs and strategies. The business scenario is also used to communicate information and opportunities to stakeholders. This is to enable informed decision-making in ranking alternatives and selecting appropriate courses of action produced and reproduced over time. In structuration, Giddens (1984) refers to this as studying modes which are grounded in the knowledgeable activities of situated actors, who then draw upon rules and resources to produce and reproduce their actions and interactions. In Table 4.5, the summary of the approach by which business scenario modelling can be carried out is presented.

4.6.5 Business Patterns

Business patterns (BP) are a collection of artefacts used to describe new processes, functions, information flows, and organisational changes as required by the business. This is primarily aimed at addressing the organisation's needs. As depicted in Figure 4.3 (EBA design flow), the business patterns depend on process modelling. The BP is based on the context, content, and value of an organisation, and consists of business event analysis, function and process decomposition, and location and integration modelling.

In addition, business patterns are used to describe and model the different units within an enterprise and communicate them to the stakeholders. This can be done while providing a foundation for organisational and technological designs. The

Table 4.5 Business Scenario

Analysis: Focus	Analysis: Artefacts	Key Questions	Business Interface
i. Visioning ii. Refine business requirements iii. What-if analysis of alternatives iv. Demonstrate the value of technology innovation opportunities	i. Business scenarios ii. Technology innovation scenarios iii. Select and rank alternatives	i. What possible business scenarios could be used to respond to environmental trends and business drivers? ii. How can technology be used to create innovations?	i. Business vision ii. Application architecture iii. Information architecture

documentation of new business patterns of an organisation enables the EBA to provide critical information for a future state. The implications of the new business patterns are potential changes to: (i) the relationship and functionality of applications in a portfolio; (ii) infrastructures that are required and guided by technical architecture; and (iii) the velocity of information that is needed for the information architecture. In the context of the EBA, documentation of business patterns is partly art and partly science. It provides further visualisation and a clearer view of the roadblocks to business and technological innovations. This is based on a subjective interpretive analysis (of accumulated knowledge) and modelling thereof, and it is used to encourage creative innovations and efforts.

4.6.6 *Implementation*

The implementation process is a fundamental component of EBA required to ensure the smooth operation of business events, processes, and activities. The implementation stage consists of two main components: appropriate planning and comprehension of migration from the current state to the desired state.

4.6.6.1 *Planning*

Implementation of the EBA has always been a challenge, which contributes to a lack of interest by some organisations. Thus, appropriate planning is required and critical. The appropriateness of planning depends on the main components and their execution. The main components at the planning stage include (i) governance framework; (ii) roles and responsibilities required to support the identified key business processes; and (iii) functioning organisational structure.

The governance reflects the information, processes, functions, and activities, as well as facilitating strategic decision-making. This is essentially a reference model through which the EBA components are founded. There are stakeholders, through whom the development and implementation tasks of EBA models are carried out. The allocation of tasks to the stakeholders is guided by their roles and responsibilities, which are geared towards a common goal. The models typically consist of current and future states of business functions, processes, and IVNs. Also, the organisational structure is critical in implementing EBA, primarily because processes are enforced through it.

4.6.6.2 *Migration*

Implementation is complete only when all desired states have been operationalised, which happens through the migration stage and process. This stage can be cumbersome due to the complexity of the various factors involved. First, among the complexity, implementation poses challenges; hence, considerable attention is advisably required. Second, the migration component is influenced and determined by factors such as skilled personnel, financial budget, timeframe, and the sequence of change, which affects processes and functional activities in an organisation. It is an exercise used for an open dialogue with users and stakeholders that will be directly affected by the proposed change resulting from the gap analysis. The migration component is used to identify areas of low and high risks. This is to identify areas that require special or more attention during implementation. The migration planning is intended to modify the generic process model of the EBA.

4.6.7 Project

The deliverables of EBA are produced through projects. The projects are ongoing, as EA remains iterative. The business requirements are used as measurement criteria to guide projects outcome. Each project constitutes and describes the entire components and processes involved from the beginning to the end in the delivery of products. This includes planning, availability of resources (such as people, technology, and finance), and time management.

Each project is unique and contextual. Thus, individual projects define roles, responsibilities, and accountability, including the estimation of cost and timelines within its context. The EBA projects are decomposed into units by the organisational structure, complexity, and priority defined at the time. In the projects, the units are often influenced mainly by the goals and objectives of the organisation, as well as the environmental trends.

4.6.8 Gap Analysis

The purpose of the gap analysis is to assess the current state of the business architecture against the desired state as reflected in the business vision and requirements. It is therefore used to assess the impact of change on the environment and the elements which could manifest into risks, weaknesses, strengths, and opportunities. The assessment is an iterative and ongoing process in an evolutionary pattern to achieve changing business goals. It is reflected by a checklist and accompanying action plans that must include status (current state) and target date.

As shown in Table 4.6, the assessment is in four main categories: scope, ownership, status, and target. Using the assessment approach of the gap analysis, the categories conform to two main factors: enterprise planning and business analysis. Each factor has entities which change from time to time, depending on the environment or organisation. The outcome helps to engineer change in terms of how and why things happen in the manner that they do during the development and implementation of the EBA in an organisation. It is therefore of utmost importance and highly recommended that the results of the assessment are stored in the EBA repository. Also, the results should be made available and accessible to the entire stakeholders' team in the organisation. The template should be used to define and

Table 4.6 EBA Conformance Checklist

No.	Conformance	Scope	Ownership	Status	Target
1	**Enterprise Planning**				
1.1	**Business vision**	Directional statements of intents that are being pursued at the time, at the organisational level	Identifies sponsors of the project, from both business and technology (IS and IT) units	Provides updates to the executive members and sponsors	Organisational roadmap with timelines
1.2	**Business requirements**	Defines the rationales, benefits, goals, and objectives, as well as limitations and boundaries	Defines stewardship, which includes accountability roles and responsibilities	Defines the communicative scheme through which information (which may lead to a decision) is shared	Specifies the intended outcome for each of the requirements
1.3	**Architecture requirements**	Defines the standards, principles, and policies	Area of specialisation, domain architects	Documentation of stages in the development and implementation	Specifies the intended architectural requirements for each business requirement
2	**Business Analysis**				
2.1	**Core process**	The most critical factors for competitive advantage	Managerial responsibilities and effects	Document change	Takes cognisance of environmental trends for competitive advantage

No.	Conformance	Scope	Ownership	Status	Target
2.2	Enterprise modelling	Short- and long-term goals and objectives	Assigns functional responsibility	Articulation and diagrammatical representation of business processes and activities	The enterprise pursuits within 3–5 year terms
2.3	Process re-engineering	Identification of influencing factors such as competitive and environmental trends	Distribution of tasks through units of analysis	Continual review to meet strategic intents	Evolutionary towards the organisational pursuits
2.4	Core information needs	Identification of drivers such as business activities	By content and context-based	Documentation and repository for business purposes	As dictated by business pursued at the time
2.5	Support services	Sustainability and maintenance of processes and activities for competitive advantage	Operation agents and managers	Manageability of the day-to-day activities	Daily and weekly tasks completion

elicit contextual content within an organisation. The categories are briefly described as follows.

i. Scope: The scope enables focus and direction within which modelling processes and activities are carried out.

i. Ownership: The ownership allows for accountability and responsibility, which assist in tracing and tracking modelling, processes and activities.

iii. Status: The status component consists of options such as completed, in progress, not started, and not applicable.

iv. Target: The target column requires specific accountability. It is primarily for management and governance purposes, for the artefacts or activities that require measurement.

Once the gap analysis is complete, the plan to migrate EBA artefacts into the new (operational) environment begins. The approach, therefore, paves the way for a sanitised environment and healthy implementation.

4.7 Summary

This chapter is directed at both academics and practitioners of information systems (IS) and information technology (IT), primarily, for three reasons. First, it is an additional resource in the areas of business architecture and enterprise architecture (EA). As revealed from existing literature, research and academic works into business architecture are scarce. The chapter may also help academics in developing the enterprise architecture curriculum. Second, the chapter methodologically advances the deployment of enterprise business architecture (EBA) in organisations. In practice, it is hard to find an organisation that understands a descriptively comprehensive approach as detailed in this chapter. Finally, the chapter practically contributes to the deployment and practice of EBA through the construction of organisations' reality exploratory, to understanding its complexities.

Practitioners, particularly architects and business managers, will find the chapter useful. One fundamental area of usefulness is in its clarification of terms, which affects the development and implementation of the concepts. Also, it provides a guide on how the concepts can be developed and implemented.

References

Amit, R., & Zott, C. (2015). Crafting business architecture: The antecedents of business model design. *Strategic Entrepreneurship Journal, 9*(4), 331–350.

Andini, S. (2021). Cloud-based information technology architecture modeling computing. *International Journal of Dynamics in Engineering and Sciences, 6*(2), 51–56.

Anthony Jnr, B. (2021). Managing digital transformation of smart cities through enterprise architecture—a review and research agenda. *Enterprise Information Systems*, *15*(3), 299–331.

Beese, J., Aier, S., Haki, K., & Winter, R. (2022). The impact of enterprise architecture management on information systems architecture complexity. *European Journal of Information Systems*, 1–21.

Byrne, D. (2017). What are ontology and epistemology. *Project Planner*, *10*, 9781526408495.

Coghlan, D., & Brydon-Miller, M. (2014). *The SAGE encyclopedia of action research* (Vols. 1–2). SAGE Publications Ltd.

Correani, A., De Massis, A., Frattini, F., Petruzzelli, A. M., & Natalicchio, A. (2020). Implementing a digital strategy: Learning from the experience of three digital transformation projects. *California Management Review*, *62*(4), 37–56.

Eid-Sabbagh, R. H., Dijkman, R., & Weske, M. (2012). Business process architecture: Use and correctness. In *Proceedings of international conference on business process management* (pp. 65–81). Springer.

Engelsman, W., Quartel, D., Jonkers, H., & van Sinderen, M. (2011). Extending enterprise architecture modelling with business goals and requirements. *Enterprise Information Systems*, *5*(1), 9–36.

Fischer, R., Aier, S., & Winter, R. (2015). A federated approach to enterprise architecture model maintenance. *Enterprise Modelling and Information Systems Architectures*, *2*(2), 14–22.

Giddens, A. (1984). *The constitution of society*. Polity Press.

Gonzalez-Lopez, F., & Bustos, G. (2019). Integration of business process architectures within enterprise architecture approaches: A literature review. *Engineering Management Journal*, *31*(2), 127–140.

Griffo, C., Almeida, J. P. A., Guizzardi, G., & Nardi, J. C. (2021). Service contract modelling in enterprise architecture: An ontology-based approach. *Information Systems*, *101*, 101454.

Gromoff, A., Kazantsev, N., Kozhevnikov, D., Ponfilenok, M., & Stavenko, Y. (2012). Newer approach to create flexible business architecture of modern enterprise. *Global Journal of Flexible Systems Management*, *13*(4), 207–215.

Hennink, M. M., Hutter, I., & Bailey, A. (2011). *Qualitative research methods*. Sage Publications.

Holm, H., Buschle, M., Lagerström, R., & Ekstedt, M. (2014). Automatic data collection for enterprise architecture models. *Software & Systems Modeling*, *13*(2), 825–841.

Hoogervorst, J. A., & Dietz, J. L. (2015). Enterprise architecture in enterprise engineering. *Enterprise Modelling and Information Systems Architectures*, *3*(1), 3–13.

Iacob, M. E., Meertens, L. O., Jonkers, H., Quartel, D. A., Nieuwenhuis, L. J., & Van Sinderen, M. J. (2014). From enterprise architecture to business models and back. *Software & Systems Modeling*, *13*(3), 1059–1083.

Iyamu, T. (2015). *Enterprise architecture: From concept to practise* (2nd ed.). Heidelberg Press.

Iyamu, T. (2022). *Enterprise architecture for strategic management of modern IT solutions*. Routledge, CRC Press.

Iyamu, T., Nehemia-Maletzky, M., & Shaanika, I. (2016). The overlapping nature of business analysis and business architecture: What we need to know. *The Electronic Journal Information Systems Evaluation*, *19*(3), 169–179.

Iyamu, T., & Shaanika, I. (2022, April 25–27). Assessing business architecture readiness, in organisations. In *The proceedings of the 24th international conference on enterprise information systems (ICEIS)* (pp. 506–514). Online Streaming. Science and Technology Publications, LDA (SciTePress).

Jayakrishnan, M., Mohamad, A. K., & Yusof, M. M. (2020). Business architecture model in strategic information system management for effective railway supply chain perspective. *International Journal of Engineering Research and Technology, 13*(11), 3927–3933.

Jonkers, H., Band, I., & Quartel, D. (2012). *The archisurance case study*. White paper, The Open Group, Spring.

Jurisica, I., Mylopoulos, J., & Yu, E. (2004). Ontologies for knowledge management: An information systems perspective. *Knowledge and Information Systems, 6*(4), 380–401.

Kang, D., Lee, J., & Kim, K. (2010). Alignment of business enterprise architectures using fact-based ontologies. *Expert Systems with Applications, 37*(4), 3274–3283.

Kotusev, S., Kurnia, S., & Dilnutt, R. (2022). The practical roles of enterprise architecture artefacts: A classification and relationship. *Information and Software Technology, 147*, 106897.

Koushik, S., & Joodi, P. (2000). E-business architecture design issues. *IT Professional, 2*(3), 38–43.

Lapalme, J. (2012). Three schools of thought on enterprise architecture. *IT Professional, 14*(6), 37–43.

Löhe, J., & Legner, C. (2014). Overcoming implementation challenges in enterprise architecture management: A design theory for architecture-driven IT management (ADRIMA). *Information Systems and e-Business Management, 12*(1), 101–137.

McDavid, D. W. (1999). A standard for business architecture description. *IBM Systems Journal, 38*(1), 12–31.

Mengmeng, Z., Honghui, C. H. E. N., & Junxian, L. I. U. (2019). Resource allocation approach to associate business-IT alignment to enterprise architecture design. *Journal of Systems Engineering and Electronics, 30*(2), 343–351.

Myrick, C. B., Hixon Jr, H. W., Koll, C. M., & Whittle Jr, R. L. (2007). *U.S. patent no. 7,162,427*. U.S. Patent and Trademark Office.

Niu, N., Da Xu, L., & Bi, Z. (2013). Enterprise information systems architecture—Analysis and evaluation. *IEEE Transactions on Industrial Informatics, 9*(4), 2147–2154.

Nogueira, J. M., Romero, D., Espadas, J., & Molina, A. (2013). Leveraging the Zachman framework implementation using action—research methodology—a case study: Aligning the enterprise architecture and the business goals. *Enterprise Information Systems, 7*(1), 100–132.

Porter, M. (2005). *Competitive advantage: Creating and sustaining superior performance*. Collier Macmillan.

Proper, H., & Lankhorst, M. M. (2015). Enterprise architecture-towards essential sensemaking. *Enterprise Modelling and Information Systems Architectures, 9*(1), 5–21.

Ren, G. J., & Glissmann, S. (2012, September 9–11). Identifying information assets for open data: The role of business architecture and information quality. In *The proceedings of the 14th international conference on commerce and enterprise computing (CEC), IEEE* (pp. 94–100). IEEE.

Roelens, B., Steenacker, W., & Poels, G. (2019). Realizing strategic fit within the business architecture: The design of a process-goal alignment modeling and analysis technique. *Software & Systems Modeling, 18*(1), 631–662.

Ross, J., Weill, P., & Robertson, D. (2006). *Enterprise architecture as a strategy: Creating a foundation for business excution*. Havard Business Press.

Rouhani, B. D., & Kharazmi, S. (2012). Presenting new solution based on business architecture for enterprise architecture. *International Journal of Computer Science Issues, 9*(3), 207–211.

Saint-Louis, P., & Lapalme, J. (2018). An exploration of the many ways to approach the discipline of enterprise architecture. *International Journal of Engineering Business Management, 10*, 1847979018807383.

Shaanika, I., & Iyamu, T. (2018). Developing the enterprise architecture for the Namibian government. *The Electronic Journal of Information Systems in Developing Countries, 84*(3), e12028.

Simon, D., Fischbach, K., & Schoder, D. (2014). Enterprise architecture management and its role in corporate strategic management. *Information Systems and e-Business Management, 12*(1), 5–42.

Spieth, P., Schneckenberg, D., & Ricart, J. E. (2014). Business model innovation—state of the art and future challenges for the field. *R&D Management, 44*(3), 237–247.

Srinivas, S., Gill, A. Q., & Roach, T. (2020). Analytics-enabled adaptive business architecture modeling. *Complex Systems Informatics and Modeling Quarterly, 23*, 23–43.

Srinivas, S., Gill, A. Q., & Roach, T. (2021). Can business architecture modeling be adaptive? *IT Professional, 23*(2), 81–88.

Tamm, T., Seddon, P. B., & Shanks, G. (2022). How enterprise architecture leads to organisational benefits. *International Journal of Information Management, 67*, 102554.

Versteeg, G., & Bouwman, H. (2006). Business architecture: A new paradigm to relate business strategy to ICT. *Information Systems Frontiers, 8*(2), 91–102.

Whittle, R., & Myrick, C. B. (2016). *Enterprise business architecture: The formal link between strategy and results*. CRC Press.

Zachman, J. A. (1996). *Concepts of the framework for enterprise architecture*. Zachman International, Inc. Los Angeles, CA.

Chapter 5

Information Architecture in the Enterprise

5.1 Introduction

Persistently, the terms data architecture and information architecture are loosely and interchangeably used in both academic and business (organisation) domains. Iyamu (2022) dedicates a chapter to this subject, providing a distinction between the two concepts. Therefore, this book does not attempt to repeat such work but focuses solely on information architecture. enterprise information architecture (EIA) is one of the domains of enterprise architecture (EA), as explained in Chapter 1. Other domains of EA are business, application, and technical architectures (Iyamu, 2022; Gong & Janssen, 2019; Kappelman & Zachman, 2013; Zachman, 1987). As established in the previous chapters, the different domains of EA are interrelated and depend on each other. The EIA focuses on solving the challenges of relevance, context, and ambiguity of the design, use, and exchange of information in organisations. Primarily, this entails governance through principles. This chapter focuses on how principles can be applied in the design, development, and implementation of the EIA domain in an organisation.

The EIA enables the management of change in information exchange, service, and its strategic use in an organisation. The change is enforced through four dimensions, essentially: the description of the structure of a system (Burford & Resmini, 2017); the categorisation of the artefacts associated with a system; the definition of flow, value chain, and usage; and the management of information linking systems within an organisation or between organisations. Fahim et al. (2021) summate that information architectures enable communication between actors and among internal and external entities. Burke (2007) adds that EIA provides the framework

DOI: 10.1201/9781003390879-5

for planning and implementing rich, standards-based, digital information infra-structure with well-integrated services and activities.

Thus, on an emboldening front, many organisations are increasingly inter-ested in deploying EIA to provide categorisation, classification, and definition of information required to periodically perform the organisation's events, processes, and activities. From another angle of interest, some organisations are continually engrossed in the intent to employ EIA to manage and share information in ensur-ing that the business goals and objectives are supported by applications and data as required for competitive and sustainable purposes. Loomba et al. (2022) explain how information architecture is used to support data workflows within context, while Fahim et al. (2021) analyse how information architecture enables the integra-tion of capability between entities.

The categorisation, classification, and common definition of business informa-tion needs and their associated functions facilitate roles, definitions and model-lings of optimal system information flow. According to Gill and Chew (2019), EIA ensures that information has a common definition and that the information is secure. In addition, common terminology enables the consistent use of the seman-tics of meaning associated with solutions of information systems (IS), information technology (IT), and the entire organisation. This could be facilitated through the concept of reuse and mediation of local variations to a common ground. Also, this is an approach that can ultimately help an organisation in addressing some of its challenges towards achieving its business objectives and goals by providing employ-ees and other stakeholders with improved access to quality information.

Despite the relevance and increasing interest, there is little academic work on EIA (Almeida et al., 2020). This could be attributed to Kotusev et al. (2021), who argued that the status and practical operationalisation of EIA remain largely unclear. Considerably, an understanding of how EIA evolves and the expected out-comes from the evolution seem to remain unclear and challenging for both academ-ics and organisations in research and practice (Haki et al., 2020). What seems clear is that addressing information architecture issues is important to enabling effective-ness and efficient flow of information from the providers to the users, including the management (Singla & Aggarwal, 2020). This chapter aims to propose a fresh and different approach, which is to deploy EIA through the design, development, and implementation stages that are defined and guided by principles.

To many organisations, information is fundamental and shapes the outcome of their events and activities. According to Iyamu (2011, p. 7), "principles are defined as guiding statements of position which communicate the fundamental elements, truths, rules, or qualities that must be exhibited by the organisation". For this book, this definition is adopted in the context of EIA. The primary aim of principles is to enforce and enable an organisation to take an incremental and iterative approach to transition to formal modelling. Principles influence immediate and consistent deci-sion-making in organisations (Kotusev & Kurnia, 2021; Haki & Legner, 2021). Thus, the cruciality of principle needs to be embraced since the processes involved in the design, development, and implementation of EIA can be challenging. Liao and Wang (2021) argue that by applying architecture principles and the associated governance, an organisation can handle major tasks and achieve substantial changes in the processes and activities of the business.

Essentially, the formulation of the EIA principle is that first, the business needs and organisational requirements are the key drivers for the formulation of EIA principles; and second, the formulation of principles is guided by format to ensure value and consistency. The format is used to describe such attributes as the name and rationale of each principle. Other attributes that a principle can constitute are statement and implication. Within context, the attributes ensure the validity, completeness, comparability, relevance, and consistency of each principle. The formulation of principles is influenced by action, which manifests from interaction and relationship between the involved actors (employees) to deter and establish the business needs. To ensure and enforce uniformity and consistency, these actions are guided by strict rules which in some contexts necessitate use of obligatory passage points (OPPs).

In the formulation of principles, OPP can be adopted to guide the actors' actions as they collate business needs and align them with IT solutions, discretely and comprehensively. OPP acts as a compulsory set of rules and regulations within a legitimate entity. Iyamu and Dewald (2012) refer to OPP as a situation that forces actors to satisfy the interests that have been attributed to them by the focal actor (employer). The focal actor defines the OPP through which other actors must pass, by which the focal actor becomes indispensable in the tasks allocated. Thus, the principles of EIA could as such be defined as the OPP in the implementation of performance contracts by which individuals agree to undertake tasks.

As stated previously, this chapter aims to propose a fresh perspective by examining how principles can be applied in the development and implementation of EIA. In doing so, some questions of an essential nature arise. The questions are as follow.

    i. What are the factors influencing the development and implementation of information architecture in the organisation?
   ii. How is information architecture designed, developed, and implemented in the organisation?
  iii. What are some of the contributions of information architecture in the organisation?
  iv. What are some of the challenges of information architecture in the organisation?

Therefore, the chapter focuses on the principles that enforce the requirements, design, development, and implementation of EIA in an organisation. This is viewed and accomplished through the perspective of a sociotechnical context, which consists of human and non-human actors. The chapter is organised into four sections. The introduction of the chapter is provided in the first section, followed by a detailed discussion on the architecture of information from an organisation's perspective. Next, EIA is covered holistically from a practice perspective. Finally, the chapter is summarised.

5.2 The Architecture of Information

EIA is often understood as a comprehensive strategic approach for managing enterprise information, which puts essential components into perspective (Kotusev et al., 2021). Additionally, in many organisations, EIA is acknowledged as a significant meta-discipline concerned with the design, implementation, and maintenance of information flows and exchanges (Almeida et al., 2020). EIA's increasing essentiality, among other capabilities, could be linked to rapid popularity, as it expands its significance to digital and websites of institutions where the generation, management, and distribution of information are the focal points and major activities (Singla & Aggarwal, 2020; Ruzza et al., 2017). However, the use of the concept as a coercive mechanism to enforce these elements remains challenging.

In this chapter, the architecture of information in an organisation is viewed from the sociotechnical construct of objectivism, at macro and micro interconnected levels. At the macro level, the focus is on two main aspects. First, it addresses the importance of information architecture to an organisation. The second aspect focuses on the inter-relationship between technical and non-technical actors in the design, development, and implementation of information architecture in an organisation. At the micro level, the impact of principles on the design, development, and implementation of information architecture in an organisation is examined. Ontological construct, from subjectivism, is of paramount importance in the formulation of EIA principles, purposely to support and enable activities and events such as value chains and supply chains. Within the spheres of the principles, directions are set and business needs are defined and streamlined (Atmaja et al., 2021).

EIA provides a standard-based design, which is a development and implementation methodology that assists IS and IT solutions to rapidly respond to change within an organisation. This is enforced through business processes enabled by principles, in both the short and long terms. Decorously, this is because through principles, EIA allows and is used to achieve the translation of functional requirements for the selection of standards, components, configurations, phasing, and the acquisition of products and services.

In many organisations, the EIA approach is well received. One of the rationales for such acceptance could be linked to its capability to enable the 'track-and-trace' capability of attributes of artefacts (Fahim et al., 2021). Also, the increasing interest in the concept of EIA is based on their thoughts and an understanding that EIA brings fresh perspectives to solving challenges relating to information flow, use, and management. This is because some organisations have tried other disciplines and approaches, such as project management and systems analysis, but the challenges remain. Project management and systems analysis-based approaches have been widely adopted over the last four decades in trying to solve the same problems relating to information governance, yet many of the challenges persist. Hence, some organisations see the need to explore other approaches, such as EIA. EIA is an essential tool for management to fortify their efforts in aligning short-term investments with enterprise-wide and long-term objectives (Haki et al., 2020).

The architecture of information for enterprises' purposes involves deployment (development and implementation). Both the development and implementation of EIA and its components are guided by principles. Through the principle-based approach, EIA can contribute to a vast information ecology that supports and enables business events and IT solutions towards an organisation's sustainability and competitiveness.

5.3 Developing Enterprise Information Architecture

The focus of this chapter is on EIA, but without references to other related domains, there would be a disconnection in some areas, such as implications for business value and business information requirements (Gong & Janssen, 2019). As discussed in previous chapters, there is an interconnection between EIA and other domains. A four-domain approach as shown in Figure 1.1 is proposed for organisations that are interested in the adoption of the concept. The arrows in Figure 1.1 illustrate the function of enterprise business architecture (EBA) that leads to the development and implementation of EIA (Iyamu, 2022). The enterprise technical architecture (ETA) and the other architecture disciplines: EBA, EIA, and enterprise application architecture (EAA) are also interdependent, as each evolves and new opportunities and requirements are identified (Tamm et al., 2022).

The design of EIA depends on the domain of EBA. As such, it is difficult to embark on the development of the EIA without first establishing the constituents of EBA within the organisation. The EBA defines the real-time information that passes between the key processes and the integration requirements. This is enabled by the underlying application and technical architectures across the units of the organisation. Saleh and Dewi (2020) explain why EIA is required and how the concept can be used to support the operationalisation of business processes in an organisation. Concisely, information architecture presents a holistic description of an organisation's key strategies related to business and information value network and chain (Hrynko & Grinko, 2020).

Also, the EBA is used to express the organisation's key business strategies and tactics and their impact and interaction with business functions, processes, and activities which inform the development of EIA. Typically, it consists of the current- and future-state models of the functions, processes, and information value chains of an organisation. Subsequently, the EBA leads to the development of the EIA, which precede the ETA and EAA. In addition, this is primarily because it defines the business design for sustainability and objectivity, which are some of the principles for its design. Fischer et al. (2010) refer to principles as the construction of enterprise requirements. Hence, the EBA is intended to establish the foundations and details in the development of EIA. Concisely, Anthony Jr. (2021) posits that information architecture describes the components required to manage business events and processes of an organisation.

The development of EIA begins with the establishment of the overall information ecology in the organisation that deploys it. Primarily, it is intended to address the value proposition of the information including the processes and activities of an organisation. According to Evernden and Evernden (2012), information architecture is critical in increasing productivity and improving business processes, which add value and benefits to interactions with customers. This *includes* the direction of business development, policy, and strategies required for EIA (Atmaja et al., 2021). Thus, the application portfolio decision-making is guided by the principles of both EBA and EIA. This is used for identifying the functionalities needed and opportunities for reuse. It is also applied to conceptualise the ETA principles. The principles influence and dictate the selection, design, and implementation of software packages, application components and business objects.

5.4 Creating Enterprise Information Architecture Principles

EIA is often used to provide an initial classification and definition of information required to perform the goals and functions of an organisation. However, frameworks can be complementarily employed with the concept to manage and share information and to ensure that the organisation is supported by applications. The classification and common definition of business information needs and their associated functions are therefore guided by the EIA principles. The principles are primarily employed to facilitate the systems' role definition and the modelling of the optimal information flow and management.

In addition, EIA is adopted to provide a common terminology, which is intended to enable consistent semantic meaning in information systems and across entire organisations. This is done by facilitating concept reuse and the mediation of local variations to a common ground. This ultimately helps an organisation to achieve its objectives and provides stakeholders with improved access to quality information.

Many organisations follow recommendations offered by consulting houses—such as The Open Group Architecture Framework (TOGAF) (The Open Group, 2003), Zachman Framework (Zachman, 1987), Gartner Inc., and Forrester, in their quest to create principles. In some organisations, the recommendations seem to remain either theoretical or challenging. Hence, the practice or operationalisation of the EIA principles remains low. As part of achieving the aim of this chapter, a model is formulated as presented in Table 5.1. The model can be used to create principles that extend beyond organisational boundaries to external sources and targets. Subsequently, the model can be understood to enable rapid business decision-making and information sharing within an organisation and with suppliers, partners, and customers. As shown in the Table 5.1, four steps are involved in creating an EIA principle. The steps reflect on each other; therefore, the process must be linear, one step before the other.

Naming convention and its consistence and uniformity are enactments of governance. From the architectural perspective, principles are intended to provide guidelines and rationales for constantly examining and evaluating information in the areas of design, access, security, use, and maintenance. The name of each principle must be reflective of its intended purpose. Largely, principles are derived from the vision of the organisation. When the vision of the organisation is not clear or documented, this process happens through intensive discussion (sometimes, in the form of a workshop) with senior computing (IS and IT) and business management units in the organisation. Thereafter, the principles are validated against and aligned with the structures of the organisation. The formulation of principles is therefore viewed as a starting point for subsequent decisions that influence EIA in the organisation. Each principle states what should improve and contains key actions through its rationale and implication (Fischer et al., 2010).

Thus, through principles, EIA provides governance that improves the quality of the information that should exist in an environment and how the information should be shared between actors (Afzali et al., 2019). Within an organisation, the EIA approach is expected to encourage decision-makers to explore externalisation,

Table 5.1 Model for Creating Principles

Step	Attribute	Description
No. 1	**Name**	A name that the majority of the stakeholders can relate to and reflects the information and essence of the goal and objectives of the organisation. The name should be precise. Therefore, it is recommended to avoid ambiguous wording.
No. 2	**Statement**	This is to communicate the fundamental rules as set by the organisation, in its context and relevance. The statement must be clear, concise, and unambiguous.
No. 3	**Rationale**	Primarily, this is to highlight the potential benefits and value for the organisation in adhering to a principle.
No. 4	**Implications**	Highlights the potential implications of the business and IT for executing the principle. This includes the impact and consequences of adopting the principle.

optimise information value chains, plan application portfolios, increase the velocity of information across the organisation, and further evolve the enterprise architecture. Tannady et al., 2020) explain how The Zachman Framework classifies a descriptive representation of information architecture into cells based on perspective and focus to increase information value and accelerate its velocity.

Based on focus and capability, EIA is a business-strategy–driven set of artefacts that describe and model the information value network (IVN), which includes information flows, business events, and linkages of an organisation. Thus, the EIA approach should be sponsored and endorsed by senior management in IT and business units. The approach extends beyond the organisational boundaries to external sources. In addition, it is targeted to enable rapid business decision-making and information sharing. The primary rationale and implications of the EIA include the following.

   i. A catalogue of authentic sources of information (e.g., public and private company databases, information regarding internal and external partners, and news media).
   ii. Classes of relevant business information and their value to both internal and external partners, and to both public and private organisations.
   iii. Information governance processes that support policy development and information management principles and practices, which intend to address security access, privacy, confidentiality, information quality, integrity, authenticity, archival cycles, business continuity planning, and ownership of information and processes.
   iv. Information management deliverables that address roles, responsibilities, and organisational structures for managing information content and delivery, such as information management and ownership.

The design, development, and implementation of EIA are aimed to establish the value and importance of using information effectively across the various units within an environment, as well as the need to achieve collaborative excellence with external partners and customers (citizenry). In times of conflicts or misunderstanding, particularly in a digital form, the EIA approach is also employed to gain consensus (through negotiation) between actors, such as the senior and middle management levels in an organisation. This is done within the rationale and implications associated with the principles. Some of the questions and elements that should be considered to enable a shift in such negotiations include:

   i. What is strategic versus non-strategic information, especially in terms of security?
   ii. How are the use and definition of common terms such as service, consumption, and citizens carried out in organisations?
   iii. Who has the information, and in what form and capacity?

iv. Who owns and manages the information, and how should it be leveraged for organisational benefit?
v. Who is responsible for the cost of developing IS/IT systems that create and deliver information to the users and clients within and outside the organisation?
vi. What metrics are used to measure information sharing success or failure from the perspectives of security, intelligence, revenue increase, cost decrease, and service delivery times?

However, effective management and exploitation of information through IS/IT is key to business success. This is indispensable, which means achieving the goals and objectives of the organisation is supposed to address the identified need. This is possible by providing a strategic context for the evolution of the IT solution in response to the constantly changing needs of the environment. Afzali et al. (2019) suggest that EIA defines the models, rules, and policies that define this evolution, which entails the collection, storage, retrieval, use, and exchange of information about an artefact.

EIA is required to encourage decision-makers at both business and IT units to explore the externalisation and optimisation of information value chains. This includes planning application portfolios and incremental use of the velocity of information across an enterprise in an iteration process. As a result, the development of EIA conveys a logical sequence which is based on relationships and dependencies of the elements within scope rather than a linear sequence of events. The three rationales for the logical sequence in developing EIA are as follow.

i. As the model was essentially business-driven, the EBA has to first model the impact of business visioning on the operations of the business.
ii. Because the EIA focuses on how information could best be leveraged, exploited, or otherwise used to provide business value, it is dependent on a certain amount of EBA modelling to determine how and where the business could derive its value.
iii. The approach to ETA depends on the business strategies and business information requirements, so this dependency places it logically after EBA and EIA.

EIA is intended to address the policy, governance, and information products necessary for information sharing across an organisation, with external partners and clients. This includes four objectives: (i) information management deliverables that address information management roles and responsibilities; (ii) information quality and integrity; (iii) data definition standards, data stewardship, and ownership; and (iv) information security access. These objectives form the foundation on which principles of information architecture are formulated. The principles are based on the vision of the organisation, including the strategies of each unit in an organisation, as previously explained.

However, not all principles are necessarily identified in earlier paths towards the development of models. Such omissions are reduced or eradicated via an iterative process, which can be confirmed as best practice through institutionalisation. Chapter 12 of this book covers the institutionalisation of the EA. Best practice aids consistent and improved quality of results. Therefore, the degree to which an organisation could establish principles in EIA is dependent on its process and capability to identify and apply best practices in each area.

5.5 Enterprise Information Architecture in an Organisation

Within an organisation, the practice of EIA focuses on how the concept is designed, developed, and implemented through a set of principles. The formulation of EIA principles has been previously discussed. The principles of EIA provide guides to the designers, developers, and implementers of EIA within an environment. The principles for each of the components of information architecture are derived from an organisation's vision and requirements. As explained in Table 5.1, for each principle, there is compulsorily a rationale which must be documented along with other elements, such as the statements of intent, repercussions for the intent, and allocation of tasks and accountabilities. There are four categories of principles in the EIA approach; design principles, development principles, implementation principles, and migration planning principles. Thereafter, measurement and validation, and gap analysis are undertaken.

The EIA provides fundamental principles that assist an organisation to achieve quality information for sustainability and competitiveness. According to Fischer et al. (2010), principles can be attributed to different layers in the business and IT units. The factors that influence the principles are from internal and external partners and clients' perspectives in a shared vision, change, evolutionary planning, classification and declassification, citizen empowerment, collaboration, problem coping, analysis, and restructuring organisational norms. These factors also support the implementation of processes and functions. The principles are interactive and interwoven, and they are formulated to achieve the objectives of an organisation. It begins with the design principles.

5.5.1 Design Principles

The design principles guide the boundaries and limitations, including the rationale and implication of EIA in an organisation. The design is based on both the short-term and long-term strategic intentions of an organisation. Table 5.2 depicts the guiding phenomena within which the design principles can be formulated. An organisation can customise the TOGAF format by adding the 'Ownership' column.

Table 5.2 Design Principles

Design Principles	Statement	Rationale	Implication	Ownership
Description	Indicate its identity, within which it could be associated with an objective	The justification, is an expression of the value to the organisation	For each principle, there must be an adopted standard, sometimes derived from best practices	Each principle is allocated to an individual or unit for execution and monitoring purposes

Due to the significance of principles, a more contractual formal approach is often or should be employed. Thus, the OPP in the form of a contractual agreement can be applied to formulate and enforce principles, such as the following.

i. Information must be valued as an asset and leveraged across the information value chain (IVN) to enhance competitive advantage and accelerate decision-making in the organisation.

ii. The IVN must continuously be identified and exploited within the organisation and the country in general.

iii. The information must be shared to maximise the effectiveness of decision-making throughout the organisation and to external partners, citizens, and other government departments.

iv. The security of the categories of information must take priority over all requirements within the organisation and shared service with other organisations.

v. Accessibility of information must be reviewed as frequently as possible.

vi. Information management must be unified across the organisation.

vii. The organisation's information must be managed throughout its lifecycle by the stewards who define subsequent roles.

viii. The interfaces across separate logical boundaries must be message-based and extend across the value chain to employees, partners, and customers.

ix. The organisation's information must have accessible metadata, which describes the definition, security classification, function class, ownership, and stewardship.

x. Leverage the business intelligence environment to accelerate decision-making and reduce development complexity.

Until the design is developed and implemented, it remains theoretical, which does not necessarily add actual value to the organisation. However, without design, the development of principles can be difficult or near impossible.

5.5.2 Development Principles

The aims and objectives of EIA are numerous and contextual, which means they differ from one organisation to another. On the long list of objectives are the reduction of integration complexity, control of duplication and replication, regulation of validation and correction of source, standardisation of information access, and detection and management of data isolation. Subjectively, the list of objectives is summarised into five categories (Figure 5.1): requirements, information management and control, information source, information classes, and information value network.

5.5.2.1 Requirements for Information Architecture

The principles that guide the development and implementation of the EIA are derived from the requirements and vision of an organisation, which include aims and objectives. Requirements are well documented as important (Engelsman et al., 2011), and changes make it a process-oriented activity (Jallow et al., 2017). The principles are therefore formulated to legitimise the scope and boundaries of each of the technical and non-technical artefacts. In addition, the intended deliverables are formulated in addressing roles, responsibilities, and organisational structures in managing information content, including storage, dissemination, and delivery.

5.5.2.2 Information Management and Controls

The management and control of information require principles to ensure boundaries and consistency across an organisation. Explicitly, the management and control principle facilitates information processing, consumption pattern, and its use for

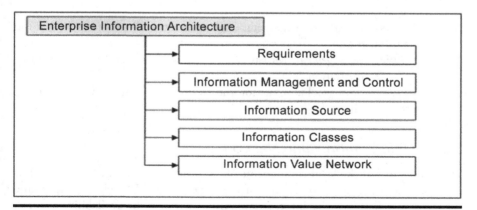

Figure 5.1 EIA Development Principles.

communication purposes (Venkatesan & Sridhar, 2019). Thus, 'management' and 'control' are statements of governance, monitoring, effectiveness, and efficiency of information use, storage, and ownership in the organisation. The principles are therefore intended to address security access, privacy, confidentiality, quality, integrity, authenticity, archival cycles, business resumption planning, and ownership of information within an organisation.

5.5.2.3 Information Sources

Within set principles, a catalogue of authentic information sources, such as the organisation's databases, internet and social media, commercial databases, news media, and government gazettes are used to establish the origins of the information on, about, and for the organisation. It also forms the basis of input for the next step (information classes, as discussed in what follows), which are used to obtain classes of relevant information and establish their value to an organisation. The governance provided by EIA can guide the filtering of the information to establish credibility and authenticity.

5.5.2.4 Information Classes

There is often a need for the classification of information in an organisation, primarily because it is an organisation's core business that is pursued at the time. The intention is to improve access to and the management of information to improve service delivery. This helps the stakeholders—including architects—to understand the value of each category. Based on the requirements, information can be classified according to the following criteria.

The functions are concerned with the following operational, managerial, and strategic activities.

i. *Business operations*: The operational (transactional) processes within the administration.
ii. *Business management*: Measurement (scorekeeping) and management of the administration.
iii. *Business strategy*: Planning for the future and identifying competitive opportunities.

5.5.2.5 Information Value Network

The IVN is one of the focal components of the principles of EIA that exist within an organisation. It helps to achieve an objective of the EIA, which is to define the sources of high-velocity information. Also, it ensures the availability of high-velocity information, and its usage by the key business processes is enabled by the underlying domains of both EAA and ETA. High-velocity information is shared within the information value network of customers, suppliers, and partners in near real-time, at both the transactional and decision support levels. This is to maximise operational effectiveness, efficiency, and high performance towards competitive advantage and to improve service delivery.

The value of information could be determined by different means—typically, the competitive advantage gained using information products. Essentially, there are three dimensions of information value: velocity, density, and reach. Velocity is the speed at which information is transmitted; reach establishes measures for assessing information, and density is concerned with the volume of information in a given space, at a time. Moving along one or more of these dimensions can increase the value of information within an organisation.

Methods and tools such as IVN analysis are used to diagnose problems or uncover opportunities to leverage IT deliverables in creating high value. Additionally, the methods can be used to assess low-cost linkages with external parties and across the lines of business (LOB). The IVN describes the linkages in a network and the value of information across the business value chain in enabling business processes, events, and procedures. Since information is an artefact of business processes, it surrounds and supports the physical value chain. Principles are therefore formulated to address components of the EIA. Table 5.2 is provided as a template for recording and guiding development principles. On that basis, this template can be populated and used to support strategic analysis over time. This leads to the implementation of the entire design, which is summarised into four areas and enforced through a set of principles.

5.5.3 *Implementation Principles*

The implementation stage enables an organisation to change from the current state to the future state, as was defined during the project initiation. As presented in Figure 5.2, the primary and key mechanisms of implementation are carried out

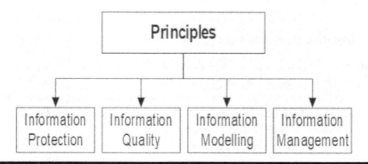

Figure 5.2 EIA Principles.

through four main components: information protection, information quality, information modelling, and information management.

5.5.3.1 Information Protection

Information shared across an organisation is regarded as corporate information. It is therefore demarcated to ensure manageability by specific units and information types. Thus, information protection against unauthorised persons is critical in organisations (Alkhodaidi & Gutub, 2022). Access and protection of information are of high priority in many organisations, especially those that rely on it in totality. As such, principles are significantly formulated to address ownership, security, and access to classification, privacy, archives, and information recovery. This is intended to support and enable the continuity of processes and activities in an environment.

5.5.3.2 Information Quality

The quality of information is primarily based on business requirements. Effectively, it is crucial to govern the requirements, which might lead to a change process (Jallow et al., 2017). Information quality is a key determinant that influences service delivery (Meilatinova, 2021). Also, the quality is principled to be governed by the requirements and vision of an organisation. The principles concentrate on the metadata, integrity, authenticity, classification, and criticality of the organisation's information.

5.5.3.3 Information Modelling

Information modelling depicts the inter-relationships and interconnectivity of objects, entities, and things. information modelling focuses on describing the required components and how they interrelate and interconnect with each other (Abualdenien & Borrmann, 2022). The principle states that an information model represents information in an understandable simplified format. Information is to be modelled according to the principles of the EIA and the application development guidelines of the organisation.

5.5.3.4 Information Management

Information management principles define the roles, responsibilities, and organisational structure required to implement the architecture of information in the organisation. Kassen (2022) suggests that information management enables the transparency and efficiency of activities. This also defines, *inter alia*, the role that users play as custodians of information, the role of the IS/IT unit, and the roles of information architects in ensuring that this principle is understood, adhered to, and effectively applied. There is an emphasis on the role of the information architect as the domain owner.

5.5.4 Migration Planning Principles

Positioning strategy and movement from one architectural phase to another is acknowledged as being a very complex issue by the architects and other stakeholders in the organisation. It is much more complex than simply bringing in a new vendor or independent consultant to provide theoretical underpinning and advisory guidance.

Certainly, one of the key decision-making processes often involved with architectural planning is the need to have a future target. Shorter-term goals could then be defined as stepping stones to strategic goals. Again, the problem is that historically, information technologists have not been very accurate in predicting products' directions and timing. As such, the migration principles are formulated based on the context of an organisation.

5.5.5 Measurement and Validation

The principles of measurement and validation are an integral component of the overall EIA approach. By way of confirmation, the principles are a set of obligations for management, administration, practices of information storage, and usage within an environment in which the EIA is deployed. There are four main components of focus areas within measurement. The components are enterprise planning, business analysis, systems analysis, and systems design. Primarily, the components are used as a conformance checklist. The components are briefly explained in Table 5.3.

Table 5.3 Conformance Components

Component	Description
Enterprise planning	This component ensures the alignment of requirements and vision with the information architecture. It specifies the core information areas, dependencies, implications, rationale, and ownership.
Business analysis	This ensures that business analysis addresses the business model, including the impacts, duplications, and changes that information has on an organisation's objectives and processes. It ensures that the business information conforms to guidance such as protection, ownership, accessibility, and classification, as defined in the information management principles.
Systems analysis	The systems analysis component covers the systems model. It ensures conformance to modelling guidelines and quality in terms of metadata, integrity, authenticity, and classification as defined by the respective principles.
Systems design	This ensures the adherence to information architecture principles and information policies, standards, management roles, and responsibilities.

The measurement constitutes a conformance checklist, an iterative process, and the domain architect who oversees the processes and activities within the scope of the EIA. The conformance checklist within an environment is a defined set of principles within the context of organisational meaning and value, as described in Table 5.3. During the implementation stage, gaps are identified and analysed for possible deficiencies, opportunities, and solutions.

The final phase of EIA deployment through a project is the gap analysis. This is conducted across all the categorised areas to determine corrective action and the development of prioritised migration plans, and finally the development of an implementation plan.

5.5.6 Gap Analysis

The gap analysis approach is used to assess the current state of the information architecture against the desired state as reflected by organisational drivers, including business and technology requirements. The assessment is an iterative process and is reflected by a conformance checklist and an accompanying action plan. As shown in Table 5.3, the assessment is to be stored and managed within the principles of conformance. Table 5.4 presents a guide for gap analysis.

Several constraints often have to be overcome to completely achieve the implementation of EIA in an environment. Some of the potential constraints include:

- i. The inherited technological environment that exists at the initiation of a process.
- ii. New information systems or technologies that constantly emerge and which must be accommodated.
- iii. Immediate concerns, such as providing IS/IT support for a new quarter, branch office, or building.
- iv. The fact that any information systems architecture is always in transition and is ever-changing and evolving.

Table 5.4   Gap Analysis

Gap Analysis	Requirement (Future State)	Action Plan	Deliverables	Roles and Responsibilities
Description	Eradicate uncontrolled data duplication and redundancy	Project to be initiated	Project scope and migration plan	Project manager information architect

5.6 Factors Influencing Enterprise Information Architecture

Information architecture is not static, and neither is the environment in which it is deployed. From time to time, some factors influence the EIA. The influencing factors are not constant but rather are variable. Also, some of the influencing factors vary from one organisation to another. However, certain factors significantly remain and apply to every environment. This includes criticality of principles, iteration, information architects, ownership and stock of knowledge.

5.6.1 Criticality of Principles

The EIS provides fundamental principles for achieving change within an environment. The principles are fundamental in that they guide areas such as the development of a shared vision, evolutionary planning, and provision for innovations, empowerment, and regular training of employees, analysis, and restructuring of organisational norms to support the implementation and ongoing learning and processes of using and managing information within an environment. Thus, the principles must be interactive and interwoven throughout the process of EIA. Principles assist with consistency; in fact, they lead to the development and deployment of consistent, multiple software- and technology-based changes in the business and the amalgamation of both the IT and the business.

5.6.2 Iterative Process

Within the scope of EIA, principles are articulated to address the aims and objectives of information in an environment. This is done in an iterative process. Some of the primary objectives include encouraging decision-makers to:

   i. Explore external trading and partnerships.
   i. Optimise information value chains.
 iii. Plan application architectures and systems portfolios.
  iv. Increase information velocity across the organisation.

Through the iterative approach, EIA is intended to identify how information flows for optimisation (increased velocity, density, and reach). Each information entity is also identified in the process. This is to define and consistently use information across the value chain. The intention is to increase the value of information across an organisation and external transactions.

Based on the objectives, EIA defines the sources of information and ensures the availability and use of this information by the key business processes. Also, it enables the underlying application and technical architectures. Similar to the EBA domain, it is expected to guide business operations that are affected by business strategies.

5.6.3 Information Architects

Within the boundaries of set principles, information architects focus on the construction of information models to meet business requirements. This includes engineering 'out' gaps where business-critical, high-velocity information is not reaching customers, suppliers and partners. Information architects also provide guidelines that concern an organisation's information assets to knowledge workers, information processors, IS/IT application developers, infrastructure managers, and management executives. However, there is always a concern in terms of the availability of skilled information architects. Primarily, the information architect focuses on process effectiveness and efficiencies arising from the elimination of non–value-adding and redundant tasks, streamlined information flow, systems placement, and business restructuring.

5.6.4 Ownership

Data, storage, process, infrastructure, and collaboration constitute some of the basics and foundations of the principles of information architecture which are allocated to individuals and groups within the IS/IT unit. Through the irreversible nature of the OPP, the principles which were formulated can be enforced. Primarily, it gives power to those people to whom the design, development, and implementation tasks were allocated to execute their responsibilities. The OPP makes each principle to be irreversible by individuals or groups, regardless of their positions in the organisation.

5.6.5 Stock of Knowledge

The stock of knowledge is not necessarily as valuable as the intended act. This is mainly because it is difficult to translate values to usefulness. However, the exact source where knowledge comes from is not easily identified. This is a major contributing factor to why managing knowledge is a challenge. As a result, the stock of knowledge is critically important, mainly because it has to be understood before its application.

The role of EIA is often misunderstood. It is difficult to differentiate between business analysts and business or information architects. According to Iyamu et al. (2016), the confusion between business analysts and architects could be of a conscious or an unconscious by people who are directly responsible. As a result, the allocation of tasks, roles, and responsibilities becomes challenging to manage.

5.7 Summary

Enterprise information architecture (EIA) offers tangible benefits to an enterprise and other stakeholders that are responsible for evolving the enterprise through its principles. The primary purpose of the principles is to *inform, guide* and manage *constraining* decisions for an enterprise, especially those related to information flow and management. The true challenge of enterprise engineering is to maintain information as a primary authoritative resource for an enterprise's information systems and information technology (IS/IT) planning. This goal can be met via the enforcement of EIA principles which add value and utility of the information to the overall architecture of the enterprise. Thus, applying EIA objectives through its principles within the context of a specific business enterprise enables an organisation to create a joint business and IS/IT planning and execution processes. The integration of business and IS/IT planning could result in a faster time to market, increased customer intimacy, and improved operational efficiency through the set principles.

The benefits as emphasised in this chapter are of paramount importance to business and IS/IT managers in organisations, as stated. Also, the chapter is important to the academic domain in that it contributes to the body of knowledge through its addition to existing literature, and it opens opportunities to researchers for further research areas such as the social construction of information, semiotics integration of information architecture into business strategy, and the ontology of information architecture.

References

Abualdenien, J., & Borrmann, A. (2022). Ensemble-learning approach for the classification of Levels of Geometry (LOG) of building elements. *Advanced Engineering Informatics, 51*, 101497.

Afzali, M., Etemad, K., Kazemi, A., & Rabiei, R. (2019). Cerebral palsy information system with an approach to information architecture: A systematic review. *BMJ Health & Care Informatics, 26*(1), e100055.

Alkhodaidi, T. M., & Gutub, A. A. (2022). Scalable shares generation to increase participants of counting-based secret sharing technique. *International Journal of Information and Computer Security, 17*(1–2), 119–146.

Almeida, M. B., Felipe, E. R., & Barcelos, R. (2020). Toward a document-centered ontological theory for information architecture in corporations. *Journal of the Association for Information Science and Technology, 71*(11), 1308–1326.

Anthony Jnr, B. (2021). Managing digital transformation of smart cities through enterprise architecture—a review and research agenda. *Enterprise Information Systems, 15*(3), 299–331.

Atmaja, S. A., Putra, I. E., Muslim, I. A., & Purnandi, H. (2021). Architecture design of e-information system marketplace with method enterprise architecture planning. *Budapest International Research and Critics Institute (BIRCI-Journal): Humanities and Social Sciences, 4*(3), 3689–3710.

Burford, S., & Resmini, A. (2017). Cross-channel information architecture for a world exposition. *International Journal of Information Management, 37*(6), 547–552.

Burke, B. (2007). *The role of enterprise architecture in technology research.* Gartner Inc. Retrieved April 14, 2010, from http://gartner.com/technology/research.jsp

Engelsman, W., Quartel, D., Jonkers, H., & van Sinderen, M. (2011). Extending enterprise architecture modelling with business goals and requirements. *Enterprise Information Systems, 5*(1), 9–36.

Evernden, R., & Evernden, E. (2012). *Information first: Integrating knowledge and information architecture for business advantage.* Routledge.

Fahim, P. B., An, R., Rezaei, J., Pang, Y., Montreuil, B., & Tavasszy, L. (2021). An information architecture to enable track-and-trace capability in Physical Internet ports. *Computers in Industry, 129*, 103443.

Fischer, C., Winter, R., & Aier, S. (2010). What is an enterprise architecture principle? In *Computer and information science 2010* (pp. 193–205). Springer.

Gill, A. Q., & Chew, E. (2019). Configuration information system architecture: Insights from applied action design research. *Information & Management, 56*(4), 507–525.

Gong, Y., & Janssen, M. (2019). The value of and myths about enterprise architecture. *International Journal of Information Management, 46*, 1–9.

Haki, K., Beese, J., Aier, S., & Winter, R. (2020). The evolution of information systems architecture: An agent-based simulation model. *Management Information Systems (MIS) Quarterly, 44*(1), 155–184.

Haki, K., & Legner, C. (2021). The mechanics of enterprise architecture principles. *Journal of the Association for Information Systems, 22*(5), 1334–1375.

Hrynko, P., & Grinko, A. (2020). Methodological approaches to modeling information architecture of the organization in the conditions of digital economy. *EUREKA: Social and Humanities, 1*(1), 27–34.

Iyamu, T. (2011). The architecture of information in organisations. *South African Journal of Information Management, 13*(1), 1–9.

Iyamu, T. (2022). *Enterprise architecture for strategic management of modern IT solutions* (1st ed.). Auerbach Publications.

Iyamu, T., & Dewald, R. (2012). The use of structuration theory and actor network theory for analysis. *International Journal of Actor-Network Theory and Technological Innovation, 9*(4), 217–228.

Iyamu, T., Nehemia-Maletzky, M., & Shaanika, I. (2016). The overlapping nature of business analysis and business architecture: What we need to know. *The Electronic Journal Information Systems Evaluation, 19*(3), 168–178.

Jallow, A. K., Demian, P., Anumba, C. J., & Baldwin, A. N. (2017). An enterprise architecture framework for electronic requirements information management. *International Journal of Information Management, 37*(5), 455–472.

Kappelman, L. A., & Zachman, J. A. (2013). The enterprise and its architecture: Ontology & challenges. *Journal of Computer Information Systems, 53*(4), 87–95.

Kassen, M. (2022). Blockchain and e-government innovation: Automation of public information processes. *Information Systems, 103*, 101862.

Kotusev, S., & Kurnia, S. (2021). The theoretical basis of enterprise architecture: A critical review and taxonomy of relevant theories. *Journal of Information Technology, 36*(3), 275–315.

Kotusev, S., Kurnia, S., & Dilnutt, R. (2021). The concept of information architecture in the context of enterprise architecture. *Aslib Journal of Information Management*, *74*(3), 432–457.

Liao, M. H., & Wang, C. T. (2021). Using enterprise architecture to integrate lean manufacturing, digitalization, and sustainability: A lean enterprise case study in the chemical industry. *Sustainability*, *13*(9), 1–26.

Loomba, J. J., Wasson, G. S., Chamakuri, R. K. R., Dash, P. K., Patterson, S. G., Potter, M. M., Krisch, E. J., Tenzer, M. M., Johnston, C. K., & Brown, D. E. (2022). The iTHRIV commons: A cross-institution information and health research data sharing architecture and web application. *Journal of the American Medical Informatics Association*, *29*(4), 631–642.

Meilatinova, N. (2021). Social commerce: Factors affecting customer repurchase and word-of-mouth intentions. *International Journal of Information Management*, *57*, 102300.

The Open Group. (2003). *The open group architecture framework version 8.1. "Enterprise Edition"*, 1–12. Retrieved from https://pubs.opengroup.org/architecture/togaf8-doc/arch/

Ruzza, M., Tiozzo, B., Mantovani, C., D'Este, F., & Ravarotto, L. (2017). Designing the information architecture of a complex website: A strategy based on news content and faceted classification. *International Journal of Information Management*, *37*(3), 166–176.

Saleh, M. P. A. Q., & Dewi, S. (2020). Design of enterprise information system architecture with Oracle Architecture Development Process (OADP) case study in Vocational High Schools. *International Journal of Quantitative Research and Modeling*, *1*(4), 217–228.

Singla, B. S., & Aggarwal, H. (2020). Effect of information architecture on the usability of a university website: A comparative study of selected websites of Punjab (India). *International Journal of Distributed Systems and Technologies (IJDST)*, *11*(1), 38–52.

Tamm, T., Seddon, P. B., & Shanks, G. (2022). How enterprise architecture leads to organisational benefits. *International Journal of Information Management*, *67*, 102554.

Tannady, H., Andry, J. F., Sudarsono, B. G., & Krishartanto, Y. (2020). Enterprise architecture using Zachman framework at paint manufacturing company. *Technology Reports of Kansai University*, *62*(4), 1869–1883.

Venkatesan, D., & Sridhar, S. (2019). A rationale for the choice of enterprise architecture method and software technology in a software driven enterprise. *International Journal of Business Information Systems*, *32*(3), 272–311.

Zachman, J. (1987). A framework for information systems. *IBM Systems Journal*, *26*(3), 276–283.

Chapter 6

The Deployment of Enterprise Application Architecture

6.1 Introduction

As has been experienced in the last two decades around the world, change in organisations is rapid and it is highly likely not going to slow down—it would rather increase. The rapid change in business needs and the evolution of technology continue to pose challenges to many organisations that wholly rely on applications for their objective logic, processes, and activities. To fulfil the ever-growing business needs, more complex, flexible, scalable, and extensible applications are needed (Jia et al., 2018; Shan & Hua, 2006). Applications are often grouped into categories, mainly to classify their functionalities and technical specifications (Malallah et al., 2021; Netto et al., 2018). Additionally, in some quarters, the categorisation is intended to understand the applications and provide appropriate governance.

Applications are employed and deployed for both technical and business purposes; hence, the categorisation. There is a difference between technical and business applications and their requirements (Shaanika & Iyamu, 2018). Technical applications refer to software (or systems) used to enable and support computer operations and capability, such as operating systems (OSs; e.g., Windows, Linux), programming languages (e.g., Java, C), network administration (e.g., network management, network monitoring), and security solutions (e.g., virtual private networks [VPNs], firewalls). Business applications are computer systems used by organisations to automate their processes, objective logic, and activities for profitability, sustainability, and competitiveness. This includes word processing, spreadsheets, enterprise

DOI: 10.1201/9781003390879-6

resource planning (ERP), and in-house solutions (applications developed uniquely for an organisation).

Regardless of the source, in-house built, buy, open source or reuse organisations implement different types of applications in their environments. Table 6.1 presents the formatting and classification of applications. Applications are deployed for various reasons using both business and technical requirements. Also, some applications require the services of other applications to carry out their function. Business applications (e.g., databases, ERP) which support the organisation for competitiveness are enabled by technical applications such as OSs. Additionally, both business and technical applications depend on each other to fulfil the organisation's needs. The dependencies make understanding the business and technical requirements critical. Hence, architecture is critically necessary for providing governance for the development, integration, reuse, and implementation of the applications within an environment. In this chapter and book, differentiation is not emphasised; both sets of technical and business applications are combined and referred to as 'applications' for enterprise architecture purposes.

Applications are sourced from in-house development, purchased off the shelf, or reused. Applications that are developed in-house are organisation-specific and are often copyrighted. Off-the-shelf applications are either proprietary or open source. Reusable applications are often open source, but can also be proprietary. Regardless of the source, whether in whole or in part, the applications should be guided by architecture within an environment for reasons such as coexistence, integration, compatibility, and flexibility.

Applications are developed, implemented, or reused in organisations primarily to automate business processes and activities to enable organisational needs towards sustainability and enhance competitiveness. According to Aerts et al. (2004), the capacity of modern enterprises to compete depends hugely on business applications. Increasingly, applications have become inevitable because of the opportunities they provide to organisations (Al-Omoush, 2022). As a result of its importance, the development, selection, reuse, and implementation of applications are acute. Despite the enormous significance associated with applications, there are various challenges encountered during development, implementation, or use. Woods and Rozanski (2010) argue that there is hardly regularity in application implementation. According to Herrmann (2022), many applications are ambiguous and lack clarification. This makes many applications difficult to coexist with or be customised or integrated into some environments; hence, the architecture of the applications is essential.

Enterprise application architecture (EAA) focuses on business functions and rational decision-making in the implementation and use of applications (Lamola, 2022). Primarily, the architecture is to provide governance and regulation on applications in the selection, development, implementation, and use within an environment. Some organisations employ EAA to address the challenges often posed and encountered in the development, selection, use, or reuse of applications. Application architecture provides a blueprint which guides application deployment and their interactions and relationships with the core business processes of an organisation. AA is a domain of the EA, which focuses on the governance and strategy aspects of applications. According to Tamm et al., 2022), EA covers both current and future states, and it focuses on the enterprise's business processes and information technology (IT) systems (or solutions) and their inter-relationships.

EA consists of four main interrelated domains as presented and discussed in Chapter 1. It begins with enterprise business architecture (EBA). In the explanation of Masuda et al. (2021), the EAA activates the EBA's process activities by guiding application development and implementation. Anthony Jnr. (2021) explains how EAA is based on business strategy and standards and guided by information architecture. Shaanika and Iyamu (2018) emphasise that the EIA provides the requirements needed to develop and implement EAA, with an impact on the processes of business users, application developers (or specialists), and IT architects. The EAA provides requirements and a guide for the enterprise's technical architecture (Iyamu, 2022).

The rationale for developing and implementing EAA might differ from one organisation to another. Harmon (2005) argues that EA is implemented primarily as a base to determine the enhancement of requirements and rationalise investments to foster competitiveness. EA is intended to bridge the gap between the business and IT units in organisations. Kang et al. (2010) suggest that EA could be used as a tool to align business and IT units in an organisation. Simply defining EA exposes gaps in business processes and strategy, IT strategy, and the relationship between the business and IT units of an organisation.

This chapter presents a systematic approach to the practice of EAA, which includes the development, implementation, and change impact on an organisation, from current to future states. The chapter also covers how EAA provides significant differences in applications' coexistence and management within an environment. The objectives and focus of this chapter are therefore twofold: (i) to present how EAA is developed and implemented distinctly; and (ii) to gain a better understanding of how EAA facilitates change, from the viewpoints of both business processes and technology solutions.

The chapter is divided into six main sections. it begins with an introduction and thereafter presents the challenges often encountered by applications in deploying EAA. This is followed by a discussion about EAA as a concept. Next, it covers the practice of the concept and details the steps in the deployment. How EAA engineers change in an environment is presented using a model, and the impact of the change is discussed. Finally, the chapter is summarised.

6.2 Application and Enterprise Architecture Application Challenges

The development, selection, reuse, implementation, and overall governance of applications continue to be challenging in many organisations, thereby making a case for more studies. The most critical challenges are attributed to the following four factors and expanded in the discussion that follows.

i. Selection, the impact of inappropriate 'fit' of applications.
ii. Integration, how applications are deployed and their influence on other applications that they are connected to within an environment.
iii. Configuration, the effect of the relationships of applications with an environment.
iv. Compatibility, the coexistence of applications with each other.

The way some applications are built makes them problematic, causing some organisations to avoid or abandon their deployment. This sometimes negatively affects business processes and activities. This also results in budget over-spend by some organisations during the implementation of such problematic applications. The need for dynamicity, scalability, and easy maintenance makes it complex and difficult to design, develop, and maintain applications.

There is often a lack of uniformity in requirements and the applications deployed in many organisations (Popli et al., 2018). This is a critical challenge that seeks redress to avoid continued prohibitive circumstances. With the rapidly growing competitive nature of many industries and sectors, the challenges will likely continue to increase, and thus, the solutions must respond by improving.

Many studies have been conducted about the significance of EAA, from both practice (business) and academic standpoints. The majority of the studies focus on the merit of EAA and justifications for adopting the concept in an enterprise (Oliveira et al., 2018). One of the many examples is by Safaei et al. (2022), who vigorously argued that EAA supported by The Open Group Architecture Framework (TOGAF) is a blueprint for applying, deploying, and enabling interactions and inter-relationships with the business processes of an organisation. None of these studies seems to provide a guide on how to develop and implement EAA in an enterprise. The lack of or the slow adoption or practice of EAA can be attributed to the lack of a practice-oriented guide (Tao et al., 2017).

Also, it is hard to find books or research studies that provide a comprehensive evaluation of EAA adoption in an organisation (Lamola, 2022). Another important point is that many of the research or academic works focus on software architecture. EAA is broader than software. It encompasses both software and application, from both business and technical perspectives. Shaanika and Iyamu (2018) summed it up as follows: both sets of software and applications are the focal point of the EAA that drives and determines the efficiency and effectiveness of the organisation. For this book, EAA is defined as a collection of integrated information systems and their components that are required for satisfying organisational needs.

Another important challenge of EAA is in its maturity in an organisation. Many organisations try to deploy EAA even when they are not ready to do so. Whilst ome organisations struggle to progress from one stage of maturity to another. Herrmann

(2022) highlights some of the challenges as disagreement and confusion about terminology which impede practitioners in the development and implementation of EAA. The application architecture can be defined to address application maturity through the matrix model (Batmetan, 2022).

6.3 Enterprise Application Architecture

EAA as one of the EA domains defines how applications are designed, how they coexist, where they reside, and how they are used to support efficiency, enable business needs, and enhance competitiveness (Iyamu, 2015). Thus, EAA is intended to provide governance for the development, selection, and implementation of applications. Consequently, this is to enable and guide integration and decision support, as well as transactions from the current to future states (Winter, 2001). According to Schekkerman (2004), the application component identifies, defines, and organises the activities that capture, manipulate, and manage business information to support mission operations.

Moreover, EAA is intended to enable a high level of distributed systems integration, the reuse of systems components, the rapid deployment of applications, and high responsiveness to changing business and technology requirements. Postma (2003) argues that the application of architecture supports a system designer to find the pieces of source codes that should be changed by translating the architecture level. EAA guides application development, implementation, and use in organisations (Safaei et al., 2022). Based on requirements, EAA is tailored to an organisation's context and application processes (Tao et al., 2017). Riwanto and Andry (2019) suggest that EAA provides an overview of interaction, communication, and information flow between applications that support business functions and processes.

Another aim of EAA is to enable and support the development and implementation of applications consistently and uniformly. From a functional angle, EAA provides architects and managers with the components' alignment of applications to enable and support business functions (Anthony Jnr, 2021). Katuu (2018) explains that one of the strengths of EAA is its support for applications to enable business capabilities. Thus, EAA is often considered a technology-based change of business processes, and an amalgamation of both business activities and technology solutions. According to Winter (2001), EAA allows for the documentation of the most important applications and their relationships, as well as the rules that are used for creating and maintaining appropriate application structures in organisations.

However, the deployment of EAA and enactment of governance is not always as easy as it is sometimes claimed. This is because applications do sometimes encounter challenges, such as integration, compatibility, and manageability (Malik & Om, 2018). This causes some applications to be cost-prohibitive, which sometimes affects response time to rapid changes in business needs (Wijaya & Prasetyo, 2020). Iyamu (2022) explains how the different understanding that some individuals and organisations have of EAA consequently shapes the description and scope. Application architecture can be viewed as the organiser of systems and their components, including the relationships among the systems as they evolve. According to Hafner and Winter (2008), application architecture represents an aggregate, enterprise-wide model of logical functionality clusters (applications), as well as information flows and control flows between applications.

Enterprise architecture frameworks such as Gartner Inc. (Burke, 2007), TOGAF, and The Zachman Framework present similar views about the EAA, including the development and implementation (Iyamu, 2022). From the EAA perspective, the frameworks focus on governance, planning and building blocks of applications (Batmetan, 2022). The frameworks are intended to assist organisations to develop and implement application architecture. The frameworks cover components such as data, functions, and networks (Zachman, 1987).

Primarily, the application architecture provides a blueprint for the deployment of applications, which also describes the relationship between applications and business processes. However, Woods and Rozanski (2010) argue that there is a disconnect between some of the activities which happen in the process of the development and implementation of EAA. The disconnect manifests in the technological mismatch and irregularity in the development, integration, reuse, implementation, and management of applications. EAA is considered the focal point of an organisation's systems development, implementation, and inventory. Riwanto and Andry (2019) suggest that EAA focuses on supporting the automation of business processes through an integrated view of applications' deployment for an enterprise. According to Shupe and Behling (2006), application architecture describes the applications which are required to support and enable the business requirements, which potentially engineer change in an organisation.

Change which affects business applications is of critical importance to the stakeholders such as business managers, application architects, and end-users. This is mainly because of the investment, value and intended contribution of the applications to the organisation. Anthony Jr. (2021) understands EAA as a concept that encompasses process and utility to transform application from the current-state to future-state purposes. From an architecture viewpoint, regardless of the sources, in-house built, preparatory or open source, every application has a trajectory within which it exists. According to Giddens (1984), a trajectory is a duality of change which brings about social-technical action and interaction between actors involved in an activity or process. Change in the applications' lifecycle is informed by business and technical requirements.

Change in applications is managed, governed, and supported by architecture, a new dimension to which the organisation must adapt. For the benefit of an organisation, it is of utmost importance from an architecture governance perspective to understand the trajectory of each application deployed in its environment. This is necessary, primarily because of the potential implications which could affect the return on investment of an organisation. Dwipriyoko et al. (2019) revealed that EAA produces change through low-cost maintenance and management of applications in an organisation that deploys it. Substantially, cost influences application deployment from technical and non-technical factors (such as processes and humans). It takes into account the need to represent situations in which different terms are practised, from familiarisation to practitioners, and to explicitly consider applications as an integral part of an organisation (Iyamu, 2015).

6.4 The Practice of Enterprise Application Architecture

There are four main phases in the deployment and practice of EAA. First, it requires requirements gathering from both technical and business viewpoints. The requirements gathering takes into account current and strategic intentions. Second, the development and implementation stages include the options to buy, build, or reuse. Finally, applying the governance of the concept determines the trajectory and type of change that circumstantially takes place. Figure 6.1 depicts the phases of EAA practice in an organisation. Each stage of the phases is covered in the discussion that follows the figure.

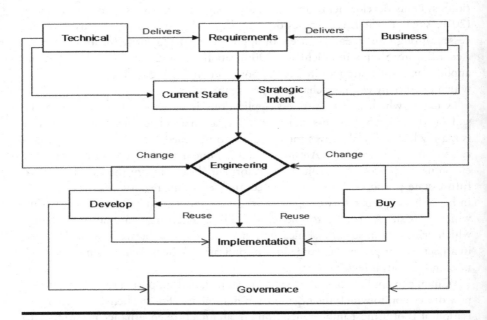

Figure 6.1   The Practice of EAA.

6.5 Requirements Gathering

EAA is problematised by a focal actor through requirements which are often unique and original from one organisation to another. The business requirements are intended to provide a clear understanding of the goals and future of the organisation for sustainability and competitiveness (Shaanika & Iyamu, 2018). Otherwise, a lack of formal, articulated, and clear requirements could manifest, create gaps, and negatively affect the environment. Thus, requirements define and determine the organisational drivers for the business strategies and value chains (processes and activities which are context-based) being pursued at the time.

The deployment of EAA requires gathering of requirements which often focus on sustainability and gaining a competitive advantage. According to Oliveira et al. (2018), the EAA domain shapes and enables requirements for the deployment of applications in an organisation. The EAA is based on and shaped by two standpoints: business and technical requirements, gathered periodically. Both perspectives share and have equal contributions to the success or failure of the EAA within an environment. Also, the contributions can be split into four classes, which are the why, where, what, and how of applications within context and relevance. The business requirements are derived from the organisational processes, objectives, and strategies. The strength and significance of the business requirements are based on the fact that it provides the 'why' (rationale) and 'where' (business focuses) as its EAA justification. The technical requirements define the 'what' (capability) and 'how' (mechanism) of the applications could be deployed in the organisation.

An additional requirement for the development, implementation, and practice of EAA is mainly to conduct 'health' checks on applications within an environment. Also, a requirement is essential to EAA in the containment of flexible integration of the heterogeneity of modern applications (Ramadoss et al., 2018). The requirements are often based on factors that result from performance statistics, availability and reliability, frequency of incidents, volume of support, and maintenance. Other requirements include the identification of needed functionalities and the strengths and opportunities for the use and reuse of applications in an organisation. Other characteristics of EAA are configuration and process. Configuration is used to provide a context-based approach to the deployment of applications in an organisation. The process is to ensure procedural step-by-step action and transitioning in the deployment of applications. EAA requirements are therefore gathered within scope and context as defined by an organisation, which subsequently leads to the development.

Each application is guided by both business and technical requirements. The architecture further helps to shape requirements that are used to formulate governance. Liao and Wang (2021) suggest that EAA applies governance to create stability and sustainability, including the digitalisation of applications in an environment. Governance is used for selecting deploying, supporting, and maintaining applications. The components of dimensions of social change (Gidden, 1984) were employed to examine and understand how EAA brings about changes in an organisation. The outcome is depicted in Figure 6.1. EAA starts by identifying the business drivers and the technical requirements. Based on the drivers and requirements, EAA focuses on providing support, direction, and priority to individuals and the coexistence of applications within an environment.

The organisational requirements, therefore, provide the scope and boundary for the development and implementation of EAA. EAA is intended to engineer and re-engineer the business processes and activities for sustainability and competitiveness through the use and reuse of applications. The bottom line is that the requirements are the determining factors and the EAA is the change agent. The dimension in which change occurs has an influence and impact on the output and performance of an organisation, wholly or partially.

In addition, the requirements help to conduct 'health' checks to detect defects in applications as change continues to occur over time. The checks are primarily aimed at identifying deficiencies and gaps within the business processes and activities. Decisions are made to change the situation, either through re-engineering or replacement, depending on the type and nature of the defects.

The iterative approach of EAA guides the deployment of applications for unique aims and objectives to produce and reproduce logics, processes, and activities of the organisation. This is initiated by the organisational drivers, period and space, primarily to increase the value chain of the organisation. Thus, competitiveness is a deterministic factor in the type of change, whether extensive or intensive, that happens within an organisation. Applications are employed based on the type of change that occurs or is required. The EAA helps to shape and reshape the deployment of applications according to environmental needs. This also includes eliminating or reducing complexity and fostering returns on investment, which influences the current state and necessitates futuristics.

6.6 Current and Future States

Applications are categorised into two main types of status: current (operational) and future (strategic). The status, whether current or strategic, has a change impact on shaping and reshaping the sustainability, growth, and competitive advantage of an organisation through applications, as defined and guided by the architecture.

6.6.1 EAA View of the Current State

The current state of applications deployed in an environment must focus on the inventory aspect for the operationalisation of business logic, processes, and activities. This includes: (i) the components which are associated with each application; (ii) the relationships between business processes, which are enabled and supported by the applications; (iii) the interface between applications; (iv) information flow,

Table 6.1 Current State Identification

Application Name (1)	Business Processes Supported (2)	Interface (3)	Information Required (4)	Technologies (5)	Lifecycle (6)
Identification of an application	Clarification of applications as they support business processes, complete with relationships	The link between applications and between applications and data	The database or file system that an application requires to carry out its functions	Technologies that support and enable an application	Lifecycle and release version of an application

which is the information about the applications shared and managed between business personnel and technologists; and (v) the infrastructure patterns—the mono- or heterogeneous enablers of the applications, including the interfaces.

The application portfolio is preferably incorporated into the architecture repository to maintain links with the business processes and activities, as well as the business and technical requirements (Shaanika & Iyamu, 2018). The current state of applications is an evolving process based on the definition, development, implementation, and practice of EAA. The EAA detects and identifies areas of deficiencies or improvement of the current applications that support key business processes (Li & Xu, 2022).

The holistic collection of information enables the architecture to support and manage applications in their current state, in the context of the environment in which they are deployed. Table 6.1 is a template that can be populated in any environment. The template is focused on capturing the information required by each application as they continue to evolve, enable and support processes and activities in an organisation that deploys it. The information is required by both the business and technical personnel (particularly, the architects) for decision-making, in response to changing needs and requirements of the organisation.

In EAA, the current state of applications is important in defining the strategic (future) direction. Some of the important factors are the facts that it helps to avoid duplication and to identify gaps. Vasconcelos and Sousa (2022) explain the essentiality of conducting gap analysis in the deployment of application architecture.

6.6.2 EAA Positioning of the Future State

EAA is intended to enable the strategic direction of applications within the context of an organisation. According to Li and Xu (2022), EAA is strategic and used to determine future applications for an organisation's purposes. It therefore enhances inventories through context-based models. The models define the relationships amongst applications, requirements (business and technical desirability) dependencies, supported business processes and activities, and required infrastructure patterns.

The current state evolves through planning and assessment, leading to strategic and technical fits of an application, from the standpoint of the computing environment. Both strategic and technical fits should be continually assessed to detect deficiencies, weaknesses, strengths, and opportunities. The strategic fit should be assessed based on an application's contribution to business value, efficiency, effectiveness, sustainability, and competitiveness, as defined by the architecture. The assessment of each application for technical fit should be guided by adherence to architecture design principles and standards. According to Fischer et al. (2010), the design principles enact the construction of an enterprise. The assessment model enables users and managers to evaluate the applications' needs, using the four categories of prioritisation, as shown in Figure 6.2: re-evaluate/reposition, maintain/evolve, phase out/replace, and the development of the application. The strategic direction determines the periodic use of the applications, which determines whether to build, buy, or reuse.

6.7 Application Development

EAA is fundamental to strategic planning, design, application development, and the production and reproduction of multiple applications. Some of the systems often have differentiated functionalities and logic. Thus, application development is influenced and determined by requirements which are both technical and non-technical.

The decision to employ an in-house built application, to purchase one off the shelf, or to reuse an existing application should be defined or based on the architecture of the environment. Hence, the development of EAA is critical if the organisation is to attain a competitive advantage for the deployment of its applications. This is primarily because the architecture influences and affects how applications exist and behave in carrying out the processes and activities of the organisation. As shown in Table 6.2, there are five primary categories of applications, which can be used by organisations. The table is a template that can be populated within an organisation. In the context of this book, it is used to illustrate viability. The applications in the categories serve distinct purposes, but they can depend on each other and can coexist within an environment.

EAA development is the master plan for the deployment, support, and maintenance of applications, in that it considers both the current and the future states of an environment when it is deployed. The development is primarily driven by requirements, as discussed in the previous section. Furthermore, the development of EAA

Table 6.2   Application Development

Planning	Analysis and Design	Programming	Middleware	Repository
Applications that carry out planning, such as financial, resource and project planning, e.g., Microsoft Project	Applications that are used for designing and analysis, such as Modelling Tools, and Case Tools	Programming languages, such as .NET, C++ and Java, for the development of applications, which include front-end (client/server and web-based)	Applications that are used mainly for interfacing between applications and between application and data; some of them include ADO, SDE, ODBC, and PLSQL	The repository covers the control and management of applications; this includes Visual Source Safe, Component Manager, and Oracle

is the procedural categorisation of artefacts that are involved in the deployment and implementation of applications. Table 6.2 provides an example of the artefacts. The development influences the implementation of EAA. Subsequently, the development shapes and informs the implementation of EAA in an organisation.

6.8 Application Implementation

EAA is implemented through governance, which includes principles, standards, configurations, processes, and policies. Through implementation, EAA is intended to provide the means by which adaptive applications could be planned, supported, maintained, and managed within an environment. Also, the implementation of applications drives the introduction of new initiatives from various viewpoints, such as the enabling of processes, sustainability, and competitive advantage. These rationales are aimed at periodically achieving the stability of functions, scalability, compatibility, and interoperability.

The implementation of EAA encompasses a documentary of inventory and a portfolio of events and activities of applications in an organisation. The events and activities codify organisational functional requirements and provide process and management engineering of applications. This is intended to influence the use of applications for competitiveness. The inventory involves documentation of the obsolete, current, and strategic state of applications in an environment. Fundamentally, this assists an organisation from three aspects: to assess the state of affairs, to drive competitiveness, and to promote return on investment. The application portfolio is a representation of the functionality, which is not satisfied by the current applications but is required to fulfil both business and technical requirements.

The business requirements enable events, processes, and activities, while the technical requirements guide the selection and deployment of technical applications aimed at supporting and enabling business applications in an organisational context. An example of technical applications is presented in Table 6.2. The table presents information and analytic requirements for enabling enterprise business and IT strategies. The applications (business or technology) are often classified into many categories, from sales and finance to manufacturing and human resources management. Each of the categories has numerous application products through which change is effected.

6.9 Build, Buy, Reuse

EAA is an ongoing, integrated collection of existing and planned applications and their associated components. Whether built in-house, purchased off the shelf, or reused, they are required to enable and support the ever-changing business requirements, consequent business processes and information, and technical requirements. The decision to build (in-house), buy or reuse an application is guided by EAA, which is driven by both technical and business requirements (Shaanika & Iyamu, 2018) as defined by an organisation.

Every application, whether it is in-house built, purchased, or reused is aimed to add value to the organisation. The categories of applications (build, buy, or reuse) are defined and guided by EAA. The model (Figure 6.2) is used to assess the status

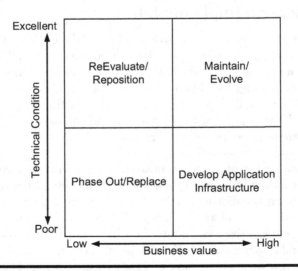

Figure 6.2　Application Assessment.

of an application. The model indicates the direction of each application as it is employed in the organisations. The components (directions) of the figure are to re-evaluate or reposition, maintain or evolve, phase out or replace, and develop an application.

Vertical and horizontal arrows along the axes of Figure 6.2 indicate ranges of poor to excellent and low to high, respectively. Within this, there is pre-evaluation/repositioning, phasing out/replacement, application infrastructure development, and maintenance/evolution, into four quadrants. The explanation that follows is exemplary of how the model can be applied in an organisation. Every organisation is unique to a certain degree, which deters the relevance of applications.

    i. **Phase Out/Replace:** This indicates a situation of low business value (BV) and poor technical condition (TC). The applications that are in this category should therefore be considered for replacement. This is considered to add limited business value to the organisation's competitiveness. However, some of them, including legacy or back-office applications, may not be cost-effective to replace in terms of return on investment. As a result, the priority might be considered low.

    ii. **Re-Evaluate/Reposition:** This is a situation which is of low BV but within excellent TC. The applications within this category are often newly implemented. The applications also often fit from an architecture angle of assessment. However, perhaps the scope of such an application was not properly defined or was of silo-oriented design. As a result, its significance to business value becomes a challenge, or something which is not easily achievable. The critical point is to identify and analyse the weaknesses, strengths, and opportunities for the use and reuse of these types of applications, or for the integration of their components within the organisation's requirements.

    iii. **Develop Application Infrastructure:** This is of high BV, but with poor TC. These types of applications serve the business needs and provide the organisation with significant sustainability and competitiveness, but on the technical front, applications within this category create substantial problems for coexistence and manageability. This includes information flow and integration with other applications. These types of problems or challenges could be addressed through a more adaptive application infrastructure, such as component-based, event-driven, and n-tier with message-based interfaces, as defined in EAA.

    iv. **Maintain/Evolve:** This is of high BV and excellent TC to the organisation. Applications within this category are considered to deliver value to the environment. Also, they are easier to manage technically. This is attributed to the fact that they have been architected for adaptability within the environment. The architecture is designed to ensure both high business value and excellent technical conditions when optimising the application portfolio to accommodate ever-changing requirements.

The EAA is developed and implemented to enforce change by moving the existing applications in a strategic direction. The architecture provides a process for migration by considering strategic factors, such as business and technical requirements, return on investment, and the 'technology fit' of existing and planned applications. The assessment of an application's strategic direction necessitates action plans, which are produced and reproduced over time and space based on requirements. The assessment is considered an analysis approach to reconcile applications within the environment.

i. Analysis of technical requirements against available technologies: This is to uncover any deficiency through which weaknesses and strengths are understood. Also, through the analysis, an understanding may be gained that there is a need for additional infrastructure capabilities.
ii. Reconcile application and infrastructure projects needed to satisfy the results of previous steps: This is a synchronisation effort of joint-migration planning of both the technical and business applications. Applications planning and deployment are prioritised by the results of the assessment.

The migration plan of each application requires documentation at a high-level timeline, within priorities, and for dependencies purposes. This is intended to incorporate all projects related to applications in an organisation.

6.10 Governance

EAA governance defines the overall direction of applications and how they affect change within an organisation. This is mainly because the EAA is a process that provides models and blueprints for both current and future states. It is therefore used to provide a roadmap to actualise business vision and objectives through requirements. Pilipchuk et al. (2021) argue that through governance, the EAA organises the structure and behaviour of applications to satisfy business process requirements. The primary characteristic of EAA is governance consisting of three components: principles, standards, and policies (Iyamu, 2022). Also, the governance guides both operational and strategic intents. Thus, the principles component guides the selection, design, and implementation of applications. The implementation aspect includes the integration and compatibility of applications and business objects. Within this context, the standard components of application governance dictate how applications are selected, deployed, coexist, and managed within an environment. The policies promulgate the rules and regulations using the available resources to dictate the deployment of applications within an organisation.

6.10.1 The Architecture Principles

The architecture principles set the boundary and limit of the operation in deploying (developing and implementing) applications within an environment. The principles provide configuration standards, which guide the deployment and management of application products in their relevance and within context. Also, within the principles, technologies are configured to deliver a reusable building block of technical infrastructure, such as web and application servers. The design, development, and implementation of applications are evaluated for consistency and uniformity purposes within the formulated principles.

In essence, architecture principles are formulated within comprehension and necessity, guiding the applications' deployment in an organisation (Fischer et al., 2010). This is not necessarily a prerequisite to terminate the process of applications' deployment. The basis for many principles is best practices and approaches that have consistently been demonstrated by diverse organisations to achieve similar results. Therefore, the degree to which an organisation can formulate principles that affect processes and activities is dependent on its ability to identify and apply best practices in each of its business areas. The principles lead to the formulation of policies and are applied to guide the designers, developers, and implementers of applications from an architecture standpoint.

6.10.2 The Architecture Policy

The architecture policy is a part of governance, which defines and promulgates what must be done in adherence to the EAA (Kotusev & Kurnia, 2021). The policy is therefore based on the organisation and derived from architectural principles. In response, the policy guides against constraints and complexities, therefore helping to facilitate and manage change through governance, within circumstances and environments. Governance also ensures that the information and processes involved in the design, development, and implementation of applications are protected, that quality is maintained, and that the competitive advantage is prioritised and pursued (Atmaja et al., 2021). Based on the policy, the architectural standards of the EAA are reached.

6.10.3 The Architecture Standards

Change to the organisation's goals, combined with other unyielding competitive forces such as environmental trends, can cause tremendous confusion and complexity in an organisation. This is one of the motivations for the architectural standards. It provides a stabilising environment of consistency, uniformity, and continuity. As in many cases, definitions of artefacts are sometimes different. Architectural standardisation is defined as documented technical specifications and requirements or criteria which are intended for consistency and unification, used as rules and guidelines, and followed to ensure that materials, products, processes, and services are fit for their purposes.

The primary role of standards, from the EAA perspective, is to organise applications and their components, deployment, and use. This includes rules which assist architects to identify the common use of technologies, eliminating redundancy as much as possible and promoting competitive advantage. The EAA reflects on process orientation, development, and operationalisation of deliverables of information systems and business processes. The importance and need to standardise events and artefacts continue to increase. This is mainly because standardisation assists in addressing complex and vital issues such as selection, compliance, and evaluations of applications.

6.11 Enterprise Architecture Application Engineering Change

The rapidity with which change in applications occurs in an organisation can be based on requirements. In other words, the rapidity of change ignites how criteria are extracted to give direction and priority to each of the business processes and activities that can be enabled and supported by applications in an organisation. Table 6.1 is a template to extract requirements from the organisational strategy and proceed to the detailed features of the applications. The speed or frequency with which an application is used determines how its support and maintenance are prioritised and provided within an environment.

The criteria and prioritisation, as defined in Table 6.3, are intended to reduce or eliminate guesswork and inconsistencies that might arise in the course of interpretation. This increases the positive impact of strategic applications on processes and activities—and therefore on the priority that should be placed on them. Furthermore, the prioritisation matrix (Table 6.3) is aimed at evaluating and

Table 6.3   EAA Change Criteria

Category	5 – Strategic	4 – Operational	3 – Tactical	2 – Managed-Out	1 – Optional
5 - Requirements					
4 - Strategic Objectives					
3 - Operational Necessity					
2 - Opportunity					
1 - Nice to Have					

managing the deployment of applications that persists in the face of rapid change from organisational requirements. additionally, it is a mechanism that can be used to identify and resolve applications' conflicts, as well as build consensus on strategic directions within the shortest possible time (Daoudi et al., 2022).

As shown in Table 6.3, the decision to deploy, use, and maintain applications in an organisation should be based on priorities. The prioritisation of applications is a building block process of the matrix which helps determine and prioritise the need and demand for applications in an organisation. Zimmermann (2017) suggests that existing EAA can be measured through the matrix model to determine its status in an organisation. The matrix contextualises the current and future states, including the operationalisation and possible opportunities during the deployment of applications. The measurement scores as defined by the matrix (Figure 6.3) are summed up to assist the prioritisation process purposely for decision-making. The increasing number of the total score indicates from an architecture standpoint, the value of an application to the organisation's needs, objectives, and goals.

The lower the total score, the less attention is required or should be associated with the application. The scores from the prioritisation matrix are calculated with associated values. The total score determines the level at which an application should be prioritised in an organisation. From the measurement, the total scores are grouped in ranges of five to leave room for expansion and maturity:

20–25: This is considered as most critical to the organisation. It is needed as soon as it is practical. It is expected to be of high value to an organisation. It is therefore considered to be driven by the strategy of the organisation.

15–19: This is the second highest level of prioritisation. It is considered to be very important to the organisation. It could be used as an indicator of sustainability and competitive advantage. As such, it does require high attention.

10–14: This is the middle-range indicator for the prioritisation of applications. Within this range, the application is considered to be essential to the processes and activities of the organisation. It is necessarily required to improve the efficiency and effectiveness of the organisation's operations.

5–9: At this range, the application is required only for continuity purposes. It is assessed to have a marginal improvement in the processes and activities of the organisation. Applications which are within this range are often required for purposes such as by laws, regulations, or directives.

0–4: This is the lowest of the priority ranges. At this range, the applications are considered to have little or no impact on the organisation's processes and activities, and could be considered optional.

The criteria for prioritisation allow the nature and degree of failure to be examined and understood by the stakeholders, including architects, IS/IT managers and business promoters. The criteria as tabulated in Table 6.3 are aimed to facilitate change to evolving requirements. The use of the criteria and prioritisation model makes decisions more discrete, consistent, and comprehensive in the execution of EAA.

6.12 Enterprise Application Architecture Change Process

The aforementioned prioritisation criteria are the responsibility of both the architects and IT managers. Some of the responsibilities are the following.

i. IT managers identify and document the requirements for each of the processes and activities supported and enabled by applications in their organisations.
ii. The architects define the architectural criteria for each of the processes and activities that are enabled and supported by each application within their environments.
iii. The architects provide options for both IT managers and technical and business benefits to facilitate informed decision-making aimed at attaining competitive advantage.
iv. In collaboration with the architects, the IT managers make decisions on prioritising application deployment, support, and maintenance. This is done following the needs of the business.
v. The decision is communicated to the IT relationship managers or business analysts, who drill down the communication and documentation to the various IT and business unit representatives. This is according to their roles and responsibilities. The communication and documentation indicate the priorities of the applications.
vi. The deployment of prioritised applications is enforced by IT managers. This includes the decision to develop, buy, or reuse applications.
vii. A prioritised plan is put together to support, maintain, and manage the affected applications within a specific timeframe and budget.

6.13 Enterprise Application Architecture Change Implication

EAA involves a process of different dimensions, from the requirements gathering to the governance stages. This is a dimension that engineers change in the reproduction of events, processes, and activities as requirements continue to evolve rapidly. The change process is intended to address identified business and technological challenges, thereby paving the way for competitiveness. Within that premise, when there is a change in an organisation's vision, resources including IT solutions are refocused on achieving the new or expected outcome.

EAA is designed, developed, implemented, and practised to fulfil the changing needs of technology and business through different dimensions. Change involves adaptations in practices, which include resources, know-how and skills. In change, the focus and belief are more about three main factors: (i) what is important; (ii) what are the values; and (iii) the change must be within context and relevant. In addition, it requires the interaction, connectedness, and sharing of power across different components that comprise an application.

Change requires the development of the organisational capacity to respond to changing needs and conditions. Typically, the goal is not to master a single innovation, but rather for ongoing learning and developing collaborative work cultures as defined by the architecture. Changing the application profile to meet the requirements of an organisation requires adaptability, flexibility, and collaboration, which are usually defined in EAA. From an application perspective, the architecture addresses and provides a shared view of how the business works and what it works with, to the actors (stakeholders) who are enrolled in the concept of use and manageability.

6.14 The Impact of Change

In line with the definition previously provided, EAA logically consists of principles, standards, and models that are derived from organisational business and technical requirements. The principles, standards, and models of EAA include the following.

   i. Guide the engineering of an organisation's information systems.
   ii. Allow applications to integrate and coexist on the same platform.
   iii. Apply and enable rapid change in an organisation's business processes.

The interpretation of the rules creates signification and symbolic meaningful systems that provide ways for architects to develop and implement EAA in the manner they deem fit. The architects reflexively apply their stocks of knowledge and information gathered from their communication with other stakeholders, including colleagues and clients.

From the EAA viewpoint, the dispensability of technologies and organisations' competitiveness are the two primary factors that influence change within an organisation. Dispensability inevitably enables change in technologies to take place. As enabling technologies become obsolete, they are dispensed to ensure compatibility and integration of newer technologies in the deployment of applications within an environment. Change is constant. As the speed of competition amongst organisations continues to increase, business processes change to enable and support competitiveness. EAA addresses these needs by providing a strategic context for the evolution of IT solutions in response to the constantly changing needs of business environments.

Applications are often modified and revitalised based on either technical or business requirements, or both. The modification of existing applications is based on future functionalities resulting from a change in processes and activities. This is enabled and supported by requirements and guides the conduct of 'health' checks on applications. Health checks examine the dependencies and interrelatedness of applications within an environment.

As shown in Figure 6.1, EAA involves dependency and interrelated processes and activities. The figure depicts a top-down flow of processes and how EAA can distinctly be developed, implemented, and practised in an organisation. The events are engineered by the EAA, and they change the current situation from transitioning to the desired state. Change does not necessarily mean replacement, and certain artefacts are reused within the ambit of its governance.

6.15 Summary

This chapter presents enterprise application architecture (EAA) as an approach to respond to change, even when requirements continue to change or evolve at a rapid rate. It shows that EAA is an adaptable and flexible approach which can be employed with other methods or approaches, such as the dimensions of change. It also demonstrates how dimensions can be enforced through governance components, standards, principles, and policies to effect change within any environment. Through change, EAA helps to interrogate prevailing business paradigms to bring about freshness and new technological realities.

Through change, EAA can enable and support a more effective and efficient operational practice that facilitates improved competitiveness and sustainability. Through EAA implementation, the information technology (IT) and business units engage in an intensive learning experience. Thus, the former develops a thorough understanding of the business domain, while the latter reflects on current practices to understand the potential of IT in transforming the environment. Thus, the primary reason for developing and implementing EAA is therefore to provide the technical foundation for effective IT and business strategies. Hence, it is posited that EAA has the additional ability to assist in managing change as a change agent.

References

Aerts, A. T. M., Goossenaerts, J. B., Hammer, D. K., & Wortmann, J. C. (2004). Architectures in context: On the evolution of business, application software, and ICT platform architectures. *Information & Management, 41*(6), 781–794.

Al-Omoush, K. S. (2022). Understanding the impact of intellectual capital on E-business entrepreneurial orientation and competitive agility: An empirical study. *Information Systems Frontiers, 24*(2), 549–562.

Anthony Jnr, B. (2021). Managing digital transformation of smart cities through enterprise architecture—a review and research agenda. *Enterprise Information Systems, 15*(3), 299–331.

Atmaja, S. A., Putra, I. E., Muslim, I. A., & Purnandi, H. (2021). Architecture design of e-information system marketplace with method enterprise architecture planning. *Budapest International Research and Critics Institute (BIRCI-Journal): Humanities and Social Sciences, 4*(3), 3689–3710.

Batmetan, J. R. (2022). Model enterprise architecture for information technology services in universities. *International Journal of Information Technology and Education, 1*(4), 18–34.

Burke, B. (2007). *The role of enterprise architecture in technology research.* Gartner Inc. Retrieved April 14, 2010, from http://gartner.com/technology/research.jsp

Daoudi, W., Doumi, K., & Kjiri, L. (2022). Adaptive enterprise architecture: Complexity metrics in a mixed evaluation method. In J. Filipe, M. Śmiałek, A. Brodsky, & S. Hammoudi (Eds.), *Enterprise information systems. ICEIS 2021* (Lecture Notes in Business Information Processing, Vol. 455). Springer. https://doi.org/10.1007/978-3-031-08965-7_26

Dwipriyoko, E., Bon, A. T. B., & Sukono, F. (2019). Enterprise architecture planning as new generation cooperatives research methods. *Journal of Physics: Conference Series, 1179*(1), 012094. IOP Publishing.

Fischer, C., Winter, R., & Aier, S. (2010). What is an enterprise architecture principle? In *Computer and information science 2010* (pp. 193–205). Springer.

Giddens, A. (1984). *The constitution of society: Outline of the theory of structuration.* John Polity Press.

Hafner, M., & Winter, R. (2008, January 7–10). Processes for enterprise application architecture management. In *Proceedings of the 41st Hawaii international conference on system sciences* (HICSS) (pp. 1–10). IEEE.

Harmon, K. (2005, October 10–12). The "systems" nature of enterprise architecture. In *The proceedings of IEEE international conference on systems, man and cybernetics.* IEEE.

Herrmann, H. (2022). The arcanum of artificial intelligence in enterprise applications: Toward a unified framework. *Journal of Engineering and Technology Management, 66*, 101716.

Iyamu, T. (2015). *Information technology enterprise architecture: From concept to practice* (2nd ed.). Heidelberg Press. ISBN: 8-3-659-61206-0.

Iyamu, T. (2022). *Enterprise architecture for strategic management of modern IT solutions* (1st ed.). Auerbach Publications.

Jia, J., Mo, H., Capretz, L. F., & Chen, Z. (2018). Grouping environmental factors influencing individual decision-making behavior in software projects: A cluster analysis. *Journal of Software: Evolution and Process, 30*(1), e1913.

Kang, D., Lee, J., & Kim, K. (2010). Alignment of business enterprise architectures using fact-based ontologies. *Expert Systems with Applications, 37*(4), 3274–3283.

Katuu, S. (2018, December 10–13). The utility of enterprise architecture to records and archives specialists. In *2018 IEEE international conference on big data (big data)* (pp. 2702–2710). IEEE.

Kotusev, S., & Kurnia, S. (2021). The theoretical basis of enterprise architecture: A critical review and taxonomy of relevant theories. *Journal of Information Technology, 36*(3), 275–315.

Lamola, K. X. (2022). Employees' aptitudes and trepidations for the adoption of enterprise application architecture for supply chain management in small and medium enterprises: A case of Capricorn District Municipality. *Journal of Transport and Supply Chain Management, 16*(1), 1–16.

Li, J., & Xu, W. (2022, July 15–17). Using a practical methodology of enterprise IT strategy for digital success. In *Proceedings of the 2nd international conference on management science and software engineering (ICMSSE 2022)* (pp. 628–635). Atlantis Press.

Liao, M. H., & Wang, C. T. (2021). Using enterprise architecture to integrate lean manufacturing, digitalization, and sustainability: A lean enterprise case study in the chemical industry. *Sustainability, 13*(9), 1–26.

Malallah, H., Zeebaree, S. R., Zebari, R. R., Sadeeq, M. A., Ageed, Z. S., Ibrahim, I. M., Yasin, M. H., & Merceedi, K. J. (2021). A comprehensive study of kernel (issues and concepts) in different operating systems. *Asian Journal of Research in Computer Science, 8*(3), 16–31.

Malik, A., & Om, H. (2018). Cloud computing and internet of things integration: Architecture, applications, issues, and challenges. In Rivera, W. (Ed.), *Sustainable cloud and energy services* (pp. 1–24). Springer.

Masuda, Y., Zimmermann, A., Viswanathan, M., Bass, M., Nakamura, O., & Yamamoto, S. (2021). Adaptive enterprise architecture for the digital healthcare industry: A digital platform for drug development. *Information, 12*(2), 1–26.

Netto, M. A., Calheiros, R. N., Rodrigues, E. R., Cunha, R. L., & Buyya, R. (2018). HPC cloud for scientific and business applications: Taxonomy, vision, and research challenges. *ACM Computing Surveys (CSUR), 51*(1), 1–29.

Oliveira, A., Bischoff, V., Gonçales, L. J., Farias, K., & Segalotto, M. (2018). BRCode: An interpretive model-driven engineering approach for enterprise applications. *Computers in Industry, 96*, 86–97.

Pilipchuk, R., Seifermann, S., Heinrich, R., & Reussner, R. H. (2021, July 7–9). Challenges in aligning enterprise application architectures to business process access control requirements in evolutional changes. In *The proceedings of the 18th international conference on e-business (ICE-B)*. Online Streaming. ACM Press.

Popli, S., Jha, R. K., & Jain, S. (2018). A survey on energy efficient narrowband internet of things (NBIoT): Architecture, application and challenges. *IEEE Access, 7*, 16739–16776.

Postma, A. (2003). A method for module architecture verification and its application on a large component-based system. *Information and Software Technology, 45*, 171–194.

Ramadoss, R., Elango, N. M., Abimannan, S., & Hsu, C. H. (2018). Non-intrusive transaction aware filtering during enterprise application modernization. *The Journal of Supercomputing, 74*(3), 1157–1181.

Riwanto, R. E., & Andry, J. F. (2019). Enterprise architectures enable of business strategy and IS/IT alignment in manufacturing using TOGAF ADM framework. *International Journal of Information Technology and Business, 1*(2), 7–7.

Safaei, A., Nassiri, R., & Rahmani, A. M. (2022). Enterprise service composition models in IoT context: Solutions comparison. *The Journal of Supercomputing, 78*(2), 2015–2042.

Schekkerman, J. (2004). *How to survive in the jungle of enterprise architecture frameworks: Creating or choosing an enterprise architecture framework*. Trafford Publishing.

Shaanika, I., & Iyamu, T. (2018). Developing the enterprise architecture for the Namibian government. *The Electronic Journal of Information Systems in Developing Countries*, *84*(3), e12028.

Shan, T. C., & Hua, W. W. (2006, September 18–22). Solution architecture for n-tier applications. In *Proceedings of the IEEE international conference on services computing, 2006. SCC'06* (pp. 349–356). IEEE.

Shupe, C., & Behling, R. (2006). Developing and implementing a strategy for technology deployment. *Information Management Journal*, *40*(4), 52–57.

Tamm, T., Seddon, P. B., & Shanks, G. (2022). How enterprise architecture leads to organisational benefits. *International Journal of Information Management*, *67*, 102554.

Tao, Z. G., Luo, Y. F., Chen, C. X., Wang, M. Z., & Ni, F. (2017). Enterprise application architecture development based on DoDAF and TOGAF. *Enterprise Information Systems*, *11*(5), 627–651.

Vasconcelos, A., & Sousa, P. (2022). Enterprise architecture development framework. In *Enterprise architecture and cartography: From practice to theory; from representation to design* (pp. 159–168). Springer International Publishing.

Wijaya, A. F., & Prasetyo, M. W. (2020). Strategic planning information systems enterprise architecture planning method case study of Semarang City Public Works Department. *Journal of Information Systems and Informatics*, *2*(1), 114–122.

Winter, R. (2001, January 3–6). The current and future role of data warehousing in corporate application architecture. In *The proceedings of the 34th Hawaii international conference on system sciences (HICSS)*. IEEE.

Woods, E., & Rozanski, N. (2010, August 23–26). Unifying software architecture with its implementation. In *The proceedings of the 4th European conference on software architecture*. The ACM Digital Library.

Zachman, J. (1987). A framework for information systems. *IBM Systems Journal*, *26*(3), 276–283.

Zimmermann, O. (2017). Architectural refactoring for the cloud: A decision-centric view on cloud migration. *Computing*, *99*(2), 129–145.

Chapter 7

The Practice of Enterprise Technical Architecture

7.1 Introduction

During the last three decades, efforts to improve information systems and information technology (IS/IT) solutions, strategies, and operations have tremendously increased. This includes the determination to bridge the gap between IS/IT and business units, pragmatics assessment and accessing of IT solutions in addressing individual and organisational needs, semiotics of technology deployment, and how the technology strategy affects the vision of an organisation. Thus, an approach that focuses on improving IS/IT solutions deployment, from strategic planning to implementation, is sought by many organisations. This is to consistently effect significant technological change within an environment that deploys it. Critically needed, the role of technical solutions is to support business objectives and operations (Kang et al., 2010; Kilpeläinen, 2007). The use of the term IS/IT corroborates the explanation provided in Chapter 2.

However, there has been an improvement over the years in many areas such as systems development, project management, and technology deployment. This is across all walks of life, from healthcare to telecommunication. According to Jones et al. (2014), there has been a significant improvement in the healthcare sector using IT solutions. Despite these improvements and efforts, organisations still find it difficult to realise and comprehend returns on their IT investments from both business and technical standpoints. According to Brynjolfsson (1993), IT has made the management information systems (MIS) manager's job of justifying investments particularly difficult. Brynjolfsson further argues that the disappointment in IT has been chronicled in literature, disclosing broad negative correlations with

DOI: 10.1201/9781003390879-7

economy-wide productivity and information worker productivity. However, this makes it seem as though none of these efforts has been able to completely resolve the challenges of achieving organisations' needs in time, ensuring that value is achieved from the investments in IT solutions.

Although the argument by Brynjolfsson (1993) surfaced about three decades ago, the situation has not changed in many organisations across the world, as revealed in the literature. Dale and Scheepers (2020) claimed that interaction and relations among actors are some of the factors whose consequences can be derailing in the implementation of IT solutions. According to Petersson et al. (2022), some of the challenges of implementing IT solutions are external factors and internal capacity for strategic change and management. Identifying and resolving technical issues are some of the critical challenges in implementing IT solutions (Chen et al., 2023).

Some of the challenges encountered in deploying IT solutions, which this chapter attempts to address through enterprise technical architecture (ETA), are complexity, duplication, compatibility, deficiencies, and integration. ETA is a domain of enterprise architecture (EA) (Iyamu, 2022a), as introduced in Chapter 1. Without ETA, each of the factors continues to manifest itself in multiplicity and in posing challenges to an organisation.

   i. *Complexities of IT solutions:* The inherent complexity and new methods of interaction by stakeholders require a corroborative response. This means that existing technology infrastructure requires regular checks to reduce complexity and avoid deficiencies (Ismagilova et al., 2022).
   ii. *Duplication of IT solutions:* Owing to the size of some organisations and the emergence of IT solutions, duplications and lack of cohesion among the technologies are increasing. The ETA can be used to facilitate the integration, collaboration, standardisation, deduplication, and re-engineering of IT solutions for an organisation's purposes (Chitsa & Iyamu, 2020).
   iii. *Compatibility of modern technologies:* The ETA strengthens the refactoring of IT solutions in the areas of integration, compatibility, and virtualisation (Spijkman et al., 2021).
   iv. *Deficiency in IT solutions:* Identification of deficiencies in the technologies deployed. Through the gap analysis, new IT solutions needed for future engagements are identified (Batmetan, 2022).
   v. *Integration of IT solutions:* How technologies are intended to enable business needs. Ismagilova et al. (2022) emphasise the need for integrated design and underlying technical architecture for the efficiency and effectiveness of IT solutions in enabling and supporting an organisation's objectives and goals, which include secure communication and data processing.

As a result of these and other factors, many organisations have sought solutions by developing and implementing ETA to address these challenges. What is even more important is achieving the technical architecture objectives, in that it involves semiotics, which is the understanding between human and technical actors in the deployment of technologies. Semiotics includes the process and how the requirements are derived in the development and implementation of the architecture. According to Ross et al. (2006), the level of the operating model is critical in the integration and standardisation of delivering goods and services. In essence, without the process of modus operandi, the challenges which are encountered in the deployment of technologies could be high and even become much more prohibitive. Many organisations have therefore developed technical architecture. However, some organisations have not implemented, or struggle to implement ETA, due to various reasons such as the semiotic relationships that exist between actors, human-to-human and human-to-technology.

Additionally, the challenges go beyond the factors of derailment, including semiotics as previously identified. Shaanika and Iyamu (2018) explain how ETA has implications for both human and non-human actors, including IT architects, business users and managers, technology vendors, and IT solutions in practice. Constantinides et al. (2018) claim that there is evidence to show that value-creating interactions between the actors renew opportunities for dynamically changing both organisational structures and the technical architecture but they are not being explored productively. Technical architectures and organisational structures, therefore, must be approached as a source of strategic opportunity and should be dynamically changed over time (Foorthuis et al., 2016), which does not seem to be happening; hence, the slow or reluctant deployment of the concept.

ETA is a prevailing paradigm which questions the goals, scope, processes, and roles considered on the technology front. This includes selection, implementation, and integration, as well as the deployment, practice, and management of modern IT solutions. In the last two decades, there has been an increasing interest in technical and other domains of EA in organisations (Iyamu, 2022a; Versteeg & Bouwman, 2006). The interest does not remove the fact that there are challenges. Patel (2002) argues that there are many challenges which need to be addressed by IT solutions, such as planning and rapid business and environmental change. Thus, in an attempt to answer the questions (how can IT infrastructure be deployed and used to achieve business needs, and gain a return on investment?), ETA is employed by many organisations.

ETA provides the means through which adaptive IS/IT infrastructure can be maintained by applying a governance approach. The approach consists of sets of principles, standards, configurations, and processes. Governance is influenced and determined by factors such as organisational requirements and environmental trends. In Patel's (2002) argument, IT governance is affected by an organisation's unique culture and work practice and should therefore reflect its own goals and ambitions. The architecture ensures that the existing and new information technologies and systems are maintained and selected respectively to achieve the strategic goals of an organisation (Iyamu, 2022a; Constantinides et al., 2018; De Vries & van Rensburg, 2008). Hafner and Winter (2008) describe technical architecture as the domain which represents an aggregate, enterprise-wide model of hardware and communications components, as well as dependencies between the technology artefacts. The architecture also drives and prescribes the introduction of new technologies by focusing on functionality, scalability, compatibility, and interoperability.

This chapter introduces and puts into context the modus operandi of technical architecture, which could be adopted or used as a framework in the deployment and practice of technical architecture in organisations. The chapter presents a four-phase framework approach for the development and implementation of ETA. Like many other frameworks, it is not a definitive guide to technical architecture modelling and deployment. It could be customised within the environmental and technological contexts of an organisation. The framework begins by presenting an overview of the technical architecture deployment, including a diagrammatical representation (Figure 7.1) of the components and process that constitute the architecture.

The remainder of this chapter is structured into four main sections. The first section introduces the chapter, which includes a discussion of the problem the chapter attempts to address. Next is a literature review. Thereafter, the practice of ETA in the organisation's context is presented in its four deployment phases: (i) the objectives of ETA; (ii) the business strategy as it relates to ETA; (iii) the development of ETA in practice; and (iv) the implementation of ETA in practice. The chapter is concluded with highlights of its contributions.

7.2 Enterprise Technical Architecture

ETA enables a log of procedures and technological activities to detect crucial deficiencies in ensuring credibility and reliability in advancing an organisation's goals and objectives (Iyamu, 2022b). According to Venkatesan and Sridhar (2019), technical architecture focuses on defining and describing platforms in the technology infrastructure to support applications and their interactions. Chronically, although this seems clear, in practice there is confusion about the concept. In some quarters, technical architecture is often mistaken for enterprise architecture (Booch, 2010). This confusion continues and affects how ETA is defined and used to identify its boundaries with other EA domains. This increases many technical dependencies on the technical architecture and intensifies the challenges in applying the concept (Spijkman et al., 2021). Also, it is critical to understand the factors that influence the deployment of ETA, which can reduce confusion about the concept (Chitsa & Iyamu, 2020).

Primarily, ETA encompasses technical principles and standards for regulatory and compliance purposes (Ismagilova et al., 2022). Iyamu (2022b) proposes technical architecture as support and guide for the development and implementation of IT solutions towards eradicating complexity and enhancing flexibility. Batmetan (2022) argues that ETA is an approach used to identify the principles of technology solutions, including platforms such as operating systems, hardware, and computing network. The technical architecture view outlines specific software implementation, physical components (e.g., network and servers), their relationships, the allocation of software parts to hardware components, the dependencies among software and hardware components, and constraints (Kochanthara et al., 2021).

Technical architecture addresses both operational and strategic intents, and therefore addresses many areas from strategic planning to implementation and management of technology infrastructures in an organisation (Iyamu, 2015). ETA represents an enterprise-wide model of hardware, software, and communications components and their dependencies. Shaanika and Iyamu (2018) affirm that ETA focuses on and defines an organisation's IT strategy, consisting of the technical design that serves as the road map for the implementation of IT by actors, using a formal process and standards. According to Bolton et al. (2020), this includes legacy systems, operational metrics and security models.

Like other EA domains, ETA has been employed to guide, support, manage, and govern IT solutions in many walks of life, such as the health sector (Masuda et al., 2018; McDermott, 2016), financial institutions, and the education sector (Williamson, 2018). Among other prevailing potential benefits, this could be attributed to the practice of ETA not allowing unauthorised proxy as guided by the technical architecture framework, which defines the standard use of the technologies, the principles for implementation of the technologies, and policies of enforcing the practice of the solutions (Iyamu, 2022b). Despite these, challenges exist in the development, implementation, and practice of ETA. A practical approach is presented in the next section.

Technical architecture has been suggested as a solution to address challenges and risks, such as lack of scalability, incompatibility, and insufficient data transportation and security (Kumar et al., 2021). Based on this premise, many organisations are increasingly relying on technical architecture primarily to avoid conflicts with IT solutions (Ahlemann et al., 2021). However, challenges persist from both business artefacts and technology solutions, and from human and non-human actors. Another fundamental challenge, the silo deployment of ETA, is highlighted by Chitsa and Iyamu (2020) as a source of lack of leverage and alignment between the enabled and the enabler. Technical sophistication can also create gaps in deployment and standards immaturity (Ismagilova et al., 2022).

7.3 The Practice of Enterprise Technical Architecture

In the context of this chapter, ETA is defined as a logically consistent set of principles, standards, and models that are derived from business strategy (business vision, requirements, and contextualisation) to guide the engineering of the organisation's IT solutions across the domain's (business, information, and application) architecture. Thus, the ETA defines the standards and structure of the technology infrastructure, consisting of hardware, software, networking, and communication platforms which are necessary to support and enable business events and application needs (Shaanika & Iyamu, 2018). It is within this context that I designed and developed a model (Figure 7.1) that employs a four-phase approach that can be applied in practice, in the deployment of ETA, for an organisation's purposes.

Methodologically, ETA is an approach (or model) for both operational and strategic activities within the computing environment of an organisation (Kochanthara et al., 2021). As depicted in Figure 7.1, the four-phase approach for ETA deployment and practice is: (i) objectives, which are gathered from the influencing factors and formulated based on technology and environmental trends; (ii) requirements, which conceptualise the business-driven requirements based on the vision of an organisation; (iii) development, which defines and develops the scope of the architecture towards achieving the objectives and requirements formulated at the time; and (iv) implementation of action through procedures and processes to ensure that the objectives and requirements are fulfilled.

Based on an organisation's vision and requirements, the ETA focuses on deriving high-level requirements to give direction and priority to its domains (Dale & Scheepers, 2020; Burke, 2007; Cook, 1996). Some organisations could find the need to develop a more robust and intuitive set of ETA requirements from the business requirements. It is therefore important to understand how the objectives and requirements direct the design of the architecture to enable and support business events and activities (Tamm et al., 2022; Spewak, 1992). In response, the architecture engineer changes the environment where it is deployed, from the standpoints of both IS/IT and business units.

Change within the computing environment of any organisation occurs through the development and implementation of the ETA. In addressing the problems identified and presented in the introductory section of this chapter (complexity, duplications, compatibility, deficiencies, and integration), the architecture is often developed and implemented with five primary intentions: (i) to manage IT solutions; (ii) to change from one IT solution to another; (iii) to implement modern IT solutions; (iv) to maintain compatibility with existing technologies; and (v) to change from one business process to another.

Even though the ETA indicates that it is purely technical, some of the activities, such as objectives and requirements require interactions between human and non-human actors, only through relationships. The processes, therefore, enact the importance of a relationship between the business and IT units. The IT and business personnel need to listen to one another, communicate effectively, and learn to leverage IT solutions in building competitive advantage (Constantinides et al., 2018; Luftman et al., 1999). As shown in Figure 7.1, the four-phase approach—objectives, requirements, development, and implementation are methodological and linear in practice. Through interaction and relationships, the phases are linked with each other, and together, they provide a significant contribution to the deployment and practice of ETA in an organisation's context.

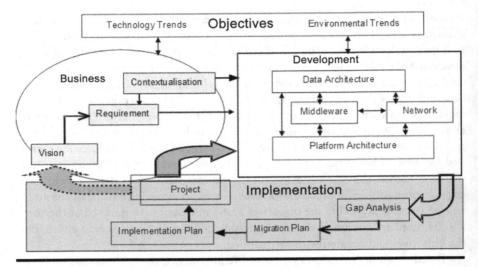

Figure 7.1   Enterprise Technical Architecture in Practice.

7.3.1 Phase One: Objectives

As shown in Figure 7.1, the objectives for the ETA approach are informed and influenced by two main factors: technology trends and environmental trends. Primarily, the objectives are to provide a baseline of the current state and future state of an organisation's computing environment (Foorthuis et al., 2016). The current and future states are further categorised into operational and strategic intents. The objectives are intended to enable, support, and manage technology activities, which bring about change within an environment.

However, there are challenges in the attempts to achieve the objectives of the ETA in many organisations. One of the challenges is gaining an accurate view of the current state against a future state. This includes: (i) facilitating the assessment of the impact technological change has on the environment; and (ii) conceptualising strategic alternatives for consideration. This leads to the main aim of the chapter, which is to provide guidelines through which the ETA approach can be deployed and practised in an environment. Conceptually, the objectives of ETA can be summarised as to do the following.

i. Effectively detect and engineer the removal of obsolete hardware from the environment.
ii. Engineer flexibility and avoid vendor dependency within the computing environment.
iii. Re-engineer IT solutions in the organisation for competitiveness.
iv. Enable IS/IT solutions by the standards and principles of the environment.

v. Periodically review the existence of IS/IT solutions by the organisation's needs.

vi. Ensure that the rapidly changing external and environmental trends are enforced to significantly change the business and technical environments of the organisation.

ETA requires continuous evaluation and iterative processes to protect the investment in IS/IT solutions. This facilitates technological checks for fit and timely updates of IT solutions within the changing environment.

7.3.2 Phase Two: Requirements

The outcome of phase one, formulation of the objectives as discussed in the preceding subsection, forms the foundation for phase two: requirements. In other words, the content of phase one is translated to address business and technological challenges within an environment. Requirements are extracted from phase one in preparation for the development and implementation of ETA to enable and re-engineer IS/IT solutions in an environment.

The business units or divisions of an organisation normally have different requirements from that of IS/IT, often far apart from each other because of individual focuses. As a result, they pose a challenge in the attempts to map the requirements from both IS/IT and business units towards an organisation's common goal. In addition, some of the stakeholders are heterogeneous in many units or divisions (networks), thereby causing a conflict of interest. Moreover, technical actors pose challenges in the areas of shared services and infrastructure.

The business strategy is the primary driver for the development and implementation of ETA (see Figure 7.1). It consists of the business vision, business requirements, and environmental context. This phase is primarily influenced by factors which include organisational processes, activities, and environmental trends (Iyamu, 2022b; Youngs et al., 1999). The trends relate to the business of the organisation, as well as relevant technologies that enable and support them.

7.3.2.1 Business Vision

The business vision is the first component of the second phase in ETA deployment. It focuses mainly on the strategic direction of the organisation, primarily for sustainability and competitiveness. The primary purpose is to provide a clear vision of the 'business future' by capturing the most important enterprise business strategies being pursued at the time (Ahlemann et al., 2021; Booch, 2010).

For visioning, a project team gathers strategic planning documents from the business units and extracts the relevant drivers. This includes information about IS/IT needs. The business drivers, information, and organisational needs are documented in the process, while environmental trends are also considered. Based on the materials gathered, the business vision document is prepared and verified with management and other stakeholders in the organisation.

7.3.2.2 Business Strategy

Business strategies are derived from the vision of the organisation and expressed as functional statements which give direction and priority to ETA, among other activities. Aerts et al. (2004) argue that a business strategy targets the goals of business processes for which the architecture is purposely developed and implemented to ensure their realisation. Generically, the business strategy includes the following.

  i. Enabling an organisation to implement its strategies over time and with minimal impact on ongoing service delivery and processes.
  ii. Enabling business scalability to respond and operate at the same rates at which business processes and activities occur.
  iii. Enabling an organisation to compete in the economy, encompassing technology and environmental trends.
  iv. Delivering flexibly packaged and priced services through multiple channels at various geographical locations.
  v. Enabling governance in the computing environment of an organisation.

7.3.2.3 Environment Context

At this stage of the ETA process, the articulation of the organisation's systems into a technical architecture context is performed. The context consists of the business vision and requirements of the organisation as captured at the time. The requirements are extracted and categorised into a set of needs, which are then used to develop the subsequent architectural products, a set of blueprints, and views of the organisation (Fernández-Cejas et al., 2022; Spijkman et al., 2021). Each view is expressed in terms of components, connections, and constraints governed by the architectural model. A key feature of the approach is the conceptual mechanism that provides traceability between views. Once information and requirements are gathered from the business strategy, the architects start with the development of the technical architecture.

7.3.3 Phase Three: ETA Development

The development of ETA, as proposed, is a four-stage approach: technical architectural requirements, classification of the domain, documentation of technologies, and formulation of governance principles. Technical architecture is developed for a specific purpose within a context. This makes it relative to the individual organisation's strategy, aims, and objectives. However, there are generic fundamentals in the development of technical architecture. They include the following four main sequential steps.

i. Technical architectural requirements.
ii. Definition of the domain.
iii. Documentation of technologies into current-to-strategic forms.
iv. Formulation of governance principles.

7.3.3.1 Technical Architectural Requirements

Technical architectural requirements are derived from the requirements contained in the business strategy. The requirements describe the basic functions required of ETA in supporting and enabling the business drivers (Shaanika & Iyamu, 2018). This is primarily to enable and support sustainability and competitiveness through governance and manageability (Ismagilova et al., 2022). The development stage also describes the components of ETA, including the inter-relationships and dependencies of the artefacts that constitute the architecture. It, therefore, gives a view of the sequence of the components involved in the development of ETA. The preceding introductory paragraphs demonstrate how ETA could be developed. This section focuses on the development, beginning with the definition.

Technical architecture describes and defines systems and software into structure and categories (Venkatesan & Sridhar, 2019). However, this is based on how ETA is defined and scoped. In this chapter, ETA is defined as a logically consistent set of principles, standards, and models with the following characteristics.

i. They are derived from business requirements.
ii. They guide the re-engineering of an organisation's information systems and technologies across various domains of the architecture.
iii. They take into account the 'full context' in which the domain of ETA is applied.
iv. They enable rapid change in an organisation's business processes and applications that enable and support them.
v. They guide the selection or the building and deployment of technologies in an organisation.

In the development, implementation, and practice of ETA, a definition is key and its importance must be emphasised. This is mainly to understand the different entities, components, and boundaries of the domain architecture, and its overall scope. This requires a mechanism to ensure that the activities are carried out according to the different classes of IS/IT standards. The classes are classifications of technical and non-technical activities that exist in a computing environment. Also, the definition guides the integrations, collaborations, and changes that ETA re-engineers through its development.

7.3.3.2 Enterprise Technical Architecture Classes

ETA consists of classes composed of both technical (IS/IT solutions) and non-technical factors, such as process and people. It also enables change by bridging the gap between strategic planning and implementation efforts, through a strategic process that is holistic in scope (Kotusev et al., 2023; Griffo et al., 2021). ETA comprises different classes: data, middleware, network, platform, and distributed architectures. Each class has unique and specific deliverables, analysis methods, processes, and participants.

Table 7.1 defines the domains, with their associated classes, descriptions, categories, and processes. This is also attributed to the fact that domain architectures are created to provide principles and standards for the use of technologies as they relate to and enable specific business objectives (Iyamu, 2022a; Fischer et al., 2010). As expressed at the beginning of the chapter and the introductory sections, ETA provides the means for maintaining adaptive infrastructures through sets of principles, standards, configurations, and processes. It also drives and guides the introduction of new technologies by focusing on function, scalability, compatibility, and interoperability in fulfilling business and technical needs. Individual templates (such as Tables 7.1–7.4) could be used to achieve the objectives of ETA within the context of an organisational need. The templates can be manual or automated but used for information capturing, validation, and processing of the architecture activities and deliverables.

The class level of ETA contains the prescriptive elements that are designed to purposely guide IS/IT re-engineering activities within an organisation. This includes analysis, design, implementation and operations management. Also, the class level provides an organisation with a means to categorise technologies that are related or depend on each other to identify reusable, conflicting, or duplicative technology. Furthermore, the class level consists of sets of principles and standards (such as industry, product, and configuration) that govern the selection and use of related technologies in specifically defined logical domains.

In the development phase, the ETA domains (data, middleware, network, platform, and distribution) are considered interconnected and interdependent. The domains, as defined in Table 7.1, evolve iteratively in the course of ETA development.

Actors enrol in the different classes, as they are guided and based on factors such as skills and areas of specialisation. However, personal interest is a strong influencing factor, as well. There are the following three main steps involved in creating the technical domain architectures.

i. Create domain architecture that represents the logical technical classes and their relationships with each other, referring to existing frameworks (Fernández-Cejas et al., 2022) and modifying them accordingly rather than continuously recreating them.

Table 7.1   Technical Architecture Classes

Classes	Description	Technology Categories	Process/ Procedural
Data Architecture	Defines the mechanics for managing, securing, and maintaining the integrity of the organisation's significant logical entities. The entities are recorded and accounted for in the business information environment. The architecture provides standards for accessing data, as well as business objects as appropriate.	Data and object repositories, data encyclopaedia, data modelling, replication and administration tools, and object-oriented databases.	Based on the business requirements, principles are formulated, within which data is classified and managed; technologies are selected and deployed.
Middleware Architecture	Defines the components that create an integrated environment between user workstations or legacy systems and server environments to improve the overall usability of the distributed infrastructures. It creates uniform mechanisms for application integration which are independent of network and platform technologies.	Remote procedure calls (RPC), messaging-oriented middleware (MOM), object request brokers (ORBs), transaction processing (TP), database (DB) gateways.	The business and technical requirements dictate the principles and standards in the selection and deployment of technologies.
Network Architecture	Provides the communication infrastructure for the distributed computing environment. It consists of logical elements, physical hardware components, carrier services, and protocols.	Network hardware, network operating systems, security, carrier and internet services.	The business and technical requirements guide the design and management of the network.

(Continued)

Table 7.1 (Continued)

Classes	Description	Technology Categories	Process/ Procedural
Platform Architecture	Defines the components of technology infrastructures, including the client and server hardware platforms, the operating systems executing on those platforms, and the database environments with their supported interfaces.	Hardware (workstations, servers), operating systems, database management Systems.	Based on the business and technology requirements, principles and standards are formulated, within which technologies are selected, deployed, and managed.
Distributed Architecture	Defines how hardware and software components are managed. It focuses on issues of configuration management, fault detection and isolation, testing, performance measurement, problem reporting, and software upgrades and controls.	Network systems, configuration, storage management and security, performance management, and capacity planning.	Based on the business and technology requirements, principles and standards are formulated, within which technologies are selected, deployed, and managed.

ii. Define domain-level principles, categorise technologies into appropriate classes, document technology's products and configure standards into appropriate groupings and product evaluations.

iii. Relate standards to appropriate and supported infrastructure patterns within the computing environment of an organisation.

Each technical architecture class provides a unique capability view of the computing environment. Within this context: (i) data and network domains provide the tools, models, techniques, and participants to manage the impact of change on the linking activities of business processes and partners (Iyamu, 2015); (ii) middleware and distributed domains enable the management of change on business system logics and applications (Belfadel et al., 2022); and (iii) the platform domain enables the management of change on technology infrastructures.

The domain architectures as presented in Table 7.1 seem to be the most appropriate groupings of technologies that are required to enable and support business drivers in organisations. The domain architectures evolve iteratively as both technical and business requirements continue to change. Primarily, the role of each of the technical domains is intended to organise technologies. The domains consist of unique rules which are meant to assist architects in identifying common uses of technologies, detecting deficiencies, and eliminating redundancy as much as possible.

7.3.3.3 Classification

Within the ETA, existing technologies are grouped into classes (see Table 7.1), which define their strategic or non-strategic status at the time. For the benefit of an organisation, a consensus is oftentimes reached amongst the key stakeholders in the following areas: employees' involvement, the authenticity of technologies, where technologies reside, and how technologies are deployed and applied. Communication among the actors on these issues helps to formulate policies for governance purposes.

Thus, the technical requirements should be defined in a technical architecture product catalogue, mainly because they contain information about various products. Table 7.2 reflects the rules that pertain to individual technologies per domain architecture. Table 7.2 can be viewed as an example of a populated template of ETA. The columns of the table may be defined as follows.

   i. **Technology category (A)** refers to each of the broad logical groupings of technologies within the domain.

   ii. **Technology (B)** refers to the actual technology that is involved in an organisational context.

   iii. **Standards (C)** are the local and international guidelines with which products comply in their selection (buy, build, or reuse).

   iv. **Products (D)** are the named vendor products, in areas such as hardware, software, networks, and protocols.

   v. **Current/Future (E)** indicates whether a product is currently in use or planned for future use in the environment.

   vi. **Architectural Status (F)** is a formal status that is at the time associated with each product as agreed upon by the architects. The indicators of architectural status include **S**trategic, **M**aintain, **O**utdated, **N**ot supported or not approved, **T**actical, and **E**valuating. The implications or what the indicators mean is summarised as follows.

     S—Strategic: All new developments will have to utilise products that are tagged strategic, according to their configurations and standards. Also, existing solutions will have to migrate to, or be replaced by, strategic products when feasible.

M—Maintain: This means that there is no room for proliferation. In other words, maintain for as long as the product is required—there should be a replacement strategy of timeframes.

O—Outdated: The product must be upgraded or replaced within a timeframe, or **Obsolete**—must therefore be removed from the environment as soon as is practical to do so.

N—Not supported or **not approved:** This applies to any products that have been evaluated but not certified for the environment.

T—Tactical: This is an interim, short-term solution for a specific period (e.g., up to 18 months). It is therefore to be replaced by product(s) with a strategic status.

E—Evaluating: A product that is being researched, is at the proof of concept phase, or is being piloted. If successful, it will be assigned tactical or strategic status; if not successful, will be assigned 'not approved' status. This goes with supporting documentation.

vii. **Configuration (G)** standards are used to describe how products are deployed and applied for organisation purposes, from both software and hardware perspectives.

    i. Software configuration standards include: (i) the release or version number, which must be adhered to; (ii) installation options and configuration settings; (iii) upgrade paths; and (iv) maintenance procedures.

    ii. Hardware configurations include: (i) the model name and number; (ii) configuration settings; (iii) installation procedures; and (iv) any related peripheral standards.

Table 7.2 Technical Architectural Grouping

Technology Category (A)	Technology (B)	Standards (C)	Products (D)	Current/ Future (E)	Architectural Status (F)	Configuration (G)
A1	B1	C1	D1	C	S	O
		C2	D2	F	E	S
	B2	C3	D3	F	S	D
		C4	D4	C	M	G
		C5	D5	C	N	F

Notes: A—Consists of one or more Bs; B—Each B could have more than one C, and D depends on the organisation; E—It is either a C or an F; If E is equal to C, then F is equal to S/N/E; and if E is equal to F, then F is equal to S/M/O/N/T.

The ETA domains are standardised primarily to ensure uniformity, assessment, evaluation, and reduced complexity. The last stage of technical architecture development is the formulation of principles, which is covered in the following subsection.

7.3.3.4 Domain Principles

Principles are guiding statements of positions that communicate fundamental elements, truths, rules, or qualities that must be exhibited by the organisation (Iyamu, 2015; Fischer et al., 2010; Patel, 2002). They are extracted and formulated from the business strategy, according to how they pertain to ETA. As shown in Table 7.3, each principle is linked to other components, which include rationale, process, and guidelines. The formation and application of principles apply to all the domains of ETA.

The primary purpose of principles is to enable an organisation to take an incremental and iterative approach (Haki & Legner, 2021) in transitioning to formal modelling while allowing it to influence decision-making immediately and consistently (Batmetan, 2022). In the ETA context, principles are used as evaluation criteria in the absence of detailed models that direct decision-making more discretely and comprehensively. For example, one type of architecture model is a technology class configuration standard that details technology products and the way they are configured together to deliver a reusable building block of technical infrastructures, such as an application server.

Principles lead to policies and procedures and are used to give guidance to the developers and implementers of ETA domains (data, middleware, network, platform, and distributed). As explained in Table 7.3, the existence of each principle is based on at least a rationale, which represents the interest of the organisation. Correspondingly, the execution of any principle follows a process or procedure and guideline, which guides orderliness within the environment. Thus, principles affect the selection, design, and implementation of software packages, application components, infrastructure deployment, and business objects processes in an organisation (Belfadel et al., 2022).

Table 7.3 Principle Formulation

Principle	Rationale	Process	Guideline
Articulate and give a name which reflects the intention and essence of the objective of the organisation	Highlight potential benefits in adhering to the principle	Formulate procedures to assist in achieving the rationale as set out by the organisation	Specify rules and regulations that must be followed in adhering to the process

7.3.4 Phase Four: Implementation

The implementation phase consists of four stages: gap analysis, migration planning, implementation planning, and project—each described in what follows. ETA is expected to enable rapid technology-related change in an organisation's business processes, as well as the applications that enable them. It is, therefore, necessary to understand the areas on which the ETA depends.

    i. The business vision of the organisation, which captures the most important business strategies being pursued at the time.

    ii. The organisational requirements which consist of high-level architectural requirements, which are derived from business strategies to give direction and priority.

    iii. The architecture which contains sets of principles mainly derived from best practices and trends, which are relative to—and consistent across—each domain architecture.

7.3.4.1 Gap Analysis

The final phase of the implementation entails a gap analysis, which is conducted across the classes of technical domains architecture. As shown in Table 7.4, gap analysis is used primarily to determine corrective action, develop prioritised migration plans, and finally draw up implementation plans.

The purpose of the gap analysis is to assess the current state of the technical architecture against the desired state as reflected by the drivers (Fernández-Cejas

Table 7.4　Implementation Plan

Requirement (Future State)	Action	Deli-verable	Res-ponsibility	Status	Target Date
Principles					
The entity that defines the rationale and motivation for the tasks; the entity guides the scope	Defines the individual and collective tasks, including the deliverables	Defines tasks to be con-ducted	Deter-mination of who does what and allocation of tasks among the actors: architect, business units, etc.	Standing: (1) not started; (2) in progress; (3) completed	Date agreed to by the primary stake-holders, including the architects

et al., 2022), which is covered during phase two (requirements—business strategy). This assessment is an iterative and ongoing process. It is reflected by a checklist (objectives and business strategy) and accompanying action plans. For two main reasons, the assessments are stored in a repository: (i) to track, trace, and monitor the action plans; and (ii) to promote and ensure accessibility and transparency of the activities, which reduces complexities. This is primarily because of the importance of the assessment to the organisation.

7.3.4.2 Migration Planning

The positioning of strategy and the movement from one architectural phase to another is a very complex issue. It is a much more complex exercise than simply consulting with vendors or employing new technology. Migration from one technology or platform to another has never been easy (Rouhani et al., 2015), and hence, planning is critical. This could be attributed to the fact that the current trends in technology and architectural direction are often geared towards higher levels of connectivity and functionality (Nikpay et al., 2017). It is true that the current movement in the industry is towards more 'open' strategies, but if this ever fully occurs in reality, the building block approach to implementation becomes a viable strategy.

Certainly, one of the key decision processes which are involved with architectural planning is the need to have a future target. Kotusev (2019) describes it as a transition roadmap, from the current state to the future state. Shorter-term goals can also be defined as stepping stones to strategic goals. One of the challenges is that, historically, information technologists have been lacking in accurate prediction of products' directions and timing. For example, who in the 1980s predicted the impact that personal computers (PCs) and mobile devices currently have on the industry and society? Or who would have predicted the explosion of the internet and mobile computing? Thus, as technologies evolve, the migration from current to future state is increasingly critical to ease implementation.

7.3.4.3 Implementation Planning

Once the inventory is defined, the first step in planning is to assess both the strategic and technical fit of the current technologies. The strategic and technical fit assessments depend on each other. However, the order in which they are carried out is discretional to the context of the environment. The strategic fit is assessed based on the technology's contributions to business value, sustainability, and competitiveness. The technical fit is assessed based on the technology's adherence to the technical architecture design principles and technology standards (Dale & Scheepers, 2020; Roelens et al., 2019). These assessments enable the technologies to be categorised as shown in Table 7.4. Also, the assessments reduce complexities and ease manageability because the technologies pass through the project.

7.3.4.4 Project

The development and implementation of technological artefacts are traditionally conducted through projects. Deployment of technologies, therefore, frequently pass through this cycle multiple times. In the process, there are continuous interactions which happen between the actors, usually comprising project implementers and the architecture team. The interactions enact the relationship between the actors. It is primarily to assess, monitor, and measure the ongoing events and activities.

Each ETA project is required to model the technology environment, including infrastructure configuration standards and guidelines, to ensure appropriate deployment. The models provide views on recommended technology based on assessing the impact of new technologies and the replacement of technologies. Similar to other EA domains, ETA is not a project, but an iterative process. The process continually ensures the operationalisation of IT solutions in an architected approach.

7.4 Summary

Enterprise technical architecture (ETA) modelling provides guidelines for information systems and information technology (IS/IT) architects and other IS/IT specialists and stakeholders such as knowledge workers, information processors, IT application developers, network administrators, and infrastructure managers. Modelling helps organisations to explore the factors that lead to the success or failure of ETA in the computing environment of the organisation.

The chapter presents a new paradigm for building ETA that improves the effectiveness of functional operations, including their efficiency and use of technology throughput in an organisation. The contributions of this chapter are from two main perspectives: methodological and practical. The methodological contribution of the chapter is through the perspective in which we gain a better understanding of the procedural development and implementation, and the importance of ETA, in the computing environment. The other main contribution is in its practicality, which constitutes a learning curve for IT architects in the development and implementation of ETA. Based on the practicality, an aggregation of ideas and experience is acquired, which architects tap into to improve their services to the organisations. Furthermore, it is generally expected to benefit the computing industry and IS researchers on the capabilities of ETA, as well as how it effects change.

An area recommended for future research, which this chapter did not cover, is the social context in the development and implementation of ETA in organisations. It would be interesting to both academics and practitioners to understand the interplay between various actors during the development and implementation of ETA in organisations.

References

Aerts, A., Goossenaerts, J., Hammer, D., & Wortmann, J. (2004). Architectures in context: On the evolution of business, application software, and ICT platform architectures. *Information & Management, 41*(2004), 781–794.

Ahlemann, F., Legner, C., & Lux, J. (2021). A resource-based perspective of value generation through enterprise architecture management. *Information & Management, 58*(1), 103266.

Batmetan, J. R. (2022). Model enterprise architecture for information technology services in universities. *International Journal of Information Technology and Education, 1*(4), 18–34.

Belfadel, A., Amdouni, E., Laval, J., Cherifi, C. B., & Moalla, N. (2022). Towards software reuse through an enterprise architecture-based software capability profile. *Enterprise Information Systems, 16*(1), 29–70.

Bolton, A., Goosen, L., & Kritzinger, E. (2020, December 16–18). Security aspects of an empirical study into the impact of digital transformation via unified communication and collaboration technologies on the productivity and innovation of a global automotive enterprise. In *Proceedings of the international conference on information security* (pp. 99–113). Springer.

Booch, G. (2010). Enterprise architecture and technical architecture. *IEEE Software, 27*(2), 96–96.

Brynjolfsson, E. (1993). The productivity paradox of information technology. *Communications of the ACM, 36*(12), 67–77.

Burke, B. (2007). *The role of enterprise architecture in technology research*. Gartner Inc. Retrieved April 14, 2010, from http://gartner.com/technology/research.jsp

Chen, R. R., Chen, K., & Ou, C. X. (2023). Facilitating interorganizational trust in strategic alliances by leveraging blockchain-based systems: Case studies of two eastern banks. *International Journal of Information Management, 68*, 102521.

Chitsa, F., & Iyamu, T. (2020). Towards enterprise technical architecture for the implementation of the South African NHIA. *Advances in Science, Technology and Engineering Systems Journal, 5*(2), 724–728.

Constantinides, P., Henfridsson, O., & Parker, G. G. (2018). Introduction—platforms and infrastructures in the digital age. *Information Systems Research, 29*(2), 381–400.

Cook, M. A. (1996). *Building enterprise information architectures: Reengineering information systems*. Prentice-Hall Inc.

Dale, M., & Scheepers, H. (2020). Enterprise architecture implementation as interpersonal connection: Building support and commitment. *Information Systems Journal, 30*(1), 150–184.

De Vries, M., & van Rensburg, A. C. J. (2008). Enterprise architecture—new business value perspectives. *South African Journal of Industrial Engineering, 19*, 1–16.

Fernández-Cejas, M., Pérez-González, C. J., Roda-García, J. L., & Colebrook, M. (2022). CURIE: Towards an ontology and enterprise architecture of a CRM conceptual model. *Business & Information Systems Engineering*, 1–29.

Fischer, C., Winter, R., & Aier, S. (2010). What is an enterprise architecture principle? In *Computer and information science 2010* (pp. 193–205). Springer.

Foorthuis, R., Van Steenbergen, M., Brinkkemper, S., & Bruls, W. A. (2016). A theory building study of enterprise architecture practices and benefits. *Information Systems Frontiers, 18*(3), 541–564.

Griffo, C., Almeida, J. P. A., Guizzardi, G., & Nardi, J. C. (2021). Service contract modeling in enterprise architecture: An ontology-based approach. *Information Systems, 101,* 101454.

Hafner, M., & Winter, R. (2008, January 7–10). Processes for enterprise application architecture management. In *The proceedings of the 41st Hawaii international conference on system sciences (HICSS)* (pp. 1–10). IEEE.

Haki, K., & Legner, C. (2021). The mechanics of enterprise architecture principles. *Journal of the Association for Information Systems, 22*(5), 1334–1375.

Ismagilova, E., Hughes, L., Rana, N. P., & Dwivedi, Y. K. (2022). Security, privacy and risks within smart cities: Literature review and development of a smart city interaction framework. *Information Systems Frontiers, 24*(2), 393–414.

Iyamu, T. (2015). *Information technology enterprise architecture: From concept to practice* (2nd ed.). Heidelberg Press. ISBN: 8-3-659-61206-0.

Iyamu, T. (2022a). *Enterprise architecture for strategic management of modern IT solutions* (1st ed.). Auerbach Publications.

Iyamu, T. (2022b). Creating a technical architecture framework for m-voting application. *African Journal of Science, Technology, Innovation and Development, 14*(1), 86–93.

Jones, S. S., Rudin, R. S., Perry, T., & Shekelle, P. G. (2014). Health information technology: An updated systematic review with a focus on meaningful use. *Annals of Internal Medicine, 160*(1), 48–54.

Kang, D., Lee, J., & Kim, K. (2010). Alignment of business enterprise architectures using fact-based ontologies. *Expert Systems with Applications, 37*(4), 3274–3283.

Kilpeläinen, T. (2007, December 5–7). Business information driven approach for EA development in practice. In *The proceedings of the 18th Australasian conference on information systems business information driven* (pp. 447–457). Association of Information Systems (AIS) Press.

Kochanthara, S., Rood, N., Saberi, A. K., Cleophas, L., Dajsuren, Y., & van den Brand, M. (2021). A functional safety assessment method for cooperative automotive architecture. *Journal of Systems and Software, 179,* 110991.

Kotusev, S. (2019). Enterprise architecture and enterprise architecture artifacts: Questioning the old concept in light of new findings. *Journal of Information Technology, 34*(2), 102–128.

Kotusev, S., Kurnia, S., & Dilnutt, R. (2023). Enterprise architecture artifacts as boundary objects: An empirical analysis. *Information and Software Technology, 155,* 107108.

Kumar, A., Sharma, S., Goyal, N., Singh, A., Cheng, X., & Singh, P. (2021). Secure and energy-efficient smart building architecture with emerging technology IoT. *Computer Communications, 176,* 207–217.

Luftman, J. N., Papp, R., & Brier, T. (1999). Enablers and inhibitors of business-IT alignment. *Communications of Association of Information Systems, 1*(11), 1–34.

Masuda, Y., Shirasaka, S., Yamamoto, S., & Hardjono, T. (2018). Architecture board practices in adaptive enterprise architecture with digital platform: A case of global healthcare enterprise. *International Journal of Enterprise Information Systems (IJEIS), 14*(1), 1–20.

McDermott, K. (2016). Achieving data liquidity across health care requires a technical architecture. *Bulletin of the Association for Information Science and Technology, 43*(1), 19–22.

Nikpay, F., Ahmad, R. B., Rouhani, B. D., Mahrin, M. N. R., & Shamshirband, S. (2017). An effective enterprise architecture implementation methodology. *Information Systems and e-Business Management, 15*(4), 927–962.

Patel, N. (2002, January 7–10). Global e-business IT governance: Radical re-directions. In *The proceeding of the 35th international conference on systems sciences (HICSS)*. IEEE.

Petersson, L., Larsson, I., Nygren, J. M., Nilsen, P., Neher, M., Reed, J. E., Tyskbo, D., & Svedberg, P. (2022). Challenges to implementing artificial intelligence in healthcare: A qualitative interview study with healthcare leaders in Sweden. *BMC Health Services Research, 22*(1), 1–16.

Roelens, B., Steenacker, W., & Poels, G. (2019). Realizing strategic fit within the business architecture: The design of a process-goal alignment modeling and analysis technique. *Software & Systems Modeling, 18*(1), 631–662.

Ross, J., Weill, P., & Robertson, D. (2006). *Enterprise architecture as strategy: Creating a foundation for business execution*. Harvard Business Press.

Rouhani, B. D., Mahrin, M. N. R., Nikpay, F., Ahmad, R. B., & Nikfard, P. (2015). A systematic literature review on enterprise architecture implementation methodologies. *Information and Software Technology, 62*, 1–20.

Shaanika, I., & Iyamu, T. (2018). Developing the enterprise architecture for the Namibian government. *The Electronic Journal of Information Systems in Developing Countries, 84*(3), e12028.

Spewak, S. H. (1992). *Enterprise architecture planning: Developing a blueprint for data, applications and technology*. John Wiley & Sons Inc.

Spijkman, T., Molenaar, S., Dalpiaz, F., & Brinkkemper, S. (2021). Alignment and granularity of requirements and architecture in agile development: A functional perspective. *Information and Software Technology, 133*, 106535.

Tamm, T., Seddon, P. B., & Shanks, G. (2022). How enterprise architecture leads to organisational benefits. *International Journal of Information Management, 67*, 102554.

Venkatesan, D., & Sridhar, S. (2019). A rationale for the choice of enterprise architecture method and software technology in a software driven enterprise. *International Journal of Business Information Systems, 32*(3), 272–311.

Versteeg, G., & Bouwman, H. (2006). Business architecture: A new paradigm from relate e-business strategy to ICT. *Information Systems Frontiers, 8*(2), 91–102.

Williamson, B. (2018). The hidden architecture of higher education: Building a big data infrastructure for the 'smarter university. *International Journal of Educational Technology in Higher Education, 15*(1), 1–26.

Youngs, R., Redmond-Pyle, D., Spaas, P., & Kahan, E. (1999). A standard for architecture description. *IBM Systems Journal, 38*(1), 32–50.

Chapter 8

Enterprise Architecture as IT Strategy

8.1 Introduction

Many organisations adopt cyclical processes to articulate and re-engineer technological responses to their business needs. The goals and objectives of some organisations are often to advance competitiveness and sustainability, in alignment with their organisational vision and strategy. In doing so, many organisations increasingly rely on information technology (IT) solutions (hardware, software, and networking) to enable and enhance their processes and capabilities. As a resource, IT solutions are employed to successfully deliver services (Roth et al., 2023). IT solutions are broad and increasingly diverse in rapidity (Abouzahra & Ghasemaghaei, 2022; Karimi-Alaghehband & Rivard, 2019). The diverse nature of IT solutions makes their selection complicated and asymmetric, which exacerbates complexities in some organisations. The increasing reliance on IT solutions and the challenges it constantly poses make the formulation of its strategy inevitable for organisations.

Thus, IT solutions are not immune to challenges and complexities which sometimes constrain processes, directly or indirectly. Among others, Giddens et al. (2023) reveal an additional challenge of users' perceptions about IT solutions use, patterns, and outcomes. In another example, Qadri et al. (2020) argue that in many organisations, the integration of IT solutions has been faced with challenges, sometimes leading to the termination of projects. Project termination is always prohibitive and sometimes threatens sustainability and competitiveness. In addressing such challenges, to fulfil the objective of IT units, through IT solutions which are designed to enable and support business goals and objectives, organisations seek approaches such as enterprise architecture (EA). EA facilitates the activities of an organisation from decision-making and strategic standpoints (Kurnia et al., 2021).

DOI: 10.1201/9781003390879-8

Iyamu (2022) explains how EA is used as a tool for integrating information systems and technologies within an environment.

EA and IT strategy are critical concepts in the organisations that deploy them. Critically, it is worth noting that the understandings and meaning which technologists and other stakeholders associate with EA and IT strategy shape, influence, and determine the deployment and outcome of its use in an organisation. This is mainly because of the huge reliability and high expectations of the organisations that deploy them. According to Ross et al. (2006), enterprise architecture is the organising logic for business processes and IT infrastructure, reflecting the integration and standardization requirements of the company's operating model. As a result, the expectations and alignment between the two concepts require a better understanding and common meaning to achieve their goals, objectives, and values (Saleem & Fakieh, 2020; Chung & McLeod, 2002). This is important because actors' different understandings and interpretations of the concepts of EA and IT strategy pose potential risks, such as incompatibility and duplication in their development, implementation, and practice.

The development, implementation, and practice of EA greatly depend on the approach employed (Kaisler & Armour, 2017; Khoury & Simoff, 2004; Zachman, 1996). Through its domains, EA establishes a current state and defines the future state across the business and IT units (Syynimaa, 2018), making it a strategic approach (Iyamu, 2022). Technical and non-technical factors such as technology, process, and people are the focal actors in the EA approach. These factors are strategic in nature, to various degrees. Strategy is directional, from one state to the other. People are the main instrument and focal actor of strategy, which is inseparable from technology, process, rules, and regulations (Hylving & Bygstad, 2019; Pereira & Sousa, 2004).

IT strategy defines the necessary autonomy that enables and supports common business processes, information systems, and information technology (IS/IT) infrastructures, periodically within an organisation. Iyamu and Adelakun (2008) define IT strategy as the technical design which serves as the road map over a period for the implementation of IT solutions by people, using a formal process. The authors further argue that an IT strategy consists of artefacts which determine the solutions based on the organisation's goals and objectives, as extracted from the information systems strategy. One of the vital solutions is integration, primarily because it enables the coexistence of technologies, including those that are heterogeneous in multiple layers (Qadri et al., 2020).

The development and implementation of EA require an in-depth understanding of technical needs and business requirements. This is due to the specialised nature of the concepts. Kilpeläinen (2007) argues that EA deployment requires high know-how by the personnel involved in the process. Many organisations progressively and wholly rely on IT solutions for their strategic and daily operations, primarily to enhance their competitiveness. In the view of Schekkerman (2004), EA clinically improves the implementation of IT solutions in an organisation. This could be viewed in that way because as business processes change, projects are initiated and technology grows, making EA an effective solution in the implementation of the IT strategy. According to Wolff and Sydor (1999), senior leadership recognises that the intelligent use of IT solutions is important for an organisation to realise its mission, goals, and objectives.

It is therefore critically important that both EA and IT strategies are aligned to consolidate efforts and resources for their efficient and effective use within an organisation. To do this, the objectives, processes, and phases of the concepts must be well understood and clearly defined. This also includes an understanding of the relationship and alignment factors that exist between EA and IT strategy. Therefore, it is important to comprehend that the goals and objectives of EA and IT strategy can be achieved through collaborative or collective efforts among EA, business, and IT units. This chapter examines how EA can be employed as an IT strategy to address the needs and challenges of both business and IT units. The focus of the chapter is geared through the individual domain to gain deeper insights into how EA can be deployed as an IT strategy in an organisation.

This chapter is organised into seven main sections. It begins with an introduction, followed by a section that presents a review of EA deployment. Next, the source of data for the chapter is explained. Subsequently, EA planning, factors influencing EA deployment, and EA as a strategy for the organisation's purposes are discussed, respectively. Finally, the chapter concludes with highlights of the contributions of the findings from the empirical study.

8.2 Enterprise Architecture Deployment

EA is a holistic approach for operational and strategic purposes of both business and IT units, encouraging organisations to explore and adopt the concept. According to Rahimi et al. (2017), organisations may adopt EA to implement IT strategies. This does not necessarily mean that problems are solved and goals are achieved. Evidently, in literature, best practices are proposed to aid organisations in the adoption of EA (Vallerand et al., 2017). The implementation of EA is critical; thus, it can be done through various programmes or using different approaches (Bui, 2017). Many of the existing studies focused on the design, implementation, and post-adoption stages (Dang, 2019). Some of the studies identified documentation (Iyamu, 2022), stakeholder participation (Dang, 2019), architectural governance (Saint-Louis & Lapalme, 2018), and culture (Shaanika & Iyamu, 2018) as some of the factors that influence EA implementation in organisations.

However, in practice, some organisations employ EA for long-term planning, whereas others prefer it for quick-fix and short-term purposes (Ahlemann et al., 2021). Thus, EA focuses on addressing enterprise-wide instead of detailed descriptions of artefacts or activities (Kotusev et al., 2023). This is in contrast because EA as a discipline is a holistic approach (Griffo et al., 2021) that facilitates broad thinking towards the development of business and IT strategies in an organisation (Georgiadis & Poels, 2021).

The interest in the concept of EA by practitioners continues to grow because of the anticipated, many claimed, benefits (Tamm et al., 2022), such as using EA as a strategic approach to define boundary objects between diverse business and IT solutions (Kotusev et al., 2023). Sukur and Lind (2022) explain how applying EA standards affect IT solutions' flexibility and enterprise agility geared towards strategy enhancement. Ahmad et al. (2022) revealed some of the factors that influence the intention to adopt EA communication, governance, and organisational structure. These are strategic in nature, which requires a holistic and enterprise-wide approach in the implementation.

The myth of EA being a silver bullet that can deal with all aspects of an enterprise is not realistic (Gong & Janssen, 2019). According to Tamm et al. (2022), the mechanisms underpinning EA benefit realisation are not fully understood and have only relatively recently begun to receive research attention. These often prove to be inherently abstract, which is a consequence of their strategic nature (Foorthuis et al., 2016). Thus, the operationalisation of EA in organisations requires different levels of adaptation of EA principles (Ajer et al., 2021). Haki and Legner (2021) argue that even when the EA principles are discussed, their suitability in context and how to apply them are often silent and pose challenges.

EA is used to enable strategies, through which business and IT models are created and activities, procedures, and events are clarified—to improve efficiency and enhance sustainability and competitiveness (Iyamu, 2022; Zhi & Zhou, 2022). EA is considered effective because it is concocted to contribute to business design, management of information flow, and integrated IT solutions (Masuda et al., 2021), which are often challenging in many organisations. Particularly concrete benefits resulting from EA have turned out to be challenging to demonstrate, not to mention the process of benefits realisation itself (Niemi & Pekkola, 2020).

Like many other frameworks, TOGAF and Gartner support the design and implementation of EA domains: business architecture, application architecture, data architecture, and technology (Jallow et al., 2017). As EA is a highly specialised discipline, it is difficult for many organisations to find and retain personnel. As a result, organisations increasingly rely on consulting firms for the implementation of EA (Bui, 2017). Despite external consultants' involvement, challenges persist, causing derailments in some aspects of it in many organisations. This negatively affects EA as a strategic tool supposedly to reduce IT solutions' implementation failure, improve sustainability, and enhance business–IT alignment within an organisation (Jusuf & Kurnia, 2017). Despite the organisations' attempts and comprehensiveness of the existing studies, it is unclear how EA is or can be employed as a strategic tool (Niemi & Pekkola, 2020).

EA, in its strategic nature, can enable effective and efficient design and evaluation of architecture domains for organisations (Jallow et al., 2017). Also, from a strategic standpoint, EA practice enables an organisation to structure the logic of a business process and ensure successful governance of IT solutions (Qazi et al., 2019). It is within this premise that some studies offer new insights into the objectives of EA, as well as its implementation (Vallerand et al., 2017). However, evidence of EA strategic benefits and success factors is limited in existing literature (Jusuf & Kurnia, 2017). This explains why EA implementation is often questioned and challenged, as its benefits are difficult to dissect in many organisations (Niemi & Pekkola, 2020; Dang, 2019). Thus, Niemi and Pekkola (2020) posed the question from where do the benefits stem?

8.3 Source of Data

The organisation Evostat Finance, which was used as a case in this study, is one of the largest financial institutions in South Africa. Evostat Finance was selected based on *prima facie* evidence that it has successfully deployed EA as an IT strategy. Thus, the case study was adopted to gain an insightful qualitative interpretation of EA and how it could be deployed to complement IT strategy in an organisation.

Evostat Finance has been in operation for more than 100 years as of the time of this study, in 2009. The organisation had about 20,000 employees on its payroll and had one of the largest IT divisions in the corporate organisations in South Africa. The organisation had nine main divisions, including IT, which was the smallest of the divisions. There were 870 employees in the IT division, split into six main departments: Systems Development, Programme Office, Infrastructure Services, Technology Management and Architecture, Human Resources, and IT Finance. Each of the departments had its roles, which were distinctively defined and managed by dedicated managers. The managers report to the CIO, who was the head of the IT division. The Technology Management and Architecture Department was headed by the CTO.

Data sources included semi-structured interviews and documentation. A total of 23 interviews were conducted. This number was reached heuristically, i.e., the decision to stop adding respondents was made when nothing new was being learnt from the interviews and a state of theoretical saturation was reached. Initially, three main questions were formulated for the interviews: (i) why was EA developed and implemented in the organisation?; (ii) how was EA developed and implemented in the organisation?; and (iii) what factors influenced the development and implementation of EA in the organisation? As the interviews progressed, more questions were generated from the participants' responses.

A set of balanced respondent demographics was a key factor in achieving a true reflection of the situations from the natural setting of the organisation. The respondents that participated in the study were from different units of the organisation. Also, the respondents were at various levels within the organisational structure, from both the Business and IT departments. They included analysts, IT architects, IT managers, IT project managers, IT executive managers and business managers.

Two criteria, knowledge and experience were used for identifying and selecting the participants: (i) knowledge: interviewees were selected based on their experience of EA, IT strategy, IT management, and organisational issues; and (ii) experience: each of the interviewees had been in the organisation for a minimum of five years, and at least three years in their current positions. These criteria were to ensure relevant and quality data.

Questions used to elicit data were threefold: (i) understanding of EA and IT strategy; (ii) why and how EA and IT strategy were complementarily developed and implemented in the organisation; and (iii) the impact of EA and IT strategy on the organisation's activities. The questions were purposely designed to achieve the following objectives: (a) to learn how the organisation could best align its technology activities and investments with its business strategy and goals; (b) to learn how IT strategy delivery could be ensured through the EA approach; and (c) to learn how the technology platforms support the organisation's growth plans and competitiveness.

An understanding was reached with the interviewees to preserve the anonymity of their identities. This enthusiastically encouraged some of them to participate in the interview process as well as to grant permission for interviews to be recorded. The recorded interviews were transcribed, interviewees were requested to confirm the content of the transcripts, and the data was then analysed using the interpretive approach.

8.4 Enterprise Architecture Planning

The analysis was carried out at two different interconnected levels. The first level focused on the conceptualisation of the development and implementation of EA. At the second level, an analysis was conducted to examine how EA is employed as an IT strategy to address business and IT needs and challenges.

The analysis explored how EA provides an organisation with a methodological approach for modelling the business and technology functions and activities performed at the time. This includes understanding whose actors performed specific functions, how the functions were performed, when and where the functions were performed, and most importantly, why the business needed to perform such functions.

First, the deployment of EA as an IT strategy is discussed conceptually and within the concept of generalisation, followed by detailed elucidation at the domains' levels. As depicted in Figure 8.1, generalisation includes the planning of activities in the process of carrying out the tasks that are involved in the deployment and practice of EA in an organisation. In the summary of Lee and Baskerville's (2003) argumentative stance, generalisability in an interpretive study is intended to formulate a theory so that it not only explains what the fieldworker has already found or observed, but also might help the same or another researcher to anticipate, or at

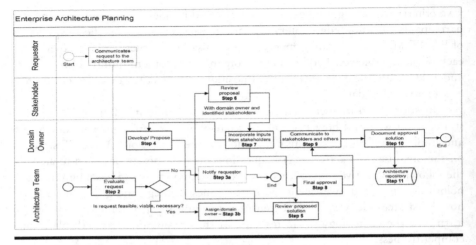

Figure 8.1 Enterprise Architecture Planning.

least not be surprised by additional observations that are subsequently made. This has led and guided me to generalise the deployment of EA for organisations. Thus, I generalise and classify the primary tasks of EA into four main groups of actors: architecture teams, domain owners, stakeholders, and requestors.

8.4.1 Requestor

In technical terms, the requestor is the sponsor (or delegate) of the tasks which are problematised by the focal actor to deploy EA in an organisation. The initiative is problematised to the stakeholders and further carried out by the architecture team, as shown in Figure 8.1. The requestor is the promoter of EA in an organisation. It is usually an executive member of the IT unit. Thus, In some quarters, EA is viewed as a mechanism employed by the IT unit (Syynimaa, 2018). As explained in Chapter 1, Tamm et al. (2022) are explicit in their discussion that EA is not only about technology but equally covers the business in an organisation. Saleem and Fakieh (2020) suggest that EA's main purpose is as a strategic tool to integrate business strategies and IT solutions.

The development and implementation of EA is iterative and periodical when it comes to fulfilling the organisational strategic mandate. The periodic space is driven by the continued business needs and the rapid changes in IT solutions. This forms part of the planning in that the requestor considers requirements such as the technology end-of-life. In some organisations, for example, the end-of-life of IT solutions such as laptops and computer servers is between three and five years, primarily to avoid compatibility and integration challenges.

EA development and implementation is done within the premise that it will have an impact and influence on both the business and IT units in the organisation. The business and information architectures lean more on the business unit, while the application and technical architectures are more on IT issues. Within this context, the requestor, through EA, codifies functional requirements. This helps the domain owners and architecture team to provide a disciplined systematic design and implementation of process engineering and performance improvement in the business, using IT solutions.

8.4.2 Stakeholder

In the deployment and practice of EA, there are two main groups of stakeholders: internal and external. According to Musukutwa (2022), the most critical aspect of EA are the stakeholders. The internal stakeholders include the managers from both business and IT units and the personnel that are directly involved in the development of EA, which requires a specialised skillset. The external stakeholders include service providers and business partners. Thus, the stakeholders are legitimately and closely involved in the processes and activities of the architects in the deployment and practice of EA in an organisation.

Specialised skills are always needed in the deployment (development and implementation) of EA in organisations. From an empirical study, Trishan et al. (2021) revealed that people and skills are continually emphasised as important and critical factors in the deployment of EA. Let's be clear: not all IT specialists are or can be architects without the opportunity to learn and practise the tools and techniques of EA or its domains. A lack of skills results in poor performance and the inability to recognise and deliver the potential of the domain architectures. Even when the process seems to be understood, it does not guarantee the realisation of EA objectives. Thus, highly skilled and experienced architects are critical in achieving the success of EA in an organisation, and therefore form an essential aspect of planning. Chapter 13 of this book focuses on EA skills.

Usually, organisations have external partners and customers. These partners often have access to an organisation's critical information on a regular or real-time basis. Knowing that partners have access to information in the organisation consciously affects the way business is conducted. Through planning, the business architecture makes a particular contribution in this regard. Otherwise, some organisations struggle to consolidate their systems, mainly because of the uniqueness of their business functions and the selection of IT solutions. The planning should provide the capability to consider different strategies in the delivery of external services. Also, it should provide the organisation with a better method for answering many questions, including the following.

i. How do external partners contribute to the development of products and service delivery?

   ii. From what perspective can external partners contribute to increasing the value of products and services of the organisation, and how can this be achieved?
   iii. When and what information can be leveraged to create or increase value for suppliers, internal operations, and customers?

Based on the answers derived from these questions, organisations establish priorities in implementing strategies for norms and values in advancing competitiveness. Additionally, the questions contribute to requirements, towards the formulation of both business and IT strategies, in enabling products and service delivery.

8.4.3 Domain Owner

At the planning level, the domains of EA are defined, boundaries are outlined, and roles are clarified. Chapters 3–7 of this book provide a detailed explanation of the definitions and scopes of the domains. Each EA domain has distinctive deliverables based on which tasks are allocated (Iyamu, 2022). Subsequently, tasks, processes, and activities in EA deployment and practice are assigned to the specific domain for onward development and execution. Although there are owners, stakeholders must be inclusive of the domain owners' activities.

Characteristically, the ownership of EA development and implementation is prescribed and defined from a phase-based approach perspective, as depicted in Figure 8.3. Purposely, the phase-based approach is intended to convey a logical sequence that is based on relationships and dependencies among the phases, rather than a linear sequence of events. Often, the rationale for the logical sequence includes the following.

   i. Business architecture is a model that is essentially business-driven, and the modelling of the impact of the organisation's vision on the operations of the business. Girsang and Abimanyu (2021) clarify the primary role of EBA as guiding the organisation in structuring itself to manage the operations including allocation, delegation, and arrangement of authority on each function, unit, or actor in the organisation.
   ii. Information architecture focuses on how information could be best leveraged, exploited, or otherwise used to provide business value. The EIA is dependent on a certain level of EBA modelling to determine how and where the business derives its value and competitiveness. Singla and Aggarwal (2020) explain how and why information architecture is a structural design, which facilitates task completion and provides intuitive access to content in an organisation.
   iii. Application architecture depends upon the business and information architectures. This is because it comprises the necessary information and requirements to support and enable the business and to provide the business with complete solutions to satisfy the business vision and strategy. Batmetan (2022) argues that one of the objectives of the EAA is to define the applications

needed to automate the process and manage and support business functions in an organisation.

iv. This is an approach in which technical architecture depends upon the business strategies and business information, which include infrastructure requirements, governance, and procedures. In a logical, sequential order, the technical architecture comes after business, information and application architectures. According to Kochanthara et al. (2021), the technical architecture is responsible for the implementation of IT solutions and managing the dependencies among software and hardware components.

8.4.4 Architecture Team

The architecture team performs the tasks and functions of EA in an organisation. Typically, the team is divided into domains: business, information, application, and technical architectures. From experience, an organisation renamed the domains as foundation (business), services (information), application, and infrastructure (technical) architecture. An expert identifies domains by the roles, responsibilities, and deliverables defined and assigned to the teams (domains). Traditionally, each domain has a group of architects, depending on the size of the organisation. The architecture team is headed by an architecture manager, usually with the title of chief architect.

The architecture team, through its domains, develops and leads the implementation of EA in an organisation. Owing to the distinctive deliverables or tasks, each domain has a unique set of principles that reflect the collective and common will of the organisation as articulated architecturally at the time of planning and the start of development. This was to support and enable an incremental and iterative approach to transitioning to formal modelling while allowing it to influence immediate, consistent, and efficient decision-making. Also, the principles are used or intended for criteria evaluation in the absence of detailed models that direct decision-making more discretely and comprehensively in the organisation. The relationship between the EA and IT strategy domains is therefore considered strategic in fostering the goals and objectives of an organisation. The relationship is informed and enacted by actors' interactions and actions during the deployment and practice of EA in an organisation.

8.5 Factors Affecting Enterprise Architecture Deployment

From the empirical data gathered from the case study, five factors were found to be key determinants of: (i) the relationship between technical and non-technical entities; and (ii) how EA could be deployed as an IT strategy in an organisation. As shown in Figure 8.2, the factors include governance, evolution, articulation of IT

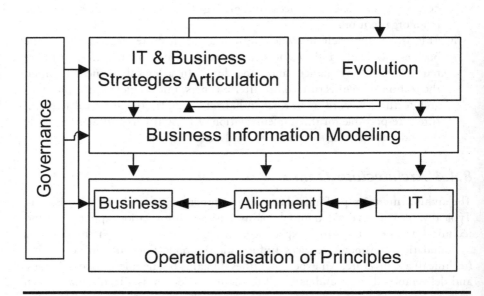

Figure 8.2   Relationship between Technical and Non-Technical Factors.

and business strategies, operationalisation of principles, and business information modelling. In Figure 8.2, the relationships that exist between the factors are also illustrated using arrows.

The factors that make EA a strategic component of the IT strategy are discussed in the following subsections.

8.5.1 Governance

Governance is considered strategic in that it shapes and transforms the current state into the future state. The implementation of IT strategy through the EA approach makes the governance of IT solutions a vital task to undertake. Through governance, according to Niemi and Pekkola (2020), EA supports decision-making and enables the strategic management of the business and IT alignment. Through governance, policies are formulated and promulgated in an organisation. The policies define the information processes required to ensure three fundamental objectives: (i) that information is protected; (ii) that information quality is maintained; and (iii) that information is modelled from current to desired states. These activities are undertaken and completed in line with the organisation's aims and objectives.

The articulation of the business requirements is a critical rationale and motivation for buy-in that is often used by the promoters of EA to portray their points in organisations. For many organisations, it is of critical importance to adopt a consistent approach to identify, deploy, and support IT solutions including business processes and information flow in an organisation. Jayakrishnan et al. (2019)

suggest that EA is a strategy that enables governance, manages the complexities of IT solutions, and transforms business models to optimise enterprise-wide systems. In many organisations, information processes and IT solutions are defined and categorised by the description and boundaries of EA. The definition allows information to be shared within an organisation and with other organisations and partners, including the general public. Information is considered critical in many organisations, primarily because it is a deterministic factor in their business processes, activities, and events. It therefore needs prioritisation and requires governance to ensure its efficient and effective use and management.

Also, EA can be used to identify and develop appropriate governance structures for the development and implementation of IT strategy in an organisation. The quality of information will therefore be governed by the principles, standards, policies, and procedures formulated by the organisation. This includes metadata integrity, the authenticity of data, and the suitability of technological activities in the organisation. According to Ismagilova et al. (2022), EA encompasses governance that provides a guide for the regulation and compliance of business design, information flow, and IT solutions. As EA activities evolve, the importance of getting the buy-in of the stakeholders increases. This spurs interaction among the stakeholders, domain owners in particular, towards gaining a deeper understanding of how roles and responsibilities are critically instrumental to the success or failure of EA deployment in organisations. Otherwise, the EA team is sure to receive less support from the stakeholders in the organisation. Governance can only be effective and efficient if deployed, evolutionarily.

8.5.2 Evolution

The evolutionary characteristic of EA ensures ongoing planning, training, and changes to business processes and IT infrastructure. This includes the analysis of the current state and organisational norms in supporting and enabling the development and implementation of IT strategy in an organisation. Jallow et al. (2017) explained, from an organisation's perspective, that to manipulate changeable requirements for architectural design and engineering of strategies, EA must be adopted as a strategic tool that evolves. The development and implementation of EA will very likely fail if its potential impacts on the business strategy are not assessed and considered. Effective business processes' use of IT strategy is a competitive differentiator and should always be considered and prioritised during business strategic planning. Thus, major organisational initiatives are articulated and assessed following the alignment between business and EA capabilities. The initiatives become operational only when the corresponding IT strategy solutions have been implemented.

As the evolution of EA continues, it is clearer that the business process design, information stream, and groupings of technologies are intended to be logical, flexible, and efficient in supporting and enabling the aims and objectives of an organisation. Business strategic planning should be established and integrated to digest the rapid changes in an organisation. Based on the underlining principles, this can be dictated by the IT strategy and facilitated, using the EA. Gong and Janssen (2019) argue that EA offers ways to steer and guide the design and evolution of an enterprise. This means that the business strategy can be linked with EA to ensure and facilitate the execution of activities in advancing the competitiveness and sustainability of the organisation.

Primarily, the success or failure of EA is hinged on the involvement of technology, people, and processes. First, this is because business activities and events follow processes which are enabled and supported using technology as defined and applied by people. Second, the architects facilitate and assist the stakeholders with an understanding and use of the principles, standards, and policies to guide processes and activities to achieve the organisation's goals and objectives. This is carried out through interaction and communicative channels, such as training and workshops. However, this often proves to be difficult in that compatibility and alignment between EA and IT strategy is not always easily articulated and understood in many organisations. Iyamu (2022) emphasises that the evolution of EA is critical for the advancement and business enhancement of IT solutions.

8.5.3 IT and Business Strategies Articulation

IT and business strategy articulation ignite the change process in organisations. Thus, change for competitiveness and sustainability is driven by the articulation of both IT and business strategies, through a recursive approach. This is primarily because change does not only affect business processes and the relationship with partners, but also affects information and technology infrastructures which enable and support the entire IS/IT in an organisation. According to Saleem and Fakieh (2020), EA is an approach that consists of multiple events and processes, to align business strategies with domain architectures. Organisations will be more successful if they can create unified business and IT strategies, which domains of EA enable and support. Unification involves establishing an architecture process that addresses the organisation's key business, information, application, and technology strategies. This includes business and technology functions and processes that enable the implementation strategy to support business competitiveness.

Effective EA deployment and practice through the domains of EBA and EIA is a competitive differentiator and should always be considered during the business strategy planning process. EA facilitates integration and alignment between business strategy and IT strategy in an organisation (Masuda et al., 2021; Fischer et al., 2010). This can add value to organisations because, in many instances, the majority of business initiatives intend to articulate the alignment of business requirements with IT capabilities, and how the capabilities could be operationalised when the corresponding IT solutions have been implemented. The approach synchronises the business strategy with the IT strategy at both unit and organisational levels.

The main challenge lies in how the aim is articulated and problematised. This is vital because it shapes the direction of the organisation's strategy (Williams et al., 2022; Al-Kharusi et al., 2021). As a result, the IT unit strategically articulates its objectives to achieve the operational excellence of the organisational goals. It therefore provides a portfolio of services, including the consolidation and management of IT solutions, to enable and fulfil the goals and objectives of an organisation. The IT strategy should be derived from the business strategy as a useful activity which defines and documents the organisational direction. This makes the business of IT an important component, and it can be better managed from the EA domains perspective. The articulation of business and IT strategies helps shape productivity and promote efficiency through the domains of EA. The domains are better defined based on operational principles in the context of an organisation.

8.5.4 Operationalisation of Principles

The operationalisation of principles guides events, processes, and activities of an organisation daily. The principles are formulated based on the business needs and technology practices of the time (Fischer et al., 2010). The primary aim is often to control processes and activities within the IT unit. The architects of the different domains define, design, and implement processes and activities within the architectural principles of their organisations. Tamm et al. (2022) suggest that EA services help improve project delivery through guiding principles and standards.

Changes to IT solutions and business processes occur continually as the objectives and requirements of the organisation evolve. Consequently, change combined with unyielding competitive forces causes tremendous confusion and complexity in many organisations. Thus, principles are increasingly important to stabilise internal and external forces (Iyamu, 2022; Li & Xu, 2022). The stabilising aspect of EA is achieved through its domains and is a major motivating factor for the institutionalisation of the concept in an organisation. Each domain has its predefined principles formulated to achieve the aims and objectives of an organisation. A good example is the business architecture, which reflects process orientation in the development and operationalisation of deliverables for competitiveness in organisations.

Architects develop principles, standards, and policies based on organisational requirements (Batmetan, 2022; Shaanika & Iyamu, 2018). This is to sanctify complexity, uniformity, and consistency in the business process design, information exchange, and selection and deployment of IT solutions. Consequently, this is also to fortify dependency on the reusability of business and technology artefacts, to increase productivity and promote quality of service. As such, the reusability principle provides governance through standards and policies in the selection, use, and management of services. For example, from an EBA perspective, principles can be used to organise the components of process orientation, services re-engineering, and operations' centres of excellence in an organisation. It brings about change to events, processes, and activities, which can be significantly addressed through principles, standards, and policies at the domain levels. This enhances the value of processes and increases the efficiency of activities in an organisation.

8.5.5 Business Information Modelling

In achieving the organisation's requirements for change and improvement towards a competitive advantage, modelling of business information is required and should be identified as a critical factor. The organisation's information modelling strives to capture and model data entities and their relationships in a top-down, enterprise, comprehensive, and detailed fashion. According to Saleem and Fakieh (2020), EA provides support to organise business models and integrate them with IT solutions. Business information modelling requires resource-intensiveness, rigorousness, and fine-grained analysis to eliminate redundancy, ensure common definitions, claim ownership, and certify access rules in achieving the needs of the users. This is intended for organisational strategies, which the IT strategy aims to address through EIA. The odds of a successful implementation of an organisation's business information modelling must therefore be within a timeframe. This helps to reflect, explore, and examine the shifting of information-sharing opportunities and challenges.

The premise that data is one of the most stable aspects of an organisation still holds, except otherwise proven, which has not happened yet. Thus, data is hugely relied upon in modelling an enterprise (organisation). Modelling increases the value of an enterprise; hence, scope is significant. Hinkelmann et al. (2016) demonstrate how modelling supports the alignment of business and IT. As such, there is always a need to focus on exposing critical linkages, externality with business partners (competitive differentiator), and internality across business units (information sharing). The data is hosted by technology as defined by the technical architecture domain. The data is or can be accessed following principles and standards set by the EAA.

Information architecture challenges the assumption of corporate modelling that all data is of value to the organisation. Also, the modelling offers an opportunity for coherence, strategic alignment, and value creation (Georgiadis & Poels, 2021). Through information value network modelling, key information that could be leveraged to create value for customers is explored and analysed for organisational competitiveness (see Chapter 5). EIA seeks to uncover information within the enterprise that defines structured modelling constructs, of which tacit knowledge is an example. Fahim et al. (2021) suggest that information is often placed in containers of chain that support the interoperability of actors' activities.

8.6 Enterprise Architecture as IT Strategy

To gain a more accurate view and better understand how EA is deployed as an IT strategy, it should be across business requirements through the domain level to the point where the transition is planned, as shown in Figure 8.3. Figure 8.3 depicts the

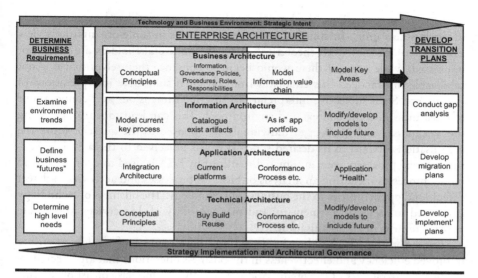

Figure 8.3   Enterprise Architecture as an IT Strategy.

primary components of business requirements and transition plans including each of the EA domains. The components are of high relevance because they shape and influence EA towards being an IT strategy. The discussion that follows should be read in conjunction with Figure 8.3 to gain a deeper understanding of the development and implementation of EA in an organisation. This is primarily within the IT strategy of the organisation that deploys them.

8.6.1 Enterprise Business Architecture as IT Strategy

The EBA relies on the organisational strategy to execute its mandates and deliverables (Srinivas et al., 2021; Jayakrishnan et al., 2020). The business strategy is developed within a specified timeframe as dictated by the current state of the environment, sustainability, and competitiveness. The development of the business strategy is based on the organisation's vision. The BA defines the 'high-velocity' (real-time) information which passes between key business processes and the integration requirements. This is enabled by the underlying EAA and ETA to achieve both the business and IT needs over time. This domain acts as an expression of the organisation's key business strategies and tactics, including their impacts on business functions and processes as defined by the domain architects at the time. Typically, the EBA domain consists of the current- and future-state models of business functions, processes, and information value chains. It leads to the development of EIA and EAA, and defines and shapes the business design.

In some organisations, the business architecture is considered successful only in the business units. In contrast, some business units in some organisations view EBA as too academic and theoretical. As such, some stakeholders are often not impressed, while some of them would begin to convince themselves that it is not achievable in practice. This emanates from personal subjective interpretations of the subject. Such subjective interpretations inscribe dimensions and connotations of uneasiness into the context and environment. This can lead to fear of exposing the weaknesses and intellect of individuals, as opposed to the quest to move the organisation forward to its desired state. This was perceived to threaten job security if many processes were automated. Uniformly, EBA is used to coordinate and model processes including an analysis of business processes and activities to detect defects and opportunities in the business of technology. The business of technology is referred to as the investment in, and manageability of, IT services to generate positive returns in an organisation.

Primarily, the EBA guides the design and development of models to ensure improved efficiency and effectiveness in the business operations that are affected by the business strategies of the organisation. Typically, the models consist of the current state and future desire of business functions, processes, and information value chains within an organisation (Roelens et al., 2019). Anthony Jr. (2021) focuses on providing value that enhances the service delivery of an organisation. The roles and responsibilities are to analyse and translate the needs of the business into specifics, as well as communicate and validate requirements for changes to business processes, policies, and requirements in an organisation.

8.6.2 Enterprise Information Architecture as IT Strategy

Information is considered the most strategic factor in the daily operations of many organisations. Thus, its architecture is essential for effective use, efficient management, and control of information exchange to improve competitiveness and solidify the sustainability of an organisation. The EIA coordinates the use, reuse, and sharing of information to enable needs of systems. It is therefore intended to strategically model, classify, and leverage the information needed to support, advance, and manage heterogeneous business and IT solutions across an organisation. From such a perspective, EIA focuses on identifying and standardising innovative ways to acquire, store, retrieve, use, and manage information in organisations (Almeida et al., 2020; Yoon et al., 2016).

Information architecture is the 'information supply chain', which is an extension of the business architecture in the development and implementation of EA. It is a business-strategy–driven set of artefacts that describe and model the enterprise's information supply chain and value chain, which is referred to as information flows, business events, and linkages. According to Iyamu (2022), EIA defines the flow, use, and governance of artefacts within an organisation; thus, EIA extends beyond the organisational boundaries to external sources and targets to enable rapid business decision-making and information sharing. Primarily, EIA includes a catalogue of authentic sources of information such as organisations, commercial databases, and research companies, classes of relevant business information and their value to the enterprise, and information governance processes to support policy development and information management principles and practices that attempt to address information security and accessibility (Soomro et al., 2016).

EIA is strategic to organisations in that it forms the core aspect of the desired state (Peeters & Widlak, 2018). For example, it is a goal of many organisations to continue to improve information quality and integrity. Additionally, EIA establishes the value and importance of using information effectively by employers and employees across lines of business (LOBs) (Gill et al., 2016). Also, the architecture helps to detect the need to achieve collaborative excellence with external partners and customers for competitive advantage.

Through governance, EIA focuses on constructing information exchanges and models to meet business evolving requirements and re-engineering. This includes detecting the gaps where business-critical high-velocity information is not reaching customers, suppliers, and partners for service delivery and competitive advantage. Thus, EIA models are increasingly essential to guide the organisation's information assets, knowledge workers, information processors, software developers, infrastructure managers, and executive managers.

Similar to EBA, the EIA encourages decision-makers to explore external trading and partnerships, from three primary standpoints: (i) to optimise information value chains; (ii) to plan EAA and systems portfolio; and (iii) to increase information velocity across the entire organisation. It also provides guidance for business operations, which particularly affect the business strategies. The EAA is sequentially developed and implemented based on the foundation of both EBA and EIA.

8.6.3 Application Architecture as IT Strategy

Application architecture determines issues related to the strategic direction of applications (information systems), such as software selection, development, and implementation, including reusability and manageability in an organisation. Accordingly, application architecture serves as a tool for identifying and driving reuse throughout the existing and planned architecture. It is therefore intended to serve as an agent in managing application strategy for information systems support, business transactions governance, and information processing re-engineering. The strategy includes the selection, deployment, collaboration, and integration of systems in an organisation.

Application architecture is the strategic arm of the IT strategy for applications' existence in the organisation. It is applied as the framework to govern how applications are designed, developed, implemented, measured, and evaluated within the organisation. It represents the required functionality to fulfil business requirements and logics, as well as to satisfy requirements of business and information architectures. As such, the architecture decision-making is guided by both business and information architectures, primarily to identify needed functionalities and opportunities which could be used to reduce complexities, improve efficiencies, and maintain application portfolios.

The application architecture is supported by technical architecture principles and standards, which affect and influence the selection, design, development, and implementation of software packages, application components, and business objects. Some of the key elements include enhancing inventories through established models for application-to-application relationships, information dependencies, supported business processes, and required infrastructure patterns. It modifies existing application models, which are based on future functionalities, processes, business strategies, and information architectures.

The scope of application architecture includes a collection of integrated information systems (applications and components; build, buy, or reuse) required to satisfy business needs. The strategic process is guided by business and information architectures in terms of needed functionalities and opportunities for reuse and by detailed technical architecture design principles and standards. This also affects and influences software selection, design, development, and implementation within the context of the organisation that deploys it. A gap between the existing applications' functionalities and the functionalities needed to satisfy business and information architecture requirements is defined by the architecture. It also develops the migration framework for moving the existing applications towards the strategic intent.

Overall, the application architecture should be viewed as an ongoing representation of the existing and planned information systems required to support the ever-changing business strategies and consequential business processes, information, and application requirements. This should be based on the IT strategy, which aims to support and enable the organisation's business.

8.6.4 Technical Architecture as IT Strategy

The organisation's strategic direction in the area of technology infrastructures is defined and determined by the technical architecture. This includes software, hardware, networks, and integration mechanisms. In many organisations, one of the most difficult challenges is implementing the technology infrastructure strategy. Unlike the business, information, and application architectures, the technical architecture is not directly tied to discrete business processes or information and application requirements resulting from new business strategies or the consequent tactics. It stands separately but is underpinned by other architecture domains.

The technical architecture creates a framework which represents the logical technical domains and their interactions and relationships with each other, referring to existing frameworks and modifying them accordingly. The framework categorises technology, product, and configuration standards. It is primarily used for product evaluation and as a reference point, rather than creating it from scratch or re-engineering the wheel. The framework is documented and guided by principles.

Technical architecture outlines the lifecycle and appropriate use of hardware and software products in organisations. It models the technology environment, which includes infrastructure configuration, standards, principles, and guidelines for the selection, deployment, integration, configuration, and management of technological artefacts within an organisation. The models provide both views of the recommended technology and a basis for assessing the impact of new or replacement technologies within the context of an organisation.

In summary, in the pursuit of strategic intents, a gap analysis is conducted in each of the domains of EA. This is also shown in Figure 8.3. The gap analysis is used to detect deficiencies and opportunities across the organisation based on the EA and IT strategy. Also, it helps to understand and document both the current and the future states.

8.7 Summary

The contribution of the study as presented in this chapter arises from implications for the decision-makers responsible for sponsorship and investment in information technology (IT) to support and enable business-changing needs and processes for competitive advantage. These decision-makers need to understand the criticality of executive managers' buy-in to dynamically deploy enterprise architecture (EA) as an IT strategy. They also need to gain a better understanding of the impact of EA as an IT strategy to be able to measure its value. It is therefore of critical importance for the stakeholders to understand that the domains of EA cannot be developed or implemented in isolation.

The other contribution of this chapter is its significance to practitioners including managers and employees within the IT units and information systems (IS) researchers. The key contribution is how EA complements IT strategy through fundamental elements. Practitioners can learn from this, and IS researchers can build on the contribution. The study demonstrates the practice of the concept rather than theorising about it.

References

Abouzahra, M., & Ghasemaghaei, M. (2022). Effective use of information technologies by seniors: The case of wearable device use. *European Journal of Information Systems*, *31*(2), 241–255.

Ahlemann, F., Legner, C., & Lux, J. (2021). A resource-based perspective of value generation through enterprise architecture management. *Information & Management*, *58*(1), 103266.

Ahmad, N. A., Drus, S. M., & Kasim, H. (2022). Factors of organizational adoption of enterprise architecture in Malaysian public sector: A multi-group analysis. *Journal of Systems and Information Technology*, *24*(4), 331–360.

Ajer, A. K. S., Hustad, E., & Vassilakopoulou, P. (2021). Enterprise architecture operationalization and institutional pluralism: The case of the Norwegian Hospital sector. *Information Systems Journal*, *31*(4), 610–645.

Al-Kharusi, H., Miskon, S., & Bahari, M. (2021). Enterprise architects and stakeholders alignment framework in enterprise architecture development. *Information Systems and e-Business Management*, *19*(1), 137–181.

Almeida, B. M., Felipe, R. E., & Barcelos, R. (2020). Toward a document-centered ontological theory for information architecture in corporations. *Journal of the Association for Information Science and Technology*, *71*(11), 1308–1326.

Anthony Jnr, B. (2021). Managing digital transformation of smart cities through enterprise architecture—a review and research agenda. *Enterprise Information Systems*, *15*(3), 299–331.

Batmetan, J. R. (2022). Model enterprise architecture for information technology services in universities. *International Journal of Information Technology and Education*, *1*(4), 18–34.

Bui, Q. (2017). Evaluating enterprise architecture frameworks using essential elements. *Communications of the Association for Information Systems*, *41*(1), 121–149.

Chung, H. M., & McLeod, G. (2002, January 7–10). Enterprise architecture, implementation, and infrastructure management. In *Proceedings of the 35th annual Hawaii international conference on system sciences* (pp. 1256–1257). IEEE.

Dang, D. (2019). Institutional logics and their influence on enterprise architecture adoption. *Journal of Computer Information Systems*, *61*(1), 42–52.

Fahim, P. B., An, R., Rezaei, J., Pang, Y., Montreuil, B., & Tavasszy, L. (2021). An information architecture to enable track-and-trace capability in Physical Internet ports. *Computers in Industry*, *129*, 103443.

Fischer, C., Winter, R., & Aier, S. (2010). What is an enterprise architecture principle? In *Computer and information science 2010* (pp. 193–205). Springer.

Foorthuis, R., Van Steenbergen, M., Brinkkemper, S., & Bruls, W. A. (2016). A theory building study of enterprise architecture practices and benefits. *Information Systems Frontiers*, *18*(3), 541–564.

Georgiadis, G., & Poels, G. (2021). Enterprise architecture management as a solution for addressing general data protection regulation requirements in a big data context: A systematic mapping study. *Information Systems and e-Business Management*, *19*(1), 313–362.

Giddens, L., Petter, S., & Fullilove, M. H. (2023). Information technology as a resource to counter domestic sex trafficking in the United States. *Information Systems Journal*, *33*(1), 8–33.

Gill, A. Q., Phennel, N., Lane, D., & Phung, V. L. (2016). IoT-enabled emergency information supply chain architecture for elderly people: The Australian context. *Information Systems*, *58*, 75–86.

Girsang, A. S., & Abimanyu, A. (2021). Development of an enterprise architecture for healthcare using TOGAF ADM. *Emerging Science Journal*, *5*(3), 305–321.

Gong, Y., & Janssen, M. (2019). The value of and myths about enterprise architecture. *International Journal of Information Management*, *46*, 1–9.

Griffo, C., Almeida, J. P. A., Guizzardi, G., & Nardi, J. C. (2021). Service contract model-ing in enterprise architecture: An ontology-based approach. *Information Systems, 101,* 101454.

Haki, K., & Legner, C. (2021). The mechanics of enterprise architecture principles. *Journal of the Association for Information Systems, 22*(5), 1334–1375.

Hinkelmann, K., Gerber, A., Karagiannis, D., Thoenssen, B., Van der Merwe, A., & Woitsch, R. (2016). A new paradigm for the continuous alignment of business and IT: Combining enterprise architecture modelling and enterprise ontology. *Computers in Industry, 79,* 77–86.

Hylving, L., & Bygstad, B. (2019). Nuanced responses to enterprise architecture manage-ment: Loyalty, voice, and exit. *Journal of Management Information Systems, 36*(1), 14–36.

Ismagilova, E., Hughes, L., Rana, N. P., & Dwivedi, Y. K. (2022). Security, privacy and risks within smart cities: Literature review and development of a smart city interac-tion framework. *Information Systems Frontiers, 24*(2), 393–414.

Iyamu, T. (2022). *Enterprise architecture for strategic management of modern IT solutions.* Routledge, CRC Press.

Iyamu, T., & Adelakun, O. (2008, July 4–7). The impact of non-technical factors on information technology strategy and e-business. In *The proceedings of the 12th pacific asia conference on information systems* (pp. 1214–1222). Association for Information Systems (AIS) Press.

Jallow, A. K., Demian, P., Anumba, C. J., & Baldwin, A. N. (2017). An enterprise architec-ture framework for electronic requirements information management. *International Journal of Information Management, 37*(5), 455–472.

Jayakrishnan, M., Mohamad, A. K., & Abdullah, A. (2019). Enterprise architecture embrace digital technology in malaysian transportation industry. *International Journal of Engineering and Advanced Technology, 8*(4), 852–859.

Jayakrishnan, M., Mohamad, A. K., & Yusof, M. M. (2020). Business architecture model in strategic information system management for effective railway supply chain perspective. *International Journal of Engineering Research and Technology, 13*(11), 3927–3933.

Jusuf, M. B., & Kurnia, S. (2017, January 4–7). Understanding the benefits and success factors of enterprise architecture. In *Proceedings of the 50th Hawaii international con-ference on system sciences (HICSS).* IEEE.

Kaisler, S., & Armour, F. (2017, January 4–7). 15 years of enterprise architecting at HICSS: Revisiting the critical problems. In *Proceedings of the 50th Hawaii international con-ference on system sciences (HICSS).* IEEE.

Karimi-Alaghehband, F., & Rivard, S. (2019). Information technology outsourcing and architecture dynamic capabilities as enablers of organizational agility. *Journal of Information Technology, 34*(2), 129–159.

Khoury, G. R., & Simoff, S. J. (2004, January 18–22). Enterprise architecture modelling using elastic metaphors. In *The proceedings of 1st Asia-Pacific conference on conceptual modelling* (pp. 65–69). IEEE.

Kilpeläinen, T. (2007, December 5–7). Business information driven approach for EA devel-opment in practice. In *The proceedings of the 18th Australasian conference on informa-tion systems business information driven* (pp. 447–457). Association of Information Systems (AIS) Press.

Kochanthara, S., Rood, N., Saberi, A. K., Cleophas, L., Dajsuren, Y., & van den Brand, M. (2021). A functional safety assessment method for cooperative automotive architecture. *Journal of Systems and Software, 179,* 110991.

Kotusev, S., Kurnia, S., & Dilnutt, R. (2023). Enterprise architecture artifacts as boundary objects: An empirical analysis. *Information and Software Technology, 155,* 107108.

Kurnia, S., Kotusev, S., Shanks, G., Dilnutt, R., & Milton, S. (2021). Stakeholder engagement in enterprise architecture practice: What inhibitors are there? *Information and Software Technology, 134,* 106536.

Lee, A., & Baskerville, R. (2003). Generalizing generalizability in information systems research. *Information Systems Research, 14*(3), 221–243.

Li, J., & Xu, W. (2022, July 15–17). Using a practical methodology of enterprise IT strategy for digital success. In *Proceedings of the 2nd international conference on management science and software engineering (ICMSSE 2022)* (pp. 628–635). Atlantis Press.

Masuda, Y., Zimmermann, A., Bass, M., Nakamura, O., Shirasaka, S., & Yamamoto, S. (2021). Adaptive enterprise architecture process for global companies in a digital IT era. *International Journal of Enterprise Information Systems (IJEIS), 17*(2), 21–43.

Musukutwa, S. C. (2022). The future of enterprise architecture. In *SAP enterprise architecture: A blueprint for executing digital transformation* (pp. 187–202). Apress.

Niemi, E., & Pekkola, S. (2020). The benefits of enterprise architecture in organizational transformation. *Business & Information Systems Engineering, 62*(6), 585–597.

Peeters, R., & Widlak, A. (2018). The digital cage: Administrative exclusion through information architecture—The case of the Dutch civil registry's master data management system. *Government Information Quarterly, 35*(2), 175–183.

Pereira, C. W., & Sousa, P. (2004). A method to define an enterprise architecture using the Zachman framework. *ACM Symposium on Applied Computing, 2004,* 1366–1371.

Qadri, Y. A., Nauman, A., Zikria, Y. B., Vasilakos, A. V., & Kim, S. W. (2020). The future of healthcare internet of things: A survey of emerging technologies. *IEEE Communications Surveys & Tutorials, 22*(2), 1121–1167.

Qazi, H., Javed, Z., Majid, S., & Mahmood, W. (2019). A detailed examination of the enterprise architecture frameworks being implemented in Pakistan. *International Journal of Modern Education & Computer Science, 11*(9), 44–53.

Rahimi, F., Gøtze, J., & Møller, C. (2017). Enterprise architecture management: Toward a taxonomy of applications. *Communications of the Association for Information Systems, 40*(7), 120–166.

Roelens, B., Steenacker, W., & Poels, G. (2019). Realizing strategic fit within the business architecture: The design of a process-goal alignment modelling and analysis technique. *Software & Systems Modeling, 18*(1), 631–662.

Ross, J., Weill, P., & Robertson, D. (2006). *Enterprise architecture as strategy: Creating a foundation for business execution.* Harvard Business Press.

Roth, T., Stohr, A., Amend, J., Fridgen, G., & Rieger, A. (2023). Blockchain as a driving force for federalism: A theory of cross-organizational task-technology fit. *International Journal of Information Management, 68,* 102476.

Saint-Louis, P., & Lapalme, J. (2018). An exploration of the many ways to approach the discipline of enterprise architecture. *International Journal of Engineering Business Management, 10,* 1847979018807383.

Saleem, F., & Fakieh, B. (2020). Enterprise architecture and organizational benefits: A case study. *Sustainability, 12*(19), 1–23.

Schekkerman, J. (2004). *How to survive in the jungle of enterprise architecture frameworks: Creating or choosing an enterprise architecture framework.* Trafford Publishing.

Shaanika, I., & Iyamu, T. (2018). Developing the enterprise architecture for the Namibian government. *The Electronic Journal of Information Systems in Developing Countries, 84*(3), e12028.

Singla, B. S., & Aggarwal, H. (2020). Effect of information architecture on the usability of a university website: A comparative study of selected websites of Punjab (India). *International Journal of Distributed Systems and Technologies (IJDST), 11*(1), 38–52.

Soomro, Z. A., Shah, M. H., & Ahmed, J. (2016). Information security management needs more holistic approach: A literature review. *International Journal of Information Management, 36*(2), 215–225.

Srinivas, S., Gill, A. Q., & Roach, T. (2021). Can business architecture modeling be adaptive? *IT Professional, 23*(2), 81–88.

Sukur, A., & Lind, M. L. (2022). Enterprise architecture to achieve information technology flexibility and enterprise agility. *International Journal of Information Systems and Social Change (IJISSC), 13*(2), 1–20.

Syynimaa, N. (2018, November 21–23). Enterprise architecture: To business or not to business? That is the question!. In *The proceedings of the international conference on enterprise information systems.* SCITEPRESS Science and Technology Publications.

Tamm, T., Seddon, P. B., & Shanks, G. (2022). How enterprise architecture leads to organisational benefits. *International Journal of Information Management, 67,* 102554.

Trishan, M., Van der Alta, M., & Aurona, G. (2021). Systematic literature review of essential enterprise architecture management dimensions. In *Proceedings of sixth international congress on information and communication technology: ICICT 2021, London, Volume 1* (pp. 381–391). Springer.

Vallerand, J., Lapalme, J., & Moïse, A. (2017). Analysing enterprise architecture maturity models: A learning perspective. *Enterprise Information Systems, 11*(6), 859–883.

Williams, J. A., Torres, H. G., & Carte, T. (2022). A review of IS strategy literature: Current trends and future opportunities. *Journal of Computer Information Systems, 62*(1), 1–11.

Wolff, S., & Sydor, K. (1999). Information systems strategy development and implementation: A nursing home perspective. *Journal of Healthcare Information Management, 13*(1), 2–12.

Yoon, K., Hulscher, L., & Dols, R. (2016). Accessibility and diversity in library and information science: Inclusive information architecture for library websites. *The Library Quarterly, 86*(2), 213–229.

Zachman, J. A. (1996). Enterprise architecture: The view beyond 2000. In *The proceedings of 7th international users group conference for warehouse repository architecture development.* Technology Transfer Institute.

Zhi, Q., & Zhou, Z. (2022). Empirically modeling enterprise architecture using ArchiMate. *Computer Systems Science & Engineering, 40*(1), 357–374.

Chapter 9

The Implementation of Enterprise Architecture in an Organisation

9.1 Introduction

As established and revealed in previous chapters of this book, enterprise architecture (EA) has many benefits and the interest in the concept continues to grow. While this chapter focuses on implementation, it revisits some of the benefits. Purposely, this is to contextualise the challenges of implementation in organisations amid the overwhelming theorised benefits of the concept. The enterprise-wide nature of EA causes it to be viewed from various perspectives, enthusing benefits from business and information to technology standpoints. This has contributed to the reason why, three decades after its emergence, there is no universal definition or implementation approach for EA (Simon et al., 2013). However, there is relatively stable clarity about the focus and meaning of the concept. Notwithstanding, this neither slows nor hampers the growing interest in EA, from both academia and business enterprises.

EA is a paradigm which promises to address and reduce the challenges encountered by the business and information systems and information technology (IS/IT) units of many organisations (Gong et al., 2020; Kappelman, 2002). From an organisation's perspective, to manipulate changeable requirements, implore governance, and engineer change, EA must be adopted as a strategic tool that evolves (Jallow et al., 2017). Bui (2017) explains that the benefit of EA is determined by how the concept is implemented in an organisation. According to Saint-Louis and Lapalme (2018), EA emerged as a discipline and practice to assist organisations in

                                         DOI: 10.1201/9781003390879-9

passing their challenges and succeeding in an increasingly dynamic environment that is often confronted with interruptions and change. This contributes to the cruciality of EA implementation. Qazi et al. (2019) explain that the implementation of EA must be strategic to ensure an effective and consistent flow of business design, information flow, and IT solutions process for improved performance purposes.

Traditionally, there are four domains of EA. However, depending on the construct and focus of an organisation, it can be expanded with a domain such as service-oriented architecture (SOA). As discussed in Chapters 3–7, the four domains are enterprise business architecture (EBA), enterprise information architecture (EIA), enterprise application architecture (EAA), and enterprise technical architecture (ETA) (Iyamu, 2022; Lankhorst, 2013). The domains are interdependent in implementation, primarily because of the interrelationship in their focuses and deliverables. It is from the domains' perspectives that EA is used to capture the interactions and interrelationships in the activities of business design, information exchange, application deployment, and technology governance (Gong et al., 2020).

In addition to the growing support and motivation for EA, Saint-Louis et al. (2019) state that EA is a strategic information asset base that defines the business process, the information necessary for operations, and the required IT solutions to support business operations. EA can be used to enact the alignment between business and IT units (Shanks et al., 2018). Strategically, EA provides support to an organisation through information models and integration of business models using IT solutions. Jayakrishnan et al. (2019) argue that EA is best practised for the implementation of strategies and roadmaps. Additionally, EA supports decision-making, transformation-based governance, and business and IT alignment through strategic management (Niemi & Pekkola, 2020). Saleem and Fakieh (2020) suggest that EA's main purpose is as a strategic tool to integrate business strategies and IT solutions. This means that EA offers ways to steer and guide the design and evolution of an enterprise (Gong & Janssen, 2019).

The deployment (development and implementation) of EA hugely depends on the activities of people, information technology (IT) solutions, and processes. The interdependency and interrelated nature of the activities make the implementation heterogeneously oriented. The rationale for EA deployment in many organisations includes alignment of business and IT units, integration of business processes, and governance of IT solutions (Belfadel et al., 2022; Saleem & Fakieh, 2020; Niemi & Pekkola, 2020). According to Alaeddini and Salekfard (2013), the process of EA deployment is iterative, through which its models and deliverables enable and support new business and technology trends, including capabilities and innovations. Many organisations have developed a blueprint for EA but were not successful in implementation due to various challenges. According to Ross et al. (2006), many of the architectural exercises end up abandoned on a shelf.

The challenges with the implementation of EA are technical and non-technical factors. The technical factors range from various angles. According to Loft et al.

(2022), in many organisations, EA implementation focuses on technology, a single component of the concept, which causes a disjoint in the wider activities of the environment. From the non-technical front, Niemi and Pekkola (2020) summarised that the benefits of EA are difficult to dissect. Also, in practice, it is difficult to align business processes with IT solutions during the implementation of EA in many organisations (Mesquita & Vasconcelos, 2022). Dale and Scheepers (2020) explain: although architects are often made responsible and accountable for EA implementation, they often depend on the business unit in most of their decisions, such as the ones that concern the selection of IT solutions and access to resources. Such dependence enables and can be a constraint as people seek power.

Power is a productive force that organises and solidifies actors into various sorts of agents that perform actions. As such, the relationship in the union between the business and EA architects of IT units is a critical factor, particularly in the areas of roles, responsibilities, and ownership which are related to EA implementation in an organisation. According to Kotusev et al. (2022), the available literature does not explain clearly what particular purposes are fulfilled by different types of EA artefacts for these stakeholders. Some of the problems encountered during the implementation of EA manifest from social context, which includes the power to or not to carry out tasks. Implementation, therefore, requires the power to enforce tasks in achieving the goals of EA. Thus, power can affect outcomes in activities, which include the allocation of tasks in the implementation of EA in an organisation. Also, the power effect can manifest and proliferate to generate other derailing factors during EA implementation.

However, there is still a need to address the challenges confronting the practice of EA, towards realising its benefits to organisations (Saleem & Fakieh, 2020). One of the challenges is that EA implementation is driven by theoretical concepts which might not hold in practice (Gong & Janssen, 2019). Another challenge, as argued by Rahmanian et al. (2023), is that although many leading-edge EA frameworks describe architecture in levels of abstraction, there are still gaps because none of the existing studies seems to have provided an accurate syntactic and semantic description of the concept. Despite the efforts by practitioners and academics, it is difficult to find organisations that have successfully fully implemented EA (Banaeianjahromi & Smolander, 2019).

This chapter proposes a framework to simplify the implementation and increase the success rate of EA. The use of the framework for EA implementation is enabled and supported by components such as guiding principles, policy, ownership, performance measurement, and conformance. The factors manifest from the interaction between people, mediated through objects of various kinds, and such interactions are in turn mediated through additional networks of objects and people. Iyamu and Dewald (2012) argue that a network grows, changes, and stabilises during the deployment of technology. This makes principles and policy vitally inevitable to guide interaction and ensure stability in the implementation of EA. Also, the activities of the actors and owners of tasks and responsibilities must conform to the implementation requirements. Due to the significant role of EA as a bridge between the business and IT units of an organisation, it is of paramount importance to measure the implementation (Zachman, 1996; Ross et al., 2006). Organisations have different requirements and methods for measuring EA within their contexts. Performance measurement is offered in this chapter as a benchmark for developing a set of criteria.

This chapter is organised into five main sections. The first section presents the literature review, exploring available related works and studies on EA and IS/IT strategy. The second section covers the research methodology adopted in the study. In the third and fourth sections, the chapter presents and discusses the analysis and empirical findings from the study, respectively. Finally, the chapter highlights the contributions of the study's empirical findings.

9.2 Enterprise Architecture in Organisations

For an organisation to be more successful, it must adapt quickly and spend less time reminiscing about the norms of its pursuits (Porter, 2008). Schekkerman (2004) argues that EA is a complete expression of an enterprise and that it is a master plan, which acts as a collaborator for alignment between the units of an organisation. EA is an approach for adapting and transforming organisations, based on business drivers, goals, and objectives enacted by architectural principles and guidelines (Haki & Legner, 2021). Through an evolutionary, iterative process, the current- and future-state definitions of the architecture are continuously developed, evaluated, and updated to ensure that EA aligns with changing business requirements and emerging technology (Girsang & Abimanyu, 2021; Nikpay et al., 2017; Alaeddini & Salekfard, 2013). It is sometimes argued that EA has 'audiences' across an organisation, fundamentally because it serves as a basis for analysis and decision-making in the business and lifecycle of IT solutions.

In some quarters, EA is considered as a set of processes that assists organisations to translate their visions into effective change by making the current state transparent and providing a strategic roadmap for the desired state (Mirsalari & Ranjbarfard, 2020). The enterprise business service is a crucial aspect of EA (Rahmanian et al., 2023). This is because strategic planning, which includes the process that determines strategy, is facilitated by EA (Grave et al., 2021). Also, many organisations employ the EA approach as a tool to increase the efficient and effective management of the business and IT solutions (Mirsalari & Ranjbarfard, 2020). Gong and Janssen (2022) state that EA is embedded with functions, processes, tools, instruments, principles, and purposes to guide the business design and governance of IT solutions, including the alignment between business and IT units.

In the last two decades, organisations have been making substantial determinations in their attempts to implement EA successfully. According to Löhe and

Legner (2014), despite considerable efforts by organisations to adopt and implement EA, the success rate has been low. Notwithstanding the rapid evolution, five years later, Abunadi (2019) makes the same observation that although there are huge contributions and interest from researchers and practitioners, respectively, the implementation success rate of EA remains low. The challenges get worse as organisations witness rising levels of IT solutions complexity, a view from the EA perspective (Ajer et al., 2021; Stroud et al., 2019). Consequently, there is still a need to better understand how EA can be effectively and better implemented in organisations (Beese et al., 2022).

At different times and from various angles, the challenges encountered during implementation have been revealed, highlighted, and argued. The bottom line is that in practice, organisations struggle to implement EA, which can be attributed to factors such as unclear requirements and benefits of the concept (Loft et al., 2022). Dale and Scheepers (2020) revealed that existing literature on EA implementation focuses on the technical and social conditions associated with the success and failure of the concept, to a lesser extent. According to Ajer and Olsen (2019), some organisations struggle to implement EA because of organisational and managerial issues and obstacles. Contemporarily, many of the EA frameworks are limited in their abilities to efficiently enable and support the adoption of emerging IT solutions and business approaches (Lnenicka & Komarkova, 2019). Some challenges in EA implementation are caused by the fragmentation of its artefacts or domains, Grave et al. (2021) argued. The challenges in the implementation of the concept begin from the point where demonstrating the business value of EA continues to prove elusive in many organisations (Shanks et al., 2018).

In addressing the implementation challenges, Nikpay et al. (2017) suggest that the first step is to identify the factors that affect the effectiveness of EA in the implementation and practices of EA. Stroud et al. (2019) suggest that documentation reveals reveal the cyclomatic complexity of an organisation, which negatively affects EA implementation. Abunadi (2019) recommends that continuous documentation and analysis of involved activities are required for the successful implementation of EA. One of the approaches suggested by Girsang and Abimanyu (2021) is to create a dedicated team to provide the solutions required for the implementation of architectures in an organisation. Gong and Janssen (2022) argue for enhancing high-level managers' EA knowledge and ensuring that communication and leadership skills of enterprise architects are the starting point to avoid EA failure. Despite these efforts, the challenges persist. Also, the problem is not isolated or unique to certain organisations or similar organisations. Many organisations continue to encounter challenges during EA implementation that have been highlighted in the literature (Oberle et al., 2023).

EA stimulates the need to design and redesign to continue improving the functioning of enterprises (Gong & Janssen, 2019). Schekkerman (2004) argues that EA is a complete expression of an enterprise and that it is a master plan which acts as a collaborator for alignment between the units of an organisation. Also, EA is intended to reduce the cost of deployment, maintenance, and management of business design and processes (Jayakrishnan et al., 2020), information flow (Fahim et al., 2021; Hauder et al., 2013), and IT solutions (Chitsa & Iyamu, 2020) in enabling business goals and objectives. Also, it could be used to achieve a significant organisational advantage over competitors in a competitive marketplace (Haki & Legner, 2021). EA enables competitiveness through process effectiveness and efficiencies that arise from the elimination of non–value-adding and redundant tasks and streamlines information flow, systems placement, and business restructuring (Loft et al., 2022; Ross et al., 2006).

Thus, the scope of EA is considered a union of the enterprise and the business engineering, including the development that is applied to it and the technical domains that support it in the organisation (Iyamu, 2015). Justifiably, the scope is often defined through pragmatism, thereby emphasising the importance of EA in an organisation, a reflection from existing literature (Kotusev et al., 2023; Grave et al., 2021; Shanks et al., 2018). However, the meanings, interactions and interpretations associated with the activities of EA implementation are significant to its outcome. Thus, Bielenia-Grajewska (2009, p. 41) emphasises that "we should remember that a person is not only determined by some factors but is also a factor himself or herself, determining the shape of the environment".

Similar to many other subjects, the implementation of EA has never been easy. This can be attributed to the fact that implementation involves and attracts social contexts, which include process, people, and culture. Law (1992) describes such a significant episode from the actor–network theory (ANT) perspective, that the activities of the actors within the networks (group or team) shape the social context and therefore if the material in the networks were to disappear, then the social order(s) would, too. Taking Law's sublimation into account, Iyamu (2015) therefore holds that a particular order is an effect generated by heterogeneous means. Latour (1996) explains how heterogeneous networks overcome issues related to identity and avoid arbitrary dichotomies and structures, and that the heterogeneity is reflected in different organisational principles that are in simultaneous action.

9.3 The Implementation of Enterprise Architecture in an Organisation

Even though the focus of this chapter is the implementation of EA, it is difficult to completely exclude the development of the concept because of its iterative nature, which spans from development to implementation and return to development. This section presents an EA implementation process model (Figure 9.1), a strategic construct that can be used for the implementation of EA in an organisation. The construct is determined by examining it from literature, business drivers, information artefacts, IT solutions, and understanding of the spheres of influence of actors

Enterprise Architecture Strategy

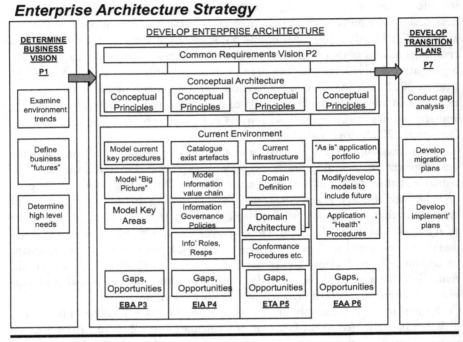

Figure 9.1   Enterprise Architecture Implementation Model.

(stakeholders) and their roles, as they draw from their stock of knowledge to exert power in the implementation of EA. Power influences the relationship between actors and manifests to shape interactions and actions of individuals and groups (Iyamu & Mgudlwa, 2018; Baron & Gomez, 2016) in the implementation of EA in organisations. Thus, power is vital and therefore examined as it enacts a relational effect that is shaped by the interaction that happens between humans and non-humans, such as automated processes, artefact design, and IT solutions selection in their heterogeneity.

This chapter affirms that the deployment of EA is often primarily based on common expectations, which is usually the minimal threshold of shared knowledge, theory, and experience that must be achieved from both business and IT perspectives. This is the case with many organisations. This belief forms the basis for the pursuit of cohesiveness and adaptiveness in efforts to achieve a common goal by many organisations. Also, for the EA to be considered successful, it must fulfil certain goals based on set criteria. The criteria are extracted from objectives as set by the organisation's sponsors and stakeholders.

From the literature, five common principles that influence the deployment of EA in many organisations were extracted: (i) business and IT strategy alignment (Mesquita & Vasconcelos, 2022; Anthony Jnr et al., 2021); (ii) reducing complexity (Tamm et al., 2022; Ajer et al., 2021; Abunadi, 2019; Banaeianjahromi &

Smolander, 2019); (iii) increasing uniformity and consistency in business, information, and IT practices (Sukur & Lind, 2022; Saleem & Fakieh, 2020; Gong & Janssen, 2019); (iv) reducing the cost of IT projects (Iyamu, 2022; Rurua et al., 2019); and (v) inscribing governance into processes and standardisation of activities and events (Haki & Legner, 2021; Fischer et al., 2010).

More than ever before, it is critical to increase the success rate of EA implementation. According to Bakar and Hussien (2018), investigating the success factors of EA implementation is essential to increase its high rate of success. Moreso, it has been proven to be very challenging as many organisations have been unsuccessful in the discipline. Empirical evidence from Iyamu (2015) revealed that of 13 organisations that participated in the study, only five were successful in the implementation of EA. Many organisations have concentrated on one or two domains, such as the EAA and ETA aspects of EA (Loft et al., 2022; Saint-Louis & Lapalme, 2018).

The process model reflects an approach that can be consistently employed by organisations to build, maintain, and apply EA. The model emphasises a holistic approach to architecture deployment (development and implementation) by recognising the perspectives and components that make for a complete view of an enterprise and EA. As such, it should be applied uniquely to an organisation's needs that depend upon organisational strategies. Halawi et al. (2019) argue that EA offers an approach for high-performing enterprises to implement their strategies (Halawi et al., 2019). Other factors include architectural maturity, prioritisation of initiatives, organisational culture, and the general computing environment (Vallerand et al., 2017).

Usually, people, technologies, and processes are the actors that constitute the team involved in the strategic implementation of EA in many organisations. Each of the actors belongs to one or more different teams or groups, referred to as networks in this chapter. For example, a systems analyst can belong to a team of business users, IT managers, and technical architects. This is structural conformance, and it varies from one organisation to another. To avoid confusion, we must note that a network in IT is different from the ANT definition of 'network'. In ANT, a network incorporates both technical and non-technical actors with linkages consisting of stabilised translations and interactions between actors (Latour, 1996). According to Wickramasinghe et al. (2009, p. 21), "This is a network of materially heterogeneous actors that is achieved by a great deal of work that both shapes those various social and non-social elements". This is different from the technology infrastructure network deployed in computing environments.

Heterogeneously, the networks of people cover areas of expertise, roles, and responsibilities, which simultaneously overlap and complement each other during the implementation of EA in many organisations. Consequently, architects work with other employees (or stakeholders) in different teams, such as the software development and network administration units. Dale and Scheepers (2020) suggest that the influence of interpersonal interactions between architects and their stakeholders through which the implementation of EA is enacted should receive more attention. The interaction allows different processes by various groups (networks) to be applied in the implementation of EA in organisations.

The processes relate and depend on each other to an exponential degree. Similar to people and technologies, processes are critical in the implementation of EA in organisations, from two main standpoints. First, the processes are employed to outline the rules and regulations within which various tasks are performed in the implementation of EA. Saleem and Fakieh (2020) argue that EA is an approach that consists of multiple processes to align strategies with domain architectures. The second aspect is that processes are used to define the roles and responsibilities, principles, policies, and standards which guide measurement and conformance. According to Banaeianjahromi and Smolander (2019), EA aims to define and describe both short-term and long-term processes relating to business artefacts and IT solutions at organisation-wide levels.

Individuals and teams interpret and translate the activities relating to IT solutions, in attempts to align them with business designs and artefacts, and information flow in the context of the organisation. The challenge is that the interpretations and translations are subjective, and often based on either an individual's comprehension or interest or both. Also, the translation of meaning is usually based on and influenced by the different units to which the individuals and teams belonged. However, in many instances, the managers dominate in the deliberation that produces the translation of meanings that are associated with objects, subjects, or activities during the implementation of EA.

Consequently, some managers can persuade their subordinates to accept their translation of activities including the meaning that they associated with processes and IT solutions. In such circumstances, some employees have no or limited choice, as the rules and regulations of many organisations are not flexible enough for alternative options or analysis. This leaves some employees with little or no room to negotiate their interests on matters of concern during the implementation of EA. By implication, the employees cannot act differently from the processes which are set or defined for them based on the translation of the activities. Otherwise, such employees are classified as non-aligned or harbouring interest against that of the organisation. In many organisations, this is the beginning of the success or failure of EA implementation.

As shown in Figure 9.1, some routines guide the development and implementation of EA in a seven-phase approach. The development stage consists of the business vision and conceptual framework. This includes documenting the current and future states of EA through its domains, EBA, EIA, EAA, and ETA. The implementation stage comprises the transition plan, gap analysis, and execution of plans in the implementation of EA.

Figure 9.1 shows a graphic illustration of EA implementation components and processes. EA is an approach that intends to address and close the gaps between: (i) the strategy and implementation of EA; and (ii) business and IT units. The gaps are a consistent challenge to an enterprise's goals, objectives, and transformation initiatives. The processes as shown in Figure 9.1 are expected to enable the prioritisation of analysis and implementation efforts. This should be based on the values delivered and therefore allows the organisation to proceed at its pace while progressing in its evolution at the same time.

The building blocks of the development and implementation, shown in the seven-phase approach in Figure 9.1, must be guided by or performed within the principles, policies, and standards set by the organisation. Al-Kharusi et al. (2021) reveal standardisation, principles, governance, communication, and change management capability as some of the factors influencing EA practice in organisations. The governance components (principles, policies, and standards) are translated by employees, led by architects and architecture managers. In some organisations, it is the sole responsibility of the chief architect or architecture manager.

The contents or tasks within the building blocks are allocated to individuals and teams, periodically. Subsequently, the execution of the tasks can be incentivised through promotions from one level to another or annual financial bonuses (Iyamu, 2015). This entices many employees to ally with their managers or architects. The alliance helps to create a stable environment and leads to obligatory passage points (OPPs), which Callon (1991) refers to as a situation that has to occur for all the actors to satisfy the interests that have been assigned to them by the focal actor, making them indispensable. An attempt to reverse or reinterpret the processes or technologies other than the managers' translation results in instability, which negatively affects EA implementation in the organisation.

Even though the EA implementation process model (Figure 9.1) is holistic in coverage and comprehension, it is not enough to deliver a successful implementation of EA on its own. Thus, it requires supporting and enabling components for enactment purposes. In alluding to the trajectory of some of the influencing factors in literature and practice (Iyamu, 2022; Al-Kharusi et al., 2021), four components are considered critical. The components are guiding principles, policy, ownership, performance measurement, and conformance. The components must be applied in the EA domains following the requirements and specifications of the organisation. Allocations of tasks are carried out and evaluated within the principles, policies, and standards of EA in the organisation. The principles, policies, and standards are formulated primarily to avoid individual interpretation and translations of meanings during EA implementation in the organisations. Examples of principles and policies are provided herein. Ideally, there should be a governance body that specialises and undertakes these tasks.

9.4 Components of Enterprise Architecture Implementation

Many organisations are confronted with complex and unwieldy challenges in assessing and articulating the components which are required in the implementation of EA in their environments. Mesquita and Vasconcelos (2022) argue that

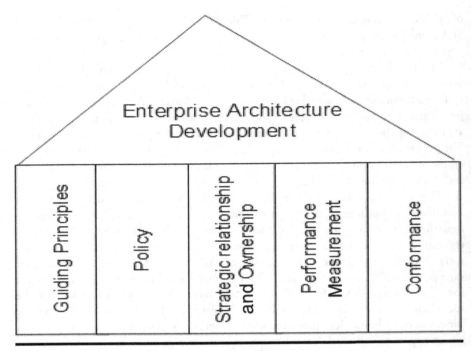

Figure 9.2   EA Implementation Components.

from the perspective of EA, it is a complex challenge to align and assess the strategic planning of an organisation. Thus, EA implementation projects remain difficult to discuss (Niemi & Pekkola, 2020). As shown in Figure 9.2, five components are considered the most critical, to aid the implementation of EA to success. These components are regarded as the key strategic components for organisations: (i) guiding principles; (ii) policy; (iii) strategic relationship and ownership; (iv) performance measurement; and (v) conformance.

9.4.1 Guiding Principles

In the context of this chapter and book, 'principles' are defined as guiding statements of positions that communicate fundamentals, vision, and mission that must be exhibited by an organisation during the implementation of EA. Also, see Chapter 5 of this book for a further complementary explanation of architecture principles. The purpose of principles is to enable an organisation to take an incremental and iterative approach to transition events and activities into formal modelling while allowing it to execute allocated tasks. In the explanation of Kotusev et al. (2023), each principle usually includes its statement, rationale, and implications, which describe guidelines and categories of solutions for implementation and practice purposes. Gallegos-Baeza et al. (2023) suggest that principles are used to conceptualise architectural activities towards solutions. The process of applying architecture principles influences decision-making immediately and consistently in the implementation of EA.

To successfully implement and maintain EA in an organisation, principles are therefore required. EA contains principles which reflect the collective and common will of the entire organisation as positioned by the business strategy (Iyamu, 2015). Thus, principles can be considered or referred to as basic philosophies that guide the process of implementing EA. Fundamentally, the principles guide the enrolment, including the execution of tasks by individuals and team employees.

Concisely, principles play a significant part in all the components of each of the domains. Also, the principles should be primarily and consistently applied to diverse EA-related activities in the various units of an organisation in achieving fruitful results from the implementation of EA (Gallegos-Baeza et al., 2023; Fischer et al., 2010). Also, the principles can be used as an evaluation criterion in the absence of detailed models that direct decision-making more discretely and comprehensively (Haki & Legner, 2021; Iyamu, 2015). Discreetly, within context, the degree to which an organisation can establish principles across EBA, EIA, ETA, and EAA is dependent on its ability to identify and apply best practices in each of the domain areas.

Owing to its significance, the principles must be derived from the principles which guide and ensure the delivery of business objectives as defined in the conceptual architecture and obligatorily related to each of the domains in the implementation of EA. Figure 9.1 shows the link between P1 (business vision) and P2 (EA conceptual architecture). The principles lead to rationale and procedures, and they also guide the designers, developers, and implementers of EA in performing their tasks and activities within the organisation's context.

In an organisation, the rationale based on which principles are formulated should be documented, along with procedures and guidelines that are associated with them (Kotusev et al., 2023). Table 9.1 is a template that can be used for recording and documenting the implementation principles in an organisation. The

Table 9.1   Implementation Principles

Principle	Rationale	Procedure	Guidelines
Elements of vision and mission are represented and identified with a name	For each of the principles, potential benefits are identified	Modus operandi and methods to consistently achieve the goals and objectives of the environment are established	Boundaries, scopes, rules, and regulations within which principles will be formulated and carried out are determined

template is populated to support strategic and operational analyses of activities in an organisation. What this significantly means is that every technology deployed in an organisation is expected to be populated into the template for assessment, evaluation, and architectural fit purposes.

There should exist at least a principle for each element of EA implementation in an organisation. Congruently, the principles must be based on the business strategy and objectives. In alignment, each principle that guides the implementation must consist of both business and IT (technical) rationale and benefits to the organisation (Anthony Jr et al., 2021). Additionally, the guidelines and procedural elements needed for EA implementation must be clearly defined. The guidelines include timeframe, roles, and responsibilities as the major factors.

During the implementation of EA, principles have a significant impact on the activities, mainly because they are considered factors of stability. Substantially, the principles provide guidelines and rationales that can be used for constant examination, re-engineering, and re-evaluation of technology plans. Nikpay et al. (2017) revealed that EA implementation often encounters a lack of support in areas such as requirements analysis, governance, and evaluation. Also, the principles are derived from an intensive discussion with senior IT and business managers, and thereafter validated in discussions with the executive (highest body) of the IT Committee. Constantinides et al. (2018) claim that there is evidence to show that value-creating interactions between the actors renew opportunities for dynamism in EA. Thus, the principles are viewed as a starting point for subsequent decisions that affect EA implementation within an organisation.

Thus, applying the principles formulated using the template (Table 9.1) significantly contributes to the successful implementation of EA in organisations. The contributions come from three main perspectives: hardware obsolescence, periodic review, and environmental change.

   i. Hardware obsolescence: This enables an organisation to effectively detect and remove obsolete hardware from their environment. This includes the removal of vendor dependence, which is prohibitive and sometimes an impediment during the re-engineering of the environment. The approach allows for more flexible use of developmental programmes for staff and minimises training costs and requirements.
   ii. Periodic review: This factor enables and allows a periodic view of IT solutions, from three standpoints. First, it ensures that the IT solutions enable and support business continuity. Second, it provides an opportunity to assess the fulfilment of business needs. Finally, it ensures that the organisation's IT solutions avoid obsolescence and complexities.
   iii. Environmental change: This factor ensures adherence to the rapidly changing external businesses and technical environments. It therefore significantly changes activities within an organisation.

Change requires an ongoing evaluation process to protect the return on investment (ROI) of business artefacts and IT solutions. There is anecdotal evidence that EA brings benefits to organisations and makes an argument for return on investment, which however does prove to be elusive (Shanks et al., 2018). This activity keeps both business artefacts and IT solutions fresh and updated to be constantly aligned with the changing needs of the organisation, which requires applying policy. Where people are involved, it is nearly impossible to change without a policy.

9.4.2 Implementation Policy

It is critically necessary to formulate and apply a set of policies to facilitate and enforce the implementation of EA. Applying policy varies from one organisation to another. Some organisations employ the implementation policy as an OPP by the management of the business and IT units. This is to enforce rules and regulations swiftly and smoothly during the implementation of EA in the organisation.

The implementation policy, therefore, sets the requirements of the EA process, and the constraints under which it must proceed and be implemented. Gellweiler (2020) claims that EA ascertains the technical goals and constraints of requirements and activities of an organisation. Essentially, there exist seven key policy statements: business strategies, iterative processes, rapid change, process re-engineering, management buy-in, accountability, and architectural fit.

i. Business strategies: EA must be driven by business strategies and consider the full context of the enterprise (and its environment) in which the concept will be applied. According to Loft et al. (2022), EA implementation assists organisations to manage complex business processes and support business strategies.

ii. Iterative processes: The EA implementation process must continuously evolve through an iterative process. Gampfer et al. (2018) argue that the iterative approach improves the results of each step, leading to evaluation processes and solutions, and to adjustment of variables until outcomes meet the requirements.

iii. Rapid change: The implementation of EA must enable rapid change in the enterprise's business processes and IT solutions deployment. Iyamu (2019) considers EA as a change agent in that it provides an organisation with the capacity to identify and make appropriate changes rapidly.

iv. Process re-engineering: The implementation of EA must guide the process re-engineering of the enterprise's events and activities, including IT solutions. Truong et al. (2021) suggest that re-engineering is EA nascent for change, reorganising, outsourcing, and realigning of activities in an organisation.

v. Management buy-in: EA must be understood and supported by senior management and the lines of business to succeed in an organisation. Management buy-in of EA is a critical factor as it helps to establish the documentation and the processes in the implementation and practice of the concept (Banaeianjahromi & Smolander, 2019).

vi. Accountability: Senior management team members involved in the engineering of the enterprise's processes, design of business artefacts, and deployment of IT solutions must be accorded full accountability to ensure conformance with EA requirements. Lapalme and de Guerre (2014) explain how accountability and responsibility assist in addressing demands for complexity management that arise during EA implementation.

vii. Architectural fit: All projects are to be assessed against architectural fit at different stages of the project lifecycle. This forms part of the project quality assurance (QA) process. Iyamu (2015) associates the lack of architectural fit with challenges of integration and governance, which reflect the complexity of EA implementation.

Thus, the policy statements must be sanctioned by the executive management to solidify and imbibe legitimacy in enforcing them. The policy should be enforced through performance contracts between the organisation and employees involved in the implementation of EA in the organisation. This approach should be drilled down to all levels—employees at middle and lower ranks within the structure of the organisation. The performance contract of each individual provides legitimacy and ease of use to determine and enforce the applicable policy set by the organisation for EA implementation. The ease of use entails incentivising through annual financial bonuses and promotions from one level to another. Consequently, this can influence the strategic relationship between employees and EA promoters within the organisation.

9.4.3 Strategic Relationship and Ownership

Fundamentally, this component is critical in the implementation of EA in an organisation. Primarily, this is because it clarifies the three vital factors: ownership, accountability, and responsibility of key elements that influence the implementation. Implementation of EA increases the ownership and responsibility of business users and IT solutions (Girsang & Abimanyu, 2021; Daoudi et al., 2020). Table 9.2 is a populated example of metric cross-references that can be applied by organisations. It contains the 19 most popular and common elements that influence EA implementation from the domains' perspectives. The elements are close and can be found in both business and IT requirements. Each of the elements requires ownership to ensure accountability and responsibility. Also, each element aligns with and applies to the domains. As shown in Table 9.2, Ownership and applicability are indicated with 'O' and 'A', respectively. Strategically, the metric helps to track and trace events and activities as they occur within an organisation. Also, this can be associated with the performance of the activities in the quest to achieve organisational goals and objectives.

Table 9.2   Cross-Reference Metric

#	Elements of Implementation	EBA	EIA	EAA	ETA
1	Common Vision	O, A	A	A	A
2	Corporate Planning Processes	O, A	A	A	A
3	Visible Strategies	O, A	A	A	A
4	Enterprise Models	O, A	O, A	O, A	O, A
5	Open Standards	–	A	A	O, A
6	Technology Standards	–	A	A	O, A
7	Portability and Scalability	–	–	O, A	A, A
8	Technology Innovation	A	–	A	O, A
9	Data Management	–	O, A	A	A
10	Information Sharing	A	O, A	A	A
11	Information Protection	A	O, A	A	A
12	Architectural Governance	A	A	A	O, A
13	EA Planning and Implementation	A	A	A	A
14	'Build' or 'Buy' Applications	–	–	O, A	A
15	Message-Based Interfaces	–	A	A	O, A
16	Network Interfaces	–	–	A	O, A
17	Logical/Physical Server Boundaries	–	–	A	O, A
18	Virtual Data Centres	–	–	A	O, A
19	Infrastructure Patterns	–	–	A	O, A

9.4.4 *Performance Measurement*

Performance measurement emerges as a key aspect of EA implementation in organisations. Thus, the establishment of appropriate performance measures is fundamental as it is key to the success of EA within organisations. This is because many executive management members of organisations often believe that an enterprise must be able to assess the progression of its goals and objectives, and whether stakeholders' expectations are being achieved.

Performance measures can be built as part of tasks assigned to individual and team contracts, which is usually used as OPP in many organisations. Primarily, this is because a performance contract is guided by the rules and regulations of an organisation. It helps to guide and mitigate against constraints that could be of risk to the implementation of EA. Some of the constraints and challenges include the following.

i. Disjoint of designs and processes between business units.
ii. Use of information and adherence to laws and acts of the society.
iii. IT solutions (technologies) at end-of-life, as defined by the product owners.
iv. Inherited IT solutions that are challenging in terms of compatibility with newer technologies.
v. Constant emergence of new technologies, which can be difficult to accommodate and coexist with other technologies.
vi. EA is always in transition and ever-changing and evolving due to changes in business events, processes, and activities.

EA assists in the development of performance measurement criteria that could be linked to the business and IT strategies, objectives, and goals. This is to allow an organisation to organise documentation in support of performance measurement. In addition, it determines not only the content of reports but also the path of the data from the source to recipients of the final reports. The combination of associated reports of the performance measures becomes the basis for a data warehouse and an EA report that can be truly tailored to the enterprise's vision and a normalised practice approach. This approach can reinforce initiatives, reward behaviour, support change, and enhance strategies through conformance towards a successful EA implementation.

9.4.5 Conformance

The architecture conformance procedure applies to the stakeholders in the re-engineering of an organisation's processes, information management, and IT solutions landscape. Conformance procedures are implemented to ensure adherence to the EA process, thereby enabling the business to realise its strategic goals and objectives while maximising business value. These are some of the primary benefits organisations can derive from EA implementation.

In this context, conformance applies to business- and IT-related projects. This means that conformance applies to processes and change requests, regardless of whether they are initiated by the business or IT unit. Conformance entails reviewing existing procedures, processes, artefacts, and solutions. In some instances, the reviews can also be event-driven. For example, time-based reviews are purposely undertaken to ensure that existing processes, information management, and IT solutions align with EA goals and objectives within the organisation.

Thus, architecture conformance assessment reviews should be conducted within an organisation as regularly as possible (Iyamu, 2015). Such an approach forms part of and enhances the QA process at various stages of the systems lifecycle, as well as the project lifecycle as principled by EA in an organisation. At each stage of the lifecycle, sets of questions from each of the four architecture domains, EBA, EIA, ETA, and EAA should be formulated to enact the implementation of EA towards value addition. Also, the approach enables the QA reviewers to determine whether there has been conformance to the EA strategy within the organisation. Only those projects and change requests likely to have an architectural impact on EA implementation are required or subjected to go through detailed architectural conformance assessment reviews.

Additionally, agreed-upon performance contracts or employment policies which each employee potentially enable a degree of irreversibility in assigning tasks in the implementation of EA. This makes the process of EA implementation pave the way for the institutionalisation of the concept in an organisation. Chapter 12 of this book covers the institutionalisation of EA in an organisation. It also creates a black box in individuals performing their tasks in implementing EA. Therefore, implementation activities which are anchored in black box–like places create a stable and resilient environment.

9.5 Summary

The chapter highlights the challenges leading to the low rate of enterprise architecture (EA) implementation. It presents solutions for some of the challenges, which are, primarily, the components that support and enable the proposed EA implementation process model. Significantly, the chapter demonstrates that the success of EA in any organisation depends on how well change elements are managed.

The study contributes to the understanding of the criticality of social relationships between people, technology, and processes in implementing EA in organisations. It highlights the importance of the influence of non-technical factors in EA implementation. This helps the architects, information technology (IT) managers, and other stakeholders in terms of focus areas during the development and implementation of EA. It helps to understand better the importance of actors' heterogeneity in implementing EA, as it focuses on change. This is an important contribution that can be of interest to both information systems (IS) researchers and professionals in the area of EA.

References

Abunadi, I. (2019). Enterprise architecture best practices in large corporations. *Information*, *10*(10), 293.

Ajer, A. K. S., Hustad, E., & Vassilakopoulou, P. (2021). Enterprise architecture operationalization and institutional pluralism: The case of the Norwegian Hospital sector. *Information Systems Journal, 31*(4), 610–645.

Ajer, A. K. S., & Olsen, D. H. (2019). Enterprise architecture implementation is a bumpy ride: A case study in the Norwegian public sector. *Electronic Journal of e-Government*, *17*(2), 79–94.

Alaeddini, M., & Salekfard, S. (2013). Investigating the role of an enterprise architecture project in the business-IT alignment in Iran. *Information Systems Frontiers*, *15*, 67–88.

Al-Kharusi, H., Miskon, S., & Bahari, M. (2021). Enterprise architects and stakeholders alignment framework in enterprise architecture development. *Information Systems and e-Business Management*, *19*, 137–181.

Anthony Jnr, B., Petersen, S. A., & Krogstie, J. (2021). A model to evaluate the acceptance and usefulness of enterprise architecture for digitalization of cities. *Kybernetes: The International Journal of Systems & Cybernetics*, *52*(1), 422–447.

Bakar, N. A. A., & Hussien, S. S. (2018). Association of people factors with successful enterprise architecture implementation. *International Journal of Engineering & Technology*, *7*(4.31), 52–57.

Banaeianjahromi, N., & Smolander, K. (2019). Lack of communication and collaboration in enterprise architecture development. *Information Systems Frontiers*, *21*(4), 877–908.

Baron, L. F., & Gomez, R. (2016). The associations between technologies and societies: The utility of actor-network theory. *Science, Technology and Society*, *21*(2), 129–148.

Beese, J., Haki, K., Schilling, R., Kraus, M., Aier, S., & Winter, R. (2022). Strategic alignment of enterprise architecture management—how portfolios of control mechanisms track a decade of enterprise transformation at Commerzbank. *European Journal of Information Systems*, 1–14.

Belfadel, A., Amdouni, E., Laval, J., Cherifi, C. B., & Moalla, N. (2022). Towards software reuse through an enterprise architecture-based software capability profile. *Enterprise Information Systems*, *16*(1), 29–70.

Bielenia-Grajewska, M. (2009). Actor-network theory in intercultural communication—translation through the prism of innovation, technology, networks and semiotics. *International Journal of Actor-Network Theory and Technological Innovation*, *1*(4), 39–49.

Bui, Q. (2017). Evaluating enterprise architecture frameworks using essential elements. *Communications of the Association for Information Systems*, *41*(1), 121–149.

Callon, M. (1991). Techno-economic networks and irreversibility. In J. Law (Ed.), *A sociology of monsters. Essays on power, technology and domination* (pp. 132–164). Routledge.

Chitsa, F., & Iyamu, T. (2020). Towards enterprise technical architecture for the implementation of the South African NHI. *Advances in Science, Technology and Engineering Systems Journal*, *5*(2), 724–728.

Constantinides, P., Henfridsson, O., & Parker, G. G. (2018). Introduction—platforms and infrastructures in the digital age. *Information Systems Research*, *29*(2), 381–400.

Dale, M., & Scheepers, H. (2020). Enterprise architecture implementation as interpersonal connection: Building support and commitment. *Information Systems Journal*, *30*(1), 150–184.

Daoudi, W., Doumi, K., & Kjiri, L. (2020, May 5–7). An approach for adaptive enterprise architecture. In *Proceedings of the 22nd international conference on enterprise information systems (ICEIS) (2)* (pp. 738–745). Springer.

Fahim, P. B., An, R., Rezaei, J., Pang, Y., Montreuil, B., & Tavasszy, L. (2021). An information architecture to enable track-and-trace capability in Physical Internet ports. *Computers in Industry*, *129*, 103443.

Fischer, C., Winter, R., & Aier, S. (2010). What is an enterprise architecture principle? Towards a consolidated definition. *Computer and Information Science, 2010*, 193–205.

Gallegos-Baeza, D., Caro, A., Rodriguez, A., & Velasquez, I. (2023). Aligning business strategy and information technologies in local governments using enterprise architectures. *Information Development, 39*(1), 147–168.

Gampfer, F., Jürgens, A., Müller, M., & Buchkremer, R. (2018). Past, current and future trends in enterprise architecture—A view beyond the horizon. *Computers in Industry, 100*, 70–84.

Gellweiler, C. (2020). Types of IT architects: A content analysis on tasks and skills. *Journal of Theoretical and Applied Electronic Commerce Research, 15*(2), 15–37.

Girsang, A. S., & Abimanyu, A. (2021). Development of an enterprise architecture for healthcare using TOGAF ADM. *Emerging Science Journal, 5*(3), 305–321.

Gong, Y., & Janssen, M. (2019). The value of and myths about enterprise architecture. *International Journal of Information Management, 46*, 1–9.

Gong, Y., & Janssen, M. (2022). Why organizations fail in implementing enterprise architecture initiatives? *Information Systems Frontiers*, 1–19.

Gong, Y., Yang, J., & Shi, X. (2020). Towards a comprehensive understanding of digital transformation in government: Analysis of flexibility and enterprise architecture. *Government Information Quarterly, 37*(3), 101487.

Grave, F., van de Wetering, R., & Kusters, R. (2021). Enterprise architecture artifacts facilitating the strategy planning process for digital transformations: A systematic literature review and multiple case study. *IADIS International Journal on Computer Science and Information Systems, 16*(1), 46–62.

Haki, K., & Legner, C. (2021). The mechanics of enterprise architecture principles. *Journal of the Association for Information Systems, 22*(5), 1334–1375.

Halawi, L., McCarthy, R., & Farah, J. (2019). Where we are with enterprise architecture. *Journal of Information Systems Applied Research, 12*(3), 4–13.

Hauder, M., Schulz, C., Roth, S., & Matthes, F. (2013, June 5–8). Organizational factors influencing enterprise architecture management challenges. In *Proceedings of the 21st European conference on information systems (ECIS)*. Association of Information Systems (AIS) Press.

Iyamu, T. (2015). *Information technology enterprise architecture: From concept to practice* (2nd ed.). Heidelberg Press. ISBN: 8-3-659-61206-0.

Iyamu, T. (2019). Understanding the complexities of enterprise architecture through structuration theory. *Journal of Computer Information Systems, 59*(3), 287–295.

Iyamu, T. (2022). *Enterprise architecture for strategic management of modern IT solutions*. CRC Press.

Iyamu, T., & Dewald, R. (2012). The use of structuration theory and actor network theory for analysis. *International Journal of Actor-Network Theory and Technological Innovation, 9*(4), 217–228.

Iyamu, T., & Mgudlwa, S. (2018). Transformation of healthcare big data through the lens of actor network theory. *International Journal of Healthcare Management, 11*(3), 182–192.

Jallow, A. K., Demian, P., Anumba, C. J., & Baldwin, A. N. (2017). An enterprise architecture framework for electronic requirements information management. *International Journal of Information Management, 37*(5), 455–472.

Jayakrishnan, M., Mohamad, A. K., & Abdullah, A. (2019). Enterprise architecture embrace digital technology in Malaysian transportation industry. *International Journal of Engineering and Advanced Technology, 8*(4), 852–859.

Jayakrishnan, M., Mohamad, A. K., & Yusof, M. M. (2020). Business architecture model in strategic information system management for effective railway supply chain perspective. *International Journal of Engineering Research and Technology, 13*(11), 3927–3933.

Kappelman, L. A. (2002). We've only just begun to use IT wisely. *Management Information Systems (MIS) Quarterly, 887*, 116–125.

Kotusev, S., Kurnia, S., & Dilnutt, R. (2022). The practical roles of enterprise architecture artifacts: A classification and relationship. *Information and Software Technology, 147*, 106897.

Kotusev, S., Kurnia, S., & Dilnutt, R. (2023). Enterprise architecture artifacts as boundary objects: An empirical analysis. *Information and Software Technology, 155*, 107108.

Lankhorst, M. (2013). Beyond enterprise architecture. In Lankhorst, M. (Ed.), *Enterprise architecture at work: Modelling, communication and analysis* (pp. 303–308). Springer, Berlin, Heidelberg.

Lapalme, J. S., & de Guerre, D. W. (2014). Enterprise-in-environment adaptation: Enterprise architecture and complexity management. In *A systemic perspective to managing complexity with enterprise architecture* (pp. 216–236). IGI Global.

Latour, B. (1996). Social theory and the study of computerised work sites. In W. J. Orlikowski, G. Walsham, M. R. Jones, & J. I. DeGross (Eds.), *Information technology and changes in organisational work* (pp. 295–307). Chapman & Hall.

Law, J. (1992). Notes on the theory of the actor-network: Ordering, strategy, and heterogeneity. *Systems Practise, 5*(4), 379–393.

Lnenicka, M., & Komarkova, J. (2019). Developing a government enterprise architecture framework to support the requirements of big and open linked data with the use of cloud computing. *International Journal of Information Management, 46*, 124–141.

Loft, P., He, Y., Yevseyeva, I., & Wagner, I. (2022). CAESAR8: An agile enterprise architecture approach to managing information security risks. *Computers & Security, 122*, 102877.

Löhe, J., & Legner, C. (2014). Overcoming implementation challenges in enterprise architecture management: A design theory for architecture-driven IT management (ADRIMA). *Information Systems and e-Business Management, 12*(1), 101–137.

Mesquita, A., & Vasconcelos, A. (2022). Heuristics' library for enterprise architecture and portfolio alignment. *International Journal of Information Technology Project Management (IJITPM), 13*(1), 1–23.

Mirsalari, S. R., & Ranjbarfard, M. (2020). A model for evaluation of enterprise architecture quality. *Evaluation and Program Planning, 83*, 101853.

Niemi, E., & Pekkola, S. (2020). The benefits of enterprise architecture in organizational transformation. *Business & Information Systems Engineering, 62*(6), 585–597.

Nikpay, F., Ahmad, R. B., Rouhani, B. D., Mahrin, M. N. R., & Shamshirband, S. (2017). An effective enterprise architecture implementation methodology. *Information Systems and e-Business Management, 15*, 927–962.

Oberle, M., Yesilyurt, O., Schlereth, A., Risling, M., & Schel, D. (2023). Enterprise IT architecture greenfield design combining IEC 62264 and TOGAF by example of battery manufacturing. *Procedia Computer Science, 217*, 136–146.

Porter, M. E. (2008). The five competitive forces that shape strategy. *Harvard Business Review, 86*(1), 78–93.

Qazi, H., Javed, Z., Majid, S., & Mahmood, W. (2019). A detailed examination of the enterprise architecture frameworks being implemented in Pakistan. *International Journal of Modern Education & Computer Science, 11*(9), 44–53.

Rahmanian, M., Nassiri, R., Mohsenzadeh, M., & Ravanmehr, R. (2023). Test case generation for enterprise business services based on enterprise architecture design. *The Journal of Supercomputing, 79*(2), 1877–1907.

Ross, J., Weill, P., & Robertson, D. (2006). *Enterprise architecture as strategy: Creating a foundation for business execution.* Harvard Business Press.

Rurua, N., Eshuis, R., & Razavian, M. (2019). Representing variability in enterprise architecture: A case study. *Business & Information Systems Engineering, 61*, 215–227.

Saint-Louis, P., & Lapalme, J. (2018). An exploration of the many ways to approach the discipline of enterprise architecture. *International Journal of Engineering Business Management, 10*, 1847979018807383.

Saint-Louis, P., Morency, M. C., & Lapalme, J. (2019). Examination of explicit definitions of enterprise architecture. *International Journal of Engineering Business Management, 11*, 1–18.

Saleem, F., & Fakieh, B. (2020). Enterprise architecture and organizational benefits: A case study. *Sustainability, 12*(19), 1–23.

Schekkerman, J. (2004). *How to survive in the jungle of enterprise architecture frameworks: Creating or choosing an enterprise architecture framework.* Trafford Publishing.

Shanks, G., Gloet, M., Someh, I. A., Frampton, K., & Tamm, T. (2018). Achieving benefits with enterprise architecture. *The Journal of Strategic Information Systems, 27*(2), 139–156.

Simon, D., Fischbach, K., & Schoder, D. (2013). An exploration of enterprise architecture research. *Communications of the Association for Information Systems, 32*(1), 1–72.

Stroud, R. O., Ertas, A., & Mengel, S. (2019). Application of cyclomatic complexity in enterprise architecture frameworks. *IEEE Systems Journal, 13*(3), 2166–2176.

Sukur, A., & Lind, M. L. (2022). Enterprise architecture to achieve information technology flexibility and enterprise agility. *International Journal of Information Systems and Social Change (IJISSC), 13*(2), 1–20.

Tamm, T., Seddon, P. B., & Shanks, G. (2022). How enterprise architecture leads to organisational benefits. *International Journal of Information Management, 67*, 102554.

Truong, T. M., Lê, L. S., Paja, E., & Giorgini, P. (2021). A data-driven, goal-oriented framework for process-focused enterprise re-engineering. *Information Systems and e-Business Management, 19*(2), 683–747.

Vallerand, J., Lapalme, J., & Moïse, A. (2017). Analysing enterprise architecture maturity models: A learning perspective. *Enterprise Information Systems, 11*(6), 859–883.

Wickramasinghe, N., Bali, K. R., & Goldberg, S. (2009). The S'ANT approach to facilitate a superior chronic disease self-management model. *International Journal of Actor-Network Theory and Technological Innovation, 1*(4), 15–26.

Zachman, J. A. (1996). Enterprise architecture: The view beyond 2000. In *The proceedings of 7th international users group conference for warehouse repository architecture development.* Technology Transfer Institute.

Chapter 10

The Zachman Framework for the Implementation of Enterprise Architecture

10.1 Introduction

Enterprise architecture (EA) is a systematic approach to designing, planning, and implementing business processes and information technology (IT) solutions to address the complexity of an organisation's landscapes (Kotusev et al., 2023; Ajer et al., 2021). IT solutions include software, hardware, networks, and databases. According to Saint-Louis et al. (2019), EA offers the approach necessary for implementing IT solutions in response to the changing needs within an organisation. Anthony Jr et al. (2021) suggest that the approach is employed for managing complexities, governance of processes, and alignment of business and IT capabilities in an organisation. Based on the potential promises, EA has increasingly attracted interest and gained considerable attention from both academia and industry for the systematic designing of business processes and planning of the IT landscape (Haki & Legner, 2021).

Holistically, EA covers activities enterprise-wide, meaning from business to technology domains (Tamm et al., 2022). Iyamu (2022) argues that an architecture process addresses an organisation's key business design and processes, information flow and governance, and selection and deployment of IT solutions. The coverage manifests into competitiveness, sustainability, and adaptiveness, rather than reminiscing about the way things used to be or how they were done previously. However, EA implementation continues to be challenging in many organisations (Gong & Janssen, 2022; Rouhani et al., 2015). As a result, different EA frameworks

DOI: 10.1201/9781003390879-10

have been employed by various organisations to increase their chances of successful implementation with aim towards sustainability and competitiveness (Sukur & Lind, 2022; Safari et al., 2016). Yet, the challenges persist, which could be attributed to a low or slow rate of implementation (Adnan et al., 2021; Ajer & Olsen, 2019; Alwadain et al., 2016).

Some of the most popular EA frameworks are the FEAF, Gartner, The Open Group Architecture Framework (TOGAF), and Zachman Framework (Oberle et al., 2023). In the view of Simon et al. (2014), the Federal Enterprise Architecture Framework (FEAF) is about using reference models to facilitate communication between stakeholders. According to Lnenicka and Komarkova (2019), Gartner Inc. is more about transforming business requirements and vision into strategies, and focuses on planning and migrating from the current to desired future states. TOGAF presents EA as a generic methodology, but the descriptions of EA skills stress IT competencies (Iyamu, 2022). Bui (2017) tries to draw a line of differentiation by arguing that if the frameworks differ only incrementally or marginally based on only explanations, then, there should be an expectation of fewer contrasting benefits and challenges in their implementation.

The slow or low rate of EA implementation in organisations has been blamed on different factors, such as a lack of know-how and a lack of an understanding of the concept (Bakar & Hussien, 2018; Kappelman & Zachman, 2013). To some degree, the two factors, lack of know-how and lack of understanding cannot be separated in EA implementation. The activities of an organisation and the frameworks must be well understood to select an appropriate framework for implementing EA in an environment. One of the main reasons, as explained by Niemi and Pekkola (2017), is that EA is an approach intended to guide the development and implementation of software and the selection and implementation of technologies in a consistent, flexible, and uniform manner.

Therefore, the activities of EA must be viewed and understood from an organisation's context (Iyamu, 2022; Närman et al., 2014). Also, the concept is often employed to transform business logic, information use, and governance of IT solutions (Al-Kharusi et al., 2021; Sukur & Lind, 2022), and often aligns both the business and IT units (Shanks et al., 2018; Fritscher & Pigneur, 2015). According to Ullah and Lai (2013), alignment is a process of mutual synchronisation of business goals and IT services, which requires implementation within context. Banaeianjahromi and Smolander (2019) suggest that due to the complexities that surround the concept, it is important to understand the factors that confront the implementation and practice of EA in organisations. Perhaps the lack of understanding could be caused by the fact that the factors influencing the challenges in the implementation of EA in organisations are correlated and interwoven in the complexity of business and IT units (Gong & Janssen, 2022), and inversely connect the promoters and architects.

Thus, one of the main challenges for enterprise architects during the implementation of the EA in some organisations is to determine and understand the factors influencing the different frameworks (Moeini et al., 2020; Rouhani et al., 2015). Even though EA frameworks have a common goal, they do differ in one way or the other. Winter and Schelp (2008) argued that some EA frameworks distinguish themselves to reduce the number of artefacts per model. The differences among the frameworks have an impact on their implementation, which adds up to their complexities (Iyamu, 2019). Also, due to a lack of know-how, there has been a decline in the adoption of some frameworks, such as Gartner Inc., FEAF, and TOGAF (Simon et al., 2014). Bui (2017) suggests that a lack of know-how creates proliferation for the implementation of EA using some of the frameworks. Among the existing frameworks, a survey (Benkamoun et al., 2014) found the Zachman Framework to be the most popular.

Organisations continue to show interest in the Zachman Framework due to its premise for organisational benefits, from both business and IT perspectives. This is an indication of the fact that the Zachman Framework provides a well-guided descriptive representation of activities into dimensions (Pereira & Sousa, 2004) and can be applied in complex systems or environments (Sharma & Sarkar, 2021). Despite its popularity, the framework continues to pose challenges to architects and organisations at large (Löhe & Legner, 2014). The challenges of the Zachman Framework are more from a practical perspective (Fatolahi & Shams, 2006). Robertson-Dunn (2012) argues that some shortfalls of the Zachman Framework are from both business and IT units. Most of the studies covering the use of the Zachman Framework focus on diagrammatic representations in different ways, including comparative analysis and the application of unified modelling language (UML) (Fatolahi & Shams, 2006). Primarily, the challenges are rooted in know-how (Darmawan et al., 2022).

As a result of existing gaps and challenges, models and approaches have been proposed in recent years. Based on Zachman Framework, Pereira and Sousa (2004) proposed an approach through which EA can be successfully deployed in an organisation. Jafari et al. (2009) developed a knowledge architecture model based on the Zachman Framework. Through a methodology based on action research, Nogueira et al. (2013) proposed models for implementing the Zachman Framework. Hernández et al. (2014) propose a reference architecture model for collaborative activities, which is also based on the Zachman Framework. Nikpay et al. (2017) developed an effective model to support EA implementation. Despite all the work done in the Zachman Framework area, challenges persist. Primarily, the challenges can be attributed to two factors: lack of understanding and lack of know-how to implement and practise the framework in an organisation.

EA implementation and practice require an understanding of the concept within context. Gong and Janssen (2019) argue that EA requires contextualisation to address relevant problems within an organisation. On the lack of know-how in applying the framework within the context of organisations, Bui (2017) reveals that many organisations continue to rely on external consulting firms for the know-how to make sense of EA implementation. The implementation and practice of the Zachman Framework entail the ability to map the framework with existing artefacts and capabilities within an organisation. Thus, this chapter aims to present a different approach that guides the implementation of EA using the Zachman Framework. In achieving the aim, the human constructivism approach is employed to build and to understand: (i) how EA deliverables drive the use of the Zachman Framework; and (ii) how the Zachman Framework can be mapped with organisational activities in addressing the challenges towards the successful implementation of EA in an organisation that deploys it.

The remainder of this chapter is divided into four main sections. It begins with a review of literature relating to EA implementation and the Zachman Framework, respectively, as the background to the chapter. This is followed by a discussion of EA deliverables. Next, a guide on how the Zachman Framework can be employed to implement EA in an organisation is presented. Finally, a conclusion is drawn by highlighting the contributions of the chapter.

10.2 Enterprise Architecture

EA is regarded as an approach for strategic activities in the business and IT units of any organisation. Shanks et al. (2018) argue that there is anecdotal evidence that EA brings benefits to organisations and makes the argument for investment in the EA approach. As a strategic tool, EA enables the management of complexities and transforms the business model and governance of IT solutions to optimise enterprise-wide systems (Jayakrishnan et al., 2019). According to Saleem and Fakieh (2020), EA is considered a strategic approach because it consists of multiple events and processes to align business strategies with domain architectures. Through the transparency of activities and structured decision processes from governance and management perspectives, EA contributes to improving decision-making in an organisation (Tamm et al., 2022).

The concept of EA is employed by many organisations primarily to provide improved and enhanced integrated business processes and IT solutions for sustainability and competitiveness (Iyamu, 2022). EA activities are carried out through frameworks, a process of effectiveness and efficiency arising from eliminating non–value-adding and redundant tasks, streamlining information flow, and implementing systems strategic placement and business restructuring (Iyamu, 2015). According to Zhi and Zhou (2022), EA entails a rigorous approach to describing the structure and objectives of modelling in an organisation. EA activities are delivered through domains, covering both business and IT functions as defined by the framework (Safari et al., 2016). As shown in Figure 10.1, Aziz et al. (2005) classified EA into four architecture domains: business, information, technical, and application. Each domain has its deliverables, which determine and shape its implementation.

The business architecture defines the business viewpoint, which includes the business vision and mission needed to guide the enterprise's strategic and daily

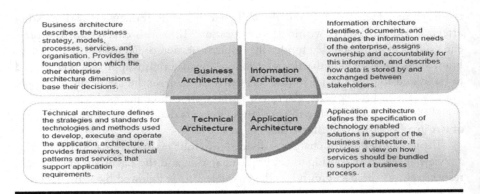

Figure 10.1 Components of the Enterprise Architecture (Aziz et al., 2005).

operations (Roelens et al., 2019). The architecture contains business strategies, performance metrics, business processes and activities, and the relationships upon which the information architecture is developed (Jayakrishnan et al., 2020; Kang et al., 2010). An organisation's information needs include policy, governance, and information products that are defined by the information architecture (Iyamu, 2019). Schekkerman (2009) elaborates on the precision and high quality of information, making it easier for an organisation to respond to changes and make informed decisions. Fundamentally, information architecture describes the structure of an enterprise's logical and physical data assets, and its data management resources that inform application architecture (Fritscher & Pigneur, 2015). Wang et al. (2008) explained application architecture as a blueprint of the individual application system to be developed and deployed, including their interactions and relationships with core business processes. The architecture also serves as a transparent communication and design tool for the application developers (Kitsios & Kamariotou, 2018). The technical architecture domain is defined to enable and support the needs of the organisation from strategic planning through implementation (Iyamu, 2015).

Each domain is a unique architecture discipline but is not independent of the others (Niemi & Pekkola, 2017). Lapalme et al. (2016) state that each domain has its distinct roles, responsibilities, and deliverables, but they are interrelated for the overall achievement of the enterprise's goals and objectives. This makes some of the frameworks challenging and complex when mapping the domains with the organisation's activities and deliverables (Gunadham & Ahmed Mohammed, 2022; Simon et al., 2014). The deliverables are based on how the EA is defined or scoped in an organisation to facilitate the many facets in a holistic way (Iyamu, 2022). The deliverables influence and determine the implementation within the goals and objectives of an organisation. According to Nogueira et al. (2013), EA implementation requires an important effort, which is not always feasible and available in many organisations. This prompts the question: how can the Zachman Framework be applied to implement the EA in an organisation? EA is thus seen as a mechanism that integrates the domains into a cohesive framework.

There are many benefits of EA, from the perspectives of both business and IT units (Foorthuis et al., 2016). Thus, EA has been implemented as an IT strategy and as a strategic approach, as covered in this book, in Chapter 8 and Chapter 9, respectively. Shanks et al. (2018) argue that EA services influence and enable dynamic capabilities in an organisation. EA offers an approach for high-performing enterprises to implement their strategies (Halawi et al., 2019). Lnenicka and Komarkova (2019) suggest that EA is considered suitable for the efficient implementation of IT solutions in an organisation. Owing to its articulated benefits, the EA approach has become an increasingly important subject in research and practice (Ajer et al., 2021). These seem to fortify the argument of Loft et al. (2022) that EA implementation can help companies manage complex business processes and support business strategies.

10.2.1 *Implementing Enterprise Architecture*

EA codifies functional requirements and provides the discipline, systematic design, and implementation of process re-engineering and performance improvement of activities through its deliverables (Chalmeta & Pazos, 2015). However, the deliverables are realised only through implementation, using any of the EA frameworks (Löhe & Legner, 2014). Rouhani et al. (2014) suggest that different methods can be used to implement EA. Many EA frameworks or methodologies have come and gone in recent years, and only four remain dominant in the field: the Zachman Framework for EA, TOGAF, FEAF, and Gartner EA Process (Oberle et al., 2023; Wang et al., 2008). The basis for considering and using EA frameworks such as TOGAF, FEAF, and ARIS was analysed by Winter and Fischer (2006). Also, a comparative study was conducted by Lim et al. (2009) to examine the basis and value of the EA frameworks in organisations. This chapter, therefore, excludes the comparison and value of using EA frameworks and focuses on the objectives to understand the deliverables and how the Zachman Framework can be employed for implementing EA in an organisation.

EA is increasingly a discipline of significant interest among scholars and practitioners across sectors. Notwithstanding, empirical studies that aim to provide a comprehensive explanation of EA benefit mechanisms are limited (Niemi & Pekkola, 2016). According to Bui (2017), EA's flexibility and conceptual nature make many organisations sceptical in attempts to modify the concept during the implementation process. Gong and Janssen (2019) explain how EA provides an overview of the IT landscape to enable its implementation at multiple and detailed levels, from both business and IT solutions perspectives. Banaeianjahromi and Smolander (2019) argued that EA is similar to a strategy, and hence, it aims to define and describe both short-term and long-term activities of business processes and IT solutions at organisation-wide levels.

However, despite the benefits and promises, many organisations continue to experience various types of challenges in the implementation of EA (Ajer et al., 2021; Niemi & Pekkola, 2020). Al-Kharusi et al. (2021) discuss some of the factors that influence business and IT units in implementing and practising EA. EA implementation complexity has a significant negative impact on factors such as efficiency, effectiveness, flexibility, and transparency, including interoperability and predictability (Beese et al., 2022). Many organisations face problems with EA implementation because it lags in achieving the objectives (Bakar & Hussien, 2018). One of the major problems is that many of the benefits of EA are intangible and the values are achieved indirectly through the domains and projects (Shanks et al., 2018). Consequently, the practice of EA remains challenging and its benefits elude many organisations (Niemi & Pekkola, 2020).

EA implementation remains challenging in both the private and public sectors (Adnan et al., 2021; Dang & Pekkola, 2017). The influence of interpersonal interactions between architects and stakeholders is a huge challenge in the implementation of EA in many organisations (Dale & Scheepers, 2020), which can be attributed to a lack of transparency in roles and responsibilities. Ajer et al. (2021) linked the challenges of EA implementation to its enterprise-wide nature because it increases demand for change on the horizon. Mesquita and Vasconcelos (2022) argue that it is a complex challenge to align and assess the strategic planning of an organisation from the EA perspective.

From both technical and non-technical perspectives, the implementation of EA remains challenging for many organisations (Iyamu, 2015). Nikpay et al. (2017) revealed that EA implementation often encounters a lack of support in areas such as requirements analysis, governance, and evaluation. Some factors affecting the implementation of EA are the need for complex maintenance and the intended comprehensive coverage of areas in an organisation (Abunadi, 2019). EA ascertains the technical goals and constraints of the requirements and activities of an organisation (Gellweiler, 2020). The benefits of EA seem clear and obvious, yet the implementation is often questioned and challenged (Niemi & Pekkola, 2020). Loft et al. (2022) claimed that the implementation of EA is intended to enable an organisation to increase accurate assessments of information modelling.

Owing to the promises, these frameworks (FEAF, Gartner, and TOGAF) are implemented in many private and public organisations across the world. However, despite the potential benefits and interest, business cases for the frameworks remain difficult to articulate (Niemi & Pekkola, 2020) and implementation challenges are continuously experienced (Ajer et al., 2021), causing EA initiatives to fail in many organisations (Gong & Janssen, 2022). Consequently, many organisations focus their interest on the Zachman Framework, as they find it easier to understand and practically implement. Also, the Zachman Framework seems to be the most popular and implemented, which can be associated with its longevity. Additionally, the framework has received more attention from the academic domain (Ajer & Olsen, 2019; Lapalme et al., 2016; Pereira & Sousa, 2004).

To support the business design, information modelling, IT solution deployment, and management of the different components of an enterprise and its interaction, different frameworks such as TOGAF and Gartner are often proposed and adopted in organisations (Rahmanian et al., 2022). Ahlemann et al. (2021) argue that EA frameworks differ and their implementation varies from one organisation to another. This makes it more difficult in practice to compare the frameworks in some organisations (Tamm et al., 2022). As a result, many organisations turn their attention to the Zachman Framework primarily because it is valuable in its reflection towards the future of business artefacts and IT solutions (Lapalme et al., 2016), and in the structuring of the enterprise modelling (Oger et al., 2022).

10.2.2 The Zachman Framework

The Zachman Framework was first published in 1987 (Zachman, 1987), then revised and extended a decade later (Zachman, 1996). The Zachman Framework defines architecture as a set of design artefacts or descriptive representations that are relevant for describing an object, such that it can be produced following requirements (quality) as well as being maintained over the period of its useful life (change). Since the introduction of the Zachman Framework by John Zachman in 1987, many organisations and individuals, including in academia have increasingly shown interest in the architecture's framework (Duarte et al., 2021; Sharma & Sarkar, 2021). The Zachman Framework has received broad acceptance from many organisations across all walks of life (Benkamoun et al., 2014). This is attributed to a distinctive focus on its integrative nature and managing change through process re-engineering, information flow and IS/IT systems in enterprises (Fritscher & Pigneur, 2015).

My understanding takes a broader view of EA, which encompasses not only the models used to describe an object in its current state but also the future state as it is affected by business strategies and consequent requirements. Leist and Zellner (2006) argued that the Zachman Framework defines different viewpoints that can be used to describe EA and stipulate the resulting specification documents for each perspective. Abu-El Seoud and Klischewski (2015) claim that the Zachman Framework ensures accuracy and consistency, and that it enables the description of architectures from stakeholders' perspectives. The framework can be applied at different levels of abstraction and enterprise-wide, for business processes, information modelling, and IT solutions, selection, and deployment.

Complementarily or as an alternative to Zachman Framework, many frameworks such as Forrester, TOGAF, DODAF, Gartner, and FEAF have been proposed for implementing EA in recent years. Some of the frameworks are difficult to apply due to the context, uniqueness, and complexity of some organisations. According to Pereira and Sousa (2004), some frameworks are generic and cannot be applied to specific environments. Also, some frameworks are truly enterprise-oriented and others are specific to the development of IT solutions only. Panetto and

Cecil (2013) conducted action research using the Zachman Framework to assist in implementing the EA framework, in which they focused on understanding the enterprise's data. The Zachman Framework has no explicit compliance rules since it is not a standard written by or for a professional organisation (Kappelman & Zachman, 2013). However, compliance can be assumed if it is used in its entirety and all the relationship rules are followed.

Strengths and weaknesses are fundamental in selecting an appropriate framework for EA implementation (Rouhani et al., 2013). Pereira and Sousa (2004) argued in their comparative study that the Zachman Framework is more suitable than others for implementing EA in an organisation. The authors' argument was based and built on the premise that the framework does not guide sequence, process, or implementation, but rather focuses on ensuring that all views are well captured, a complete system is established, and ownerships are well structured. Nogueira et al. (2013) argue that the Zachman Framework continues to be a suitable tool of great utility and value for EA, as it can be used to integrate and align both IT solutions and business goals.

As shown in Tables 10.1 and 10.2, the Zachman Framework for EA is represented by a matrix of components that maps the six interrogatives (who, what, when, where, why, and how) with six different perspectives (planner, owner, designer, builder, subcontractor, and functioning enterprise) (Zachman, 1996). The framework is a classification scheme for descriptive representations of an enterprise. According to Lim et al. (2009), the framework can be categorised as a descriptive framework primarily because it provides a brief description of all the artefacts involved.

A framework can be subjected to any type of meaning. Thus, Zachman (1987) argues that his EA framework can be viewed as a generic classification scheme used for artefact design and descriptive representations of any complex object. In Urbaczewski and Mrdalj (2006), the Zachman Framework is primarily based on the principles of classical architecture, which are found to establish a common vocabulary and set of perspectives for describing complex systems within an enterprise. Zachman (1996) argues that the classification is utilitarian in nature and is to enable focused concentration on specifics, without losing a sense of the contextual or holistic angle.

As shown in Table 10.1, the Zachman Framework depicts artefacts into rows (perspective) and columns (interrogative). In Zachman (1987), it is explained that the framework is in a graphic, simplistic form which depicts the design of artefacts that constitute the intersection between the roles and product abstractions. Owner, designer, and builder are listed as some of the roles, and the product abstractions include what it is made of (material), how it works (process), and where the components are in relation to one another (geometry).

Within the Zachman Framework, there are many models with too much depth to ever complete, which causes a problem for the architects through its complexities (Fatolahi & Shams, 2006). Also, the practical goal of the Zachman Framework to

Table 10.1   The Zachman Framework (Zachman, 1987)

Enterprise Architecture - a Framework

	Data *What*	Function *How*	Network *Where*
Objectives/ Scope (Contextual) *Planner*	List of things important to the business Entity = Class of business thing	List of processes the business performs Process = Class of business process	List of locations in which the business operates Node = Major business location
Enterprise Model (Conceptual) *Owner*	e.g. Semantic model Ent = Business entity Reln = Business relationship	e.g. Business process model Proc = Bus process I/O = Bus resources	e.g. Business logistics system Node = Business location Link = Business linkage
System Model (Logical) *Designer*	e.g. Logical data model Ent = Data entity Reln = Data relationship	e.g. Application architecture Proc = Application function I/O = User views	e.g. Distributed system architecture Node = I/S function (processor, storage, etc) Link = Line characteristics
Technology Constrained Model (Physical) *Builder*	e.g. Physical data model Ent = Segment/table/etc. Reln = Pointer/key/etc.	e.g. System design Proc = Computer function I/O = Data elements/sets	e.g. System architecture Node = Hardware/systems software Link = Line specifications
Detailed Representations (Out-of-Context) *Sub-Contractor*	e.g. Data definition Ent = Field Reln = Address	e.g. Program Pro = Language statement I/O = Control block	e.g. Network architecture Node = Address Link = Protocol
Functioning Enterprise	e.g. Data	e.g. Function	e.g. Network

Table 10.2   The Zachman Framework (Zachman, 1987)

Enterprise Architecture the "Other Three Columns"

People	Time	Motivation	
List of organizations important to the business People = Major organizations	List of events significant to the business Time = Major business event	List of business goals/ strategies Ends/means = Major business goals/critical success factors	Scope *Planner*
e.g. Work flow model People = Organization unit Work = Work product	e.g. Master schedule Time= Business event Cycle = Business cycle	e.g. Business plan End = Business objective Means = Business strategy	Enterprise Model (Conceptual) *Owner*
e.g. Human interface architecture People = Role Work = Deliverable	e.g. Processing structure Time = System event Cycle = Processing cycle	e.g. Business rule model End = Structural assertion means = Action assertion	System Model (Logical) *Designer*
e.g. Presentation architecture Work = Screen format People = User	e.g. Control structure Time = Execute Cycle = Component cycle	e.g. Rule design End = Condition Means = Action	Technology Model (Physical) *Builder*
e.g. Security architecture People = Identity Work = Job	e.g. Timing definition Time = Interrupt Cycle = Machine cycle	e.g. Rule specification End = Sub-condition Means = Step	Detailed Represen-tations (Out-of-Context) *Sub-contractor*
e.g. organization	e.g. Schedule	e.g. Strategy	Functioning Enterprise

build models has not been easy to achieve in many organisations (Löhe & Legner, 2014). The combination of the Zachman Framework and architecture process represents the strategy to selectively guide an enterprise through the selection, creation, and analysis of models (Kappelman & Zachman, 2013). Thus, only organisations that have gone through one or more EA iteration processes have a distinct advantage in managing change (Hernández et al., 2014), which has been one of the challenges for many enterprise architects (Rouhani et al., 2015). However, there is an advantage which includes the existence of models that aid the impact gained from carrying out analysis and the experience of model creation and scenario analysis. In Zachman's (1987) view, there should be a balance between the holistic, contextual view, and the pragmatic, during implementation. He then argues that this can be facilitated through a framework that has the characteristics of a classification scheme, as shown in Figure 10.2.

The Zachman Framework is built on the premise that the only way to manage change in complex objects is through the manipulation of representative renderings (models) of those objects (Lapalme et al., 2016). The framework attempts to categorise the possible types of models that an enterprise needs to describe within context and relevance (Nogueira et al., 2013). Thus, it is noted that the Zachman Framework differs slightly from some other EA frameworks in scope and definition of the EA (Urbaczewski & Mrdalj, 2006). According to Zachman (1987), the framework is considered or selected for reasons such as its ease of understanding, addressing an enterprise in its entirety, communication of complex concepts in a precise manner, abstractive nature, and independence from other tools or methodologies.

The scope of the Zachman Framework for EA is directly expansive by including the builder and subcontractor rows (Hendriana et al., 2015). The builders and subcontractors (i.e., application developers, programmers, data administrators, help desk specialists, and experts of various domains), are intended to cover the owner, planner, and designer roles more directly. Noran (2003, p. 4) briefly explains that "The Zachman Framework does not have an explicit life history concept, and thus only an implicit mapping is possible". Before the mapping can be embarked upon, EA deliverables must be established. This is to ensure that the goals are achieved and the gaps are filled.

In contrast to the benefits, such as a guide to categorise and develop the business and information artefacts (Abu-El Seoud & Klischewski, 2015) and its suitability for complex systems (Batmetan, 2022), the Zachman Framework remains problematic to many organisations. Also, despite its continuous popularity, it is difficult for many organisations to implement and practise the Zachman Framework for business purposes (Darmawan et al., 2022; Löhe & Legner, 2014). Although Duarte et al. (2021) explain how to apply the Zachman Framework by navigating to answer the "what?", "how?", and "who?" questions from Zachman's abstractions, the challenges persist in many organisations. Rahmanian et al. (2022) argue that in the framework, there is a lack of a specific modelling instrument.

10.3 Enterprise Architecture Deliverables

The strengths of EA are primarily in its deliverables, which are based on relevance and context within an organisation. Thus, the focus is on deliverables to determine and understand how the Zachman Framework can be used to implement the EA in an organisation. De Vries and Van Rensburg (2008) posited that the deliverables direct the EA objectives in an organisation's context. Through workshops comprising both business and IT personnel, deliverables are formulated for the architecture team. The deliverables are grouped into three main categories: enterprise, for holistic coverage; architecture, to target desirability; and influencing factors, to gain insights about the drivers. As shown in Figure 10.2, the categories cover both business and IT events, processes, and activities in their inter-related and interconnected nature.

10.3.1 Enterprise Factors

Some factors are at the enterprise level, meaning that they directly or indirectly affect and influence the activities of the divisions and units of the organisation

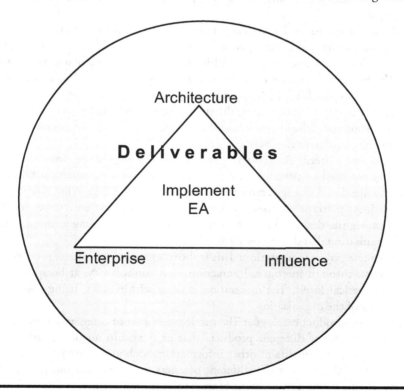

Figure 10.2   Deliverables for EA Implementation.

at the highest and horizontal levels. This is to ensure that core business divisions and their units are represented in the workshops to allow holistic coverage of the deliverables. The enterprise factors include business strategies, business information requirements, business events and scenarios, business patterns, business process integration, and business product catalogues.

    i. Enterprise business strategies (EBSs): EBSs consist of short- and long-term strategic goals and objectives. According to Kang et al. (2010), enterprise business strategies define a direction or a position upon which an enterprise should focus and develop. The EBS is often the responsibility of the senior managers in the various lines of business (LOBs) of an organisation. The EBSs enable the architecture team to design for the future and be measured against it. Therefore, the business strategies take cognisance of and address the environmental trends reflecting on the organisation.

    ii. Business information requirements (BIRs): The BIRs contain valuable information relating to business logics, processes, and activities over a period. The BIRs are intended to enable and support the EBSs, horizontally and vertically, for short- and long-term business designs, development, and growth.

    iii. Business events and scenarios: The business event defines how events are identified, handled, managed and documented, enabled and supported by IT solutions. These are done within the rules and scope of an environment. The business scenarios draw from the events and are used to communicate innovations and futuristic intents with the executive team and other employees. This is carried out using different channels within an organisation. The scenarios assist the employees and employer with informed decision-making and appropriateness of action plans.

    iv. Business pattern: A business pattern consists of a collection of artefacts that are used to describe new processes, functions, information flows, and organisational changes required at a high level of EBA's value relationships. Business patterns are used to describe and model new enterprises, communicating the desires of senior management while providing a foundation for organisational and technological-based designs.

    v. Business process integration: This is the integration of business processes and events, through interface, interaction, and connectivity, at both horizontal and vertical levels. The integration is done within rules, using the requirements of the organisation.

    vi. Business product catalogue: The catalogue is a set of categorisations and documentations of different products that exist within an organisation. Also, the catalogue consists of other information, such as requirements, rules and rationale that govern the different business products. The business product catalogue forms a component of the business architecture.

10.3.2 The Influencing Factors

The enterprise factors alone are not enough to guide EA implementation in an organisation. Fundamentally, businesses should not be conducted in isolation because they influence and are influenced by both internal and external factors. The primary influencing factors are both internal and external. They include environmental trends and drivers, enterprise value network, geographical location, and linear responsibility matrix.

    i. Environmental trends and drivers: Environmental trends consist of external factors (such as legislation and politics), market (e.g., consumers' and suppliers' supply and demand), economic, and technology trends. These factors have an impact on the organisation's processes and activities, directly or indirectly, and therefore require EA considerations.

    ii. Enterprise value network (EVN): The EVN defines the critical functions required to deliver processes and activities, leading to finished products. This includes the relationships that occur in the process which ensure that functionalities are carried out by different actors. This is critical, as some businesses are like a web of fluid with heterogeneous networks rather than a fixed distribution channel.

    iii. Geographic location: This is used to geographically identify different bases and environments where business functions, events, processes, and activities are performed or transformed. It characterises the heterogeneity of the business functions. The location artefact focuses on the past, present, and future states for modelling and visualising organisational structures and functions.

    iv. Linear responsibility matrix (LRM): This event-centric method is used for creating and documenting business functions and information flows within an environment. The LRM is a user-based tool that forms or carries out functions similar to workflow. It could be used to identify and examine roles, responsibilities, rules, and processes in a heterogeneous network environment.

10.3.3 Architecture Factors

Based on the enterprise and influencing factors, the architecture factors are developed. At this point, the decision about the driver is made. As an enabler, the IT unit should not be the driver. Thus, the non-technology factors should be decided before the architecture deliverables are embarked upon. From an architecture perspective, the factors of influence include conceptual architecture principles, architectural requirements, architecture principles, information architecture, and business application portfolios.

    i. Conceptual architecture principles: These are formulated based on the vision, goals, and objectives that were pursued at the time. The principles reflect the collective and common goals and direction of an organisation. The principles are often enforced through policies as dictated by the organisational structure. Also, the principles are a reference guide for achieving the organisation's goals and objectives to improve competitiveness and sustainability within rules, regulations, and ethics. Therefore, principles should be used as evaluation criteria in the absence of detailed models that direct decision-making more discretely and comprehensively.

    ii. Architectural requirements (ARs): ARs are a collection of business-driven requirements which are considered to be common across the line of business within the organisation. The ARs are shared and guide the development and implementation of the various domains for organisational purposes and competitiveness.

    iii. Architecture principles: The architecture principles are derived from the conceptual architecture principles. The principles provide the foundation for other governance components, such as processes, policies, and procedures. Additionally, the principles are used as guidelines during the execution of various tasks, such as requirements analysis, process and software design, software development, and hardware deployment.

    iv. Information architecture: One of the primary objectives of information architecture is to define and describe the sources of high-velocity information and ensure its availability and usage through key business processes. High-velocity information refers to the information that is shared within the EVN. The architecture consists of information obtained or accessed from customers, suppliers, partners, and employees in real time at all levels of organisational structures. The high-velocity information exists horizontally between business units and vertically between customers, suppliers, and partners.

    v. Business application portfolios (BAPs): A BAP is a collection of inventories about existing business applications in the organisation. The business application portfolio is an ongoing process guided by organisational strategies which is needed to support and manage technical functionalities, such as the coexistence and reuse of technologies and applications within the environment.

The EA is employed with the primary purpose of achieving significant objectives whose advantages are viewed through its deliverables. It therefore provides holistic coverage enterprise-wide, through which modelling functions and events are carried out, using aspects such as what, who, where, and when. In such a contextual scenario, the key questions are related to: what functions need to be performed, who should perform the functions, where the functions should be conducted, when the task should be executed, and most importantly, why the business needs to perform such functions to achieve the deliverables at the time.

10.4 Zachman Framework Mapped with Enterprise's Activities

In the process of applying the Zachman Framework, the deliverables are first discussed as presented previously. Duarte et al. (2021) argue that mapping is a decision process for stakeholders (who) to define what their actions are and how they currently structure their decisions. This is to gain a better comprehension of the benefits, rationale, and action plans towards fulfilling the implementation objectives in the context of an organisation. In doing so, the focus is on context and relevance, using Zachman's perspective and interrogative model to answer the following questions. Whose perspective (planner, owner, designer, and builder or subcontractor) do the EA deliverables intend to fulfil in the organisation? How does the interrogative (who, what, when, where, or how) components assist to understand and address the deliverables of an organisation's intents?

As shown in Figure 10.3, a three-step approach is proposed in applying the Zachman Framework for EA implementation in an organisation. The first step is to determine the deliverables established in the section before this. The second step entails mapping the Zachman Framework with the deliverables (Table 10.3). The outcome of the mapping process provides guides for cross-referencing the deliverables with the EA domains.

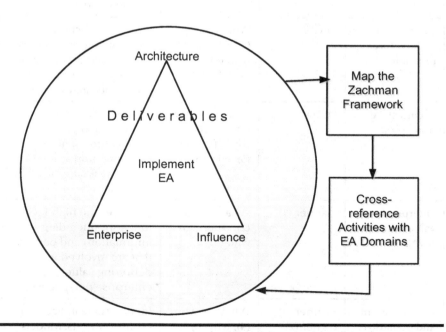

Figure 10.3   EA Implementation through the Zachman Framework.

Table 10.3 Mapping the Zachman Framework with EA Deliverables

Architecture Deliverable	Perspectives (Rows)	Interrogatives (Columns)	Implementation Activities
Environmental trends and drivers	Planner (1)	When (5), why (6)	Identifies the events, circumstances, and trends that impact the enterprise. This is carried out periodically.
Enterprise business strategies (EBSs)	Planner (1)	Why (6)	Identifies high-level motivation for an enterprise towards competitiveness and sustainability.
Business information requirements (BIRs)	Owner (2)	What (1)	Identifies the BIRs that are needed to enable and support EBSs.
Architectural requirements	Owner (2)	What (1)	Identifies EA deliverables in supporting and enabling the EBSs and BIRs.
Conceptual architecture principles	Owner (2)	What (1), how (2), where (3), who (4), when (5), why (6)	Provides direction, including rationale across the architecture domains, and guides re-engineering with the technology domain.
Architecture principles	Designer (3)	What (1), how (2), where (3), who (4), when (5), why (6)	Provides direction and guidelines to each of the architecture domains. Each direction and guideline is supported by rationale.
Enterprise value network (EVN)	Planner (1)	What (1), how (2), where (3), who (4)	Identifies the high-level functions (including information) and parties that are involved in delivering value, from the enterprise perspective.
Business event and scenarios	Planner (1), owner (2)	What (1), who (4), why (6)	Identifies the initiators of business events. Models the different outcomes from various strategies, and the changing variables.

Architecture Deliverable	Perspectives (Rows)	Interrogatives (Columns)	Implementation Activities
Location model	Planner (1)	How (2), who (4), where (3)	Identifies where major functions are or should be performed.
Business process integration	Owner (2), designer (3)	What (1), how (2), why (6), where (3), who (4)	Identifies the major processes performed by business functions. Identifies the integration of business processes and the required information across locations and users.
Business product catalogue	Owner (2), designer (3)	What (1), where (3), who (4)	Identifies business products and the related information required to support the business strategies.
Liner responsibility matrix	Planner (1), owner (2)	What (1), how (2), where (3), who (4), when (5), why (6)	Identifies roles in various tasks and allocates duties to enable and support business objectives. Specifies location and time.
Information architecture	Designer (3)	What (1), how (2), where (3), who (4), when (5), why (6)	Identifies information flows that are required to enable and support business strategies.
Application architecture	Owner (2), designer (3)	What (1), how (2), where (3), who (4), when (5), why (6)	Owner models and identifies high-level functionalities needed to satisfy EBA and designs models and maps functionalities across the enterprise, addressing business events and data reuse in various locations.
Technical architecture	Builder (4)	What (1), how (2), where (3), who (4), when (5), why (6)	Specifies the technologies and configurations to be used in different situations, enabling and supporting business processes and activities.

The EA deliverables shown in Table 10.3 are extracted from the discussion as presented in the preceding section. The EA deliverables are spanned into columns (interrogatives) and rows (perspectives), horizontally and vertically, respectively. This is in alignment with the enterprise-wide nature of EA. Many of the same (interrogative) questions apply across multiple perspectives. As a result, there is a need to assess a specific perspective across different domains of the organisation. The EA process and deliverables, while directly affecting builders and subcontractors (i.e., application developers, programmers, data administrators, service desk specialists, and technicians of the various domains), are intended to cover the owner, planner, and designer rows more directly. Table 10.3 presents a guide through which organisations could map the Zachman Framework to their activities with context and relevance. Also, the mapping helps to identify roles and responsibilities, particularly to overcome overlap challenges (Gunadham & Ahmed Mohammed, 2022).

As shown in Table 10.3, the integration of the dynamic business processes and events are established purposely to digest the rapid and evolving IT solutions and changes. The business strategy, which expresses the processes and events, is linked with EA using the Zachman Framework. The architecture involves both business artefacts and IT solutions including individuals and groups of shared responsibilities in different domains. EA exhumes the effective use of IT solutions, which are a set of competitive differentiators, for an organisation. To this extent, all major business initiatives are enabled and supported, using IT capabilities. The execution or articulation of the business strategy and application of the EA hinges on the involvement of various domains within the organisation. The owners of the activities are both business and IT units, which are enabled and supported by the EA team. The enterprise architects facilitate and assist with an understanding of the current standards and processes of EA implementation.

As presented, the development and implementation of EA are critical to the competitiveness and sustainability of organisations. EA is therefore fundamental to strategic planning, systems design, software and hardware development, and the production of multiple systems with different functionalities of architecture. Batmetan (2022) suggests that the Zachman Framework is an approach for analysing system requirements and preparing business and IT strategic plans. Regarding the mapping presented in Table 10.3, the EA can therefore be considered as the union of the enterprise, the business engineering and development, and the technical domains that support it, as depicted in Table 10.4.

Thus, the activities of EA are executed pragmatically through its domains: enterprise business vision (EBV), enterprise conceptual architecture (ECA), enterprise business architecture (EBA), enterprise information architecture (EIA), enterprise application architecture (EAA), and enterprise technical architecture (ETA). Based on the different contexts and perspectives, the activities in Table 10.3 are carried out through various interrogations, as shown in Table 10.4. The mapping considers the different user perspectives, levels of decision, and types of data (Iyamu, 2022).

Table 10.4 Enterprise Activities Cross-Referenced with EA Domains

Model	EBV	ECA	EBA	EIA	EAA	ETA
Environmental trends and drivers	✓					
Enterprise business strategies (EBSs)	✓					
Business information requirements (BIRs)	✓		✓	✓		
Enterprise value networks (EVNs)			✓	✓		
Conceptual architecture principles		✓				
Architectural requirements (ARs)	✓					
Domain architecture principles			✓	✓	✓	✓
Business events and scenarios			✓			
Location models			✓			
Business process integration	✓		✓	✓		
Business product catalogue			✓			
Linear responsibility matrix			✓			
EIA models				✓		
Application portfolios					✓	
ETA domain architecture standards/ configurations						✓

As shown in Table 10.4, each model is associated with domains. Through the domains, the models are guided towards achieving their individual goals and objectives, which are enabled by specific criteria. The criteria are used as checking lists in fulfilling those objectives before they are considered to be complete or successful.

10.5 Summary

This chapter brings a different and fresh perspective to the use of the Zachman Framework in the implementation of enterprise architecture (EA) in organisations. The chapter is therefore of significant benefit to both business and academic domains through its contributions, which are from both theoretical and practical perspectives. It is highly likely that the chapter can be of use to students who aspire to be architects. Another important contribution of the chapter is that it can be used as training material for both students and those in organisations.

From a theoretical viewpoint, the chapter advances the concept of EA. Practically, the mapping approach can be employed in addressing the challenges experienced in applying the Zachman Framework for EA implementation, with which many professionals and organisations have been confronted for many years. From an academic perspective, this chapter contributes an answer to the questions which are being asked in EA literature about how to apply the Zachman Framework in an organisation. For organisations, the chapter helps enterprise architects and IT managers to better understand the complex factors in mapping organisational activities with the Zachman Framework.

References

Abu-El Seoud, M., & Klischewski, R. (2015, August 30–September 2). Mediating citizen-sourcing of open government applications—a design science approach. In *The proceedings of 14th IFIP WG 8.5 international conference on electronic government (EGOV)* (Vol. 14, pp. 118–129). Springer International Publishing.

Abunadi, I. (2019). Enterprise architecture best practices in large corporations. *Information*, *10*(10), 1–26.

Adnan, H. R., Kurnia, S., Hidayanto, A. N., & Dilnutt, R. (2021, July 12–14). Enterprise architecture implementation challenges in the healthcare sector: A reflection from the literature. In *The proceedings of the Pacific Asia conference on information systems (PACIS)*. Association of Information Systems (AIS) Press.

Ahlemann, F., Legner, C., & Lux, J. (2021). A resource-based perspective of value generation through enterprise architecture management. *Information & Management*, *58*(1), 103266.

Ajer, A. K. S., Hustad, E., & Vassilakopoulou, P. (2021). Enterprise architecture operationalization and institutional pluralism: The case of the Norwegian Hospital sector. *Information Systems Journal*, *31*(4), 610–645.

Ajer, A. K. S., & Olsen, D. H. (2019). Enterprise architecture implementation is a bumpy ride: A case study in the Norwegian public sector. *Electronic Journal of e-Government*, *17*(2), 79–94.

Al-Kharusi, H., Miskon, S., & Bahari, M. (2021). Enterprise architects and stakeholders alignment framework in enterprise architecture development. *Information Systems and e-Business Management*, *19*(1), 137–181.

Alwadain, A., Fielt, E., Korthaus, A., & Rosemann, M. (2016). Empirical insights into the development of a service-oriented enterprise architecture. *Data & Knowledge Engineering*, *105*, 39–52.

Anthony Jnr, B., Petersen, S. A., & Krogstie, J. (2021). A model to evaluate the acceptance and usefulness of enterprise architecture for digitalization of cities. *Kybernetes: The International Journal of Systems & Cybernetics*, *52*(1), 422–447.

Aziz, S., Obitz, T., Modi, R., & Sarkar, S. (2005). Enterprise architecture: A governance framework. In *Part I: Embedding architecture into the organisation*. InfoSyS Technologies Ltd.

Bakar, N. A. A., & Hussien, S. S. (2018). Association of people factors with successful enterprise architecture implementation. *International Journal of Engineering & Technology*, *7*(4.31), 52–57.

Banaeianjahromi, N., & Smolander, K. (2019). Lack of communication and collaboration in enterprise architecture development. *Information Systems Frontiers*, *21*(4), 877–908.

Batmetan, J. R. (2022). Model enterprise architecture for information technology services in universities. *International Journal of Information Technology and Education*, *1*(4), 18–34.

Beese, J., Haki, K., Schilling, R., Kraus, M., Aier, S., & Winter, R. (2022). Strategic alignment of enterprise architecture management—how portfolios of control mechanisms track a decade of enterprise transformation at Commerzbank. *European Journal of Information Systems*, 1–14.

Benkamoun, N., ElMaraghy, W., Huyet, A. L., & Kouiss, K. (2014). Architecture framework for manufacturing system design. *Procedia CIRP*, *17*, 88–93.

Bui, Q. (2017). Evaluating enterprise architecture frameworks using essential elements. *Communications of the Association for Information Systems*, *41*(1), 121–149.

Chalmeta, R., & Pazos, V. (2015). A step-by-step methodology for enterprise interoperability projects. *Enterprise Information Systems*, *9*(4), 436–464.

Dale, M., & Scheepers, H. (2020). Enterprise architecture implementation as interpersonal connection: Building support and commitment. *Information Systems Journal*, *30*(1), 150–184.

Dang, D. D., & Pekkola, S. (2017). Systematic literature review on enterprise architecture in the public sector. *Electronic Journal of e-Government*, *15*(2), 130–154.

Darmawan, A. K., Masykur, F., Muhsi, M., Umam, B. A., & Rofiuddin, R. (2022, August 10–11). Proposing enterprise architecture for smart regencies in Indonesia: A perspective of Zachman Framework (ZF). In *Proceedings of international conference on ICT for smart society (ICISS)* (pp. 1–7). Virtual Conference. IEEE.

De Vries, M., & Van Rensburg, A. C. (2008). Enterprise architecture-new business value perspectives. *South African Journal of Industrial Engineering*, *19*(1), 1–16.

Duarte, S. P., de Sousa, J. P., & de Sousa, J. F. (2021). A conceptual framework for an integrated information system to enhance urban mobility. *International Journal of Decision Support System Technology (IJDSST)*, *13*(4), 33–49.

Fatolahi, A., & Shams, F. (2006). An investigation into applying UML to the Zachman framework. *Information Systems Frontiers*, *8*(2), 133–143.

Foorthuis, R., Van Steenbergen, M., Brinkkemper, S., & Bruls, W. A. (2016). A theory building study of enterprise architecture practices and benefits. *Information Systems Frontiers*, *18*(3), 541–564.

Fritscher, B., & Pigneur, Y. (2015). A visual approach to business IT alignment between business model and enterprise architecture. *International Journal of Information System Modeling and Design (IJISMD)*, *6*(1), 1–23.

Gellweiler, C. (2020). Connecting enterprise architecture and project portfolio management: A review and a model for IT project alignment. *International Journal of Information Technology Project Management (IJITPM)*, *11*(1), 99–114.

Gong, Y., & Janssen, M. (2019). The value of and myths about enterprise architecture. *International Journal of Information Management*, *46*, 1–9.

Gong, Y., & Janssen, M. (2022). Why organizations fail in implementing enterprise architecture initiatives? *Information Systems Frontiers*, 1–19.

Gunadham, T., & Ahmed Mohammed, E. M. (2022). Solving challenges in an electronic banking services company by implementing enterprise architecture 252 frameworks. *Journal of Information and Knowledge Management (JIKM), 12*(2), 252–261.

Haki, K., & Legner, C. (2021). The mechanics of enterprise architecture principles. *Journal of the Association for Information Systems, 22*(5), 1334–1375.

Halawi, L., McCarthy, R., & Farah, J. (2019). Where we are with enterprise architecture. *Journal of Information Systems Applied Research, 12*(3), 4–13.

Hendriana, Y., Umar, R., & Pranolo, A. (2015). Modelling and design e-commerce SMI sector using Zachman framework. *International Journal of Computer Science and Information Security, 13*(8), 9–14.

Hernández, J. E., Lyons, A. C., Poler, R., Mula, J., & Goncalves, R. (2014). A reference architecture for the collaborative planning modelling process in multi-tier supply chain networks: A Zachman-based approach. *Production Planning & Control, 25*(13–14), 1118–1134.

Iyamu, T. (2015). *Information technology enterprise architecture: From concept to practice* (2nd ed.). Heidelberg Press. ISBN: 8-3-659-61206-0.

Iyamu, T. (2019). Understanding the complexities of enterprise architecture through structuration theory. *Journal of Computer Information Systems, 59*(3), 287–295.

Iyamu, T. (2022). *Enterprise architecture for strategic management of modern IT solutions.* Routledge, CRC Press.

Jafari, M., Akhavan, P., & Nouranipour, E. (2009). Developing an architecture model for enterprise knowledge: An empirical study based on the Zachman framework in Iran. *Management Decision, 47*(5), 730–759.

Jayakrishnan, M., Mohamad, A. K., & Abdullah, A. (2019). Enterprise architecture embrace digital technology in Malaysian transportation industry. *International Journal of Engineering and Advanced Technology, 8*(4), 852–859.

Jayakrishnan, M., Mohamad, A. K., & Yusof, M. M. (2020). Business architecture model in strategic information system management for effective railway supply chain perspective. *International Journal of Engineering Research and Technology, 13*(11), 3927–3933.

Kang, D., Lee, J., & Kim, K. (2010). Alignment of business enterprise architectures using fact-based ontologies. *Expert Systems with Applications, 37*(4), 3274–3283.

Kappelman, L. A., & Zachman, J. A. (2013). The enterprise and its architecture: Ontology & challenges. *Journal of Computer Information Systems, 53*(4), 87–95.

Kitsios, F., & Kamariotou, M. (2018). Business strategy modelling based on enterprise architecture: A state of the art review. *Business Process Management Journal, 25*(4), 606–624.

Kotusev, S., Kurnia, S., & Dilnutt, R. (2023). Enterprise architecture artefacts as boundary objects: An empirical analysis. *Information and Software Technology, 155*, 107108.

Lapalme, J., Gerber, A., Van der Merwe, A., Zachman, J., De Vries, M., & Hinkelmann, K. (2016). Exploring the future of enterprise architecture: A Zachman perspective. *Computers in Industry, 79*, 103–113.

Leist, S., & Zellner, G. (2006, April 23–27). Evaluation of current architecture frameworks. In *The proceedings of the 2006 ACM symposium on applied computing* (pp. 1546–1553). ACM Press.

Lim, N., Lee, T. G., & Park, S. G. (2009, May 27–29). A comparative analysis of enterprise architecture frameworks based on EA quality attributes. In *The proceedings of the 10th international conference on software engineering, artificial intelligences, networking and parallel/distributed computing* (pp. 283–288). IEEE.

Lnenicka, M., & Komarkova, J. (2019). Developing a government enterprise architecture framework to support the requirements of big and open linked data with the use of cloud computing. *International Journal of Information Management, 46*, 124–141.

Loft, P., He, Y., Yevseyeva, I., & Wagner, I. (2022). CAESAR8: An agile enterprise architecture approach to managing information security risks. *Computers & Security, 122*, 102877.

Löhe, J., & Legner, C. (2014). Overcoming implementation challenges in enterprise architecture management: A design theory for architecture-driven IT management (ADRIMA). *Information Systems and e-Business Management, 12*(1), 101–137.

Mesquita, A., & Vasconcelos, A. (2022). Heuristics' library for enterprise architecture and portfolio alignment. *International Journal of Information Technology Project Management (IJITPM), 13*(1), 1–23.

Moeini, M., Simeonova, B., Galliers, R. D., & Wilson, A. (2020). Theory borrowing in IT-rich contexts: Lessons from IS strategy research. *Journal of Information Technology, 35*(3), 270–282.

Närman, P., Buschle, M., & Ekstedt, M. (2014). An enterprise architecture framework for multi-attribute information systems analysis. *Software & Systems Modeling, 13*(3), 1085–1116.

Niemi, E. I., & Pekkola, S. (2016). Enterprise architecture benefit realization: Review of the models and a case study of a public organization. *ACM SIGMIS Database: The DATABASE for Advances in Information Systems, 47*(3), 55–80.

Niemi, E. I., & Pekkola, S. (2017). Using enterprise architecture artefacts in an organisation. *Enterprise Information Systems, 11*(3), 313–338.

Niemi, E. I., & Pekkola, S. (2020). The benefits of enterprise architecture in organizational transformation. *Business & Information Systems Engineering, 62*, 585–597.

Nikpay, F., Ahmad, R. B., Rouhani, B. D., Mahrin, M. N. R., & Shamshirband, S. (2017). An effective enterprise architecture implementation methodology. *Information Systems and e-Business Management, 15*, 927–962.

Nogueira, J. M., Romero, D., Espadas, J., & Molina, A. (2013). Leveraging the Zachman framework implementation using action—research methodology—a case study: Aligning the enterprise architecture and the business goals. *Enterprise Information Systems, 7*(1), 100–132.

Noran, O. (2003). An analysis of the Zachman framework for enterprise architecture from the GERAM perspective. *Annual Reviews in Control, 27*(2), 163–183.

Oberle, M., Yesilyurt, O., Schlereth, A., Risling, M., & Schel, D. (2023). Enterprise IT architecture greenfield design combining IEC 62264 and TOGAF by example of battery manufacturing. *Procedia Computer Science, 217*, 136–146.

Oger, R., Lauras, M., Montreuil, B., & Benaben, F. (2022). A decision support system for strategic supply chain capacity planning under uncertainty: Conceptual framework and experiment. *Enterprise Information Systems, 16*(5), 1793390.

Panetto, H., & Cecil, J. (2013). Information systems for enterprise integration, interoperability and networking: Theory and applications. *Enterprise Information Systems, 7*(1), 1–6.

Pereira, C. M., & Sousa, P. (2004, March 14–17). A method to define an enterprise architecture using the Zachman framework. In *The proceedings of the ACM symposium on applied computing* (pp. 1366–1371). ACM Press.

Rahmanian, M., Nassiri, R., Mohsenzadeh, M., & Ravanmehr, R. (2022). Test case generation for enterprise business services based on enterprise architecture design. *The Journal of Supercomputing*, 1–31.

Robertson-Dunn, B. (2012). Beyond the Zachman framework: Problem-oriented system architecture. *IBM Journal of Research and Development*, *56*(5), 10–19.

Roelens, B., Steenacker, W., & Poels, G. (2019). Realizing strategic fit within the business architecture: The design of a process-goal alignment modeling and analysis technique. *Software & Systems Modeling*, *18*(1), 631–662.

Rouhani, B. D., Mahrin, M. N. R., Nikpay, F., & Nikfard, P. (2013). A comparison enterprise architecture implementation methodologies. In *The proceedings of international conference on informatics and creative multimedia (ICICM)* (pp. 1–6). IEEE.

Rouhani, B. D., Mahrin, M. N. R., Nikpay, F., Nikfard, P., & Najafabadi, M. K. (2015). Factors that affect the effectiveness of enterprise architecture implementation methodology. *International Journal of Social, Education, Economics and Management Engineering*, *9*(1), 19–25.

Rouhani, B. D., Mahrin, M. N. R., Nikpay, F., & Rouhani, B. D. (2014). Current issues on enterprise architecture implementation methodology. In *New perspectives in information systems and technologies* (Vol. 2, pp. 239–246). Springer International Publishing.

Safari, H., Faraji, Z., & Majidian, S. (2016). Identifying and evaluating enterprise architecture risks using FMEA and fuzzy VIKOR. *Journal of Intelligent Manufacturing*, *27*(2), 475–486.

Saint-Louis, P., Morency, M. C., & Lapalme, J. (2019). Examination of explicit definitions of enterprise architecture. *International Journal of Engineering Business Management*, *11*, 1847979019866337.

Saleem, F., & Fakieh, B. (2020). Enterprise architecture and organizational benefits: A case study. *Sustainability*, *12*(19), 1–23.

Schekkerman, J. (2009). *How to manage the enterprise architecture practice*. Trafford Publishing.

Shanks, G., Gloet, M., Someh, I. A., Frampton, K., & Tamm, T. (2018). Achieving benefits with enterprise architecture. *The Journal of Strategic Information Systems*, *27*(2), 139–156.

Sharma, S., & Sarkar, P. (2021). Capturing knowledge transfer using Zachman framework in bio-inspired design process. In *Design for tomorrow—Volume 2: Proceedings of ICoRD 2021* (pp. 563–574). Springer.

Simon, D., Fischbach, K., & Schoder, D. (2014). Enterprise architecture management and its role in corporate strategic management. *Information Systems and e-Business Management*, *12*(1), 5–42.

Sukur, A., & Lind, M. L. (2022). Enterprise architecture to achieve information technology flexibility and enterprise agility. *International Journal of Information Systems and Social Change (IJISSC)*, *13*(2), 1–20.

Tamm, T., Seddon, P. B., & Shanks, G. (2022). How enterprise architecture leads to organisational benefits. *International Journal of Information Management*, *67*, 102554.

Ullah, A., & Lai, R. (2013). A systematic review of business and information technology alignment. *ACM Transactions on Management Information Systems (TMIS)*, *4*(1), 1–30.

Urbaczewski, L., & Mrdalj, S. (2006). A comparison of enterprise architecture frameworks. *Issues in Information Systems*, *7*(2), 18–23.

Wang, X., Ma, F., & Zhou, X. (2008, October 12–17). Aligning business and IT using enterprise architecture. In *The proceedings of the 4th international conference on wireless communications, networking and mobile computing* (pp. 1–5). IEEE.

Wang, X., Zhou, X., & Jiang, L. (2008). A method of business and IT alignment based on enterprise architecture. In *Service operations and logistics, and informatics, IEEE international conference on* (Vol. 1, pp. 740–745). IEEE.

Winter, R., & Fischer, R. (2006, October 16–20). Essential layers, artefacts, and dependencies of enterprise architecture. In *The proceedings of the 10th IEEE international enterprise distributed object computing conference workshops (EDOCW'06)* (pp. 30–30). IEEE.

Winter, R., & Schelp, J. (2008, March 16–20). Enterprise architecture governance: The need for a business-to-IT approach. In *The proceedings of the ACM symposium on applied computing* (pp. 548–552). ACM Press.

Zachman, J. A. (1987). A framework for information systems architecture. *IBM Systems Journal, 26*(3), 276–292.

Zachman, J. A. (1996, November). Enterprise architecture: The view beyond 2000. In *Conference proceedings, warehouse repository architecture development 7th international users group conference.* Technology Transfer Institute.

Zhi, Q., & Zhou, Z. (2022). Empirically modeling enterprise architecture using ArchiMate. *Computer Systems Science Engineering, 40*(1), 357–374.

Chapter 11

A Readiness-Based Approach for Enterprise Business Architecture Practice

11.1 Introduction

This chapter covers the practice-based enterprise business architecture (EBA) model. It explores models aimed at assessing the readiness of the environment for EBA deployment. A model is selected and a study is conducted to give empirical credence to the readiness assessment of the concept. The model has been neither validated nor tested, which is a gap that the study covers, as presented in this chapter. Thus, we began this chapter with a momentary introduction to the concept of business architecture.

As established in previous chapters, EBA is a domain of enterprise architecture (EA) covering the non-technical activities of an organisation (Kim et al., 2013). Other domains of EA are information, application, and technology (Iyamu, 2015). The focus of this chapter is on EBA, with a particular focus on validating its readiness assessment model (RAM) (Zondani & Iyamu, 2021). Al-Ghamdi and Saleem (2016) explain how the concept of EBA deals more with business processes and modelling than with the technical and technological aspects. EBA is derived from the business strategy and is mainly concerned with human resources, business processes, and rules (Kitsios & Kamariotou, 2019). Al-Ghamdi (2017) described business architecture as the strategic tool that enables organisations to drive business operations and determinants

DOI: 10.1201/9781003390879-11

for information technology (IT) solutions, for competitiveness purposes. These facets, strategies, operationalisations, and process models are the reasons why organisations (or enterprises) show interest in and emphasise the concept.

Furthermore, the deliverables of EBA are said to inform the design and development of other architectural domains, including information, application, and technology. Al-Ghamdi and Saleem (2016) argued that even though EBA focuses on business processes, it eventually gets incorporated with the technical infrastructure, data architecture, hardware, and software of the organisation. Thus, EBA provides a roadmap for aligning business needs with IT infrastructures. This aspect of EBA enacts the fact that business environments should not be studied in isolation but through context (Gonzales-Lopez & Bustos, 2019). The practice of EBA provides the context that allows for a better understanding, performance, and control of business operations (Gonzales-Lopez & Bustos, 2019). Organisations that have implemented EBA are expected to reap benefits such as strategic alignment, customer-centric focus, and faster speed to market (Whittle & Myrick, 2016).

However, many organisations have not been able to implement the concept of EBA. As a result, they lose out on the benefits that would have fostered their competitiveness. The lack of implementation of the concept can be attributed to two main factors: (i) there are not many cases, which limits references and learning from practice, and consequently, it makes some organisations reluctant to embark on the process (Hadaya & Gagnon, 2017); and (ii) many of the organisations that have implemented or attempted to implement the concept have failed or failed to realise or articulate the benefits (Gromoff et al., 2017). These factors are because of a lack of readiness assessment (Zondani & Iyamu, 2021; Aji & Widodo, 2019).

Given the strategic significance of EBA, there has always been a need for assessment to determine an organisation's readiness for the implementation of the concept. Unfortunately, there seem to be no RAMs tailored for EBA that can guide this process. Many of the assessment models found in the literature focus on enterprise architecture (EA) as a whole and not on EBA as a domain (Zondani & Iyamu, 2021; Javanbakht et al., 2009). A study by Bakar and Kama (2016) developed an enterprise architecture implementation and priority assessment model comprising 27 assessment criteria. Jahani et al. (2010) presented a model based on an analysis of nine factors and 34 indicators to assess organisations' readiness when implementing EA. Due to the lack of EBA assessment models, organisations find themselves deploying EBA even when the environment is not fit. Jahani et al. (2010) noted that assessment models are critical as they enable organisations to determine to what extent they are ready before practising EA concepts and, if they were not ready, to better understand the gaps.

It is not sufficient to merely have an assessment model. The assessment model needs to be validated from theory to practice. According to Iyamu (2018), being theoretical about EA concepts with no practicality provides limited knowledge which is not sufficient to apply architectural concepts in organisations. The validation of models from theory to practice enables organisations to measure the value and costs of practising EBA. Otherwise, organisations that are interested in EBA will continue to be challenged with implementation and practice stages (Aji & Widodo, 2019). This chapter presents the result from the validation of an assessment model that specifically focuses on EBA readiness developed by Zondani and Iyamu (2021).

There are three main theoretical, empirical, and practical contributions from this research. From the theoretical front, it demonstrates the significance of the RAM and explains how its capability leads to organisational benefits. From the empirical perspective, we conducted tests in five South African companies targeting business architects and other senior managers such as the chief technology officer (CTO) and architecture managers. Extracts from the transcripts enhance the validity of the model. Finally, from a practical angle, we developed a model to assess the readiness of an environment before embarking on the development and implementation of EBA in an organisation. In addition, we provide business and IT managers with evidence from the test, which will lead the managers to realistic opportunities for organisational benefits.

This chapter is structured into seven main sections, sequentially. The first section introduces the paper. The second section presents a literature review which tries to unpack the gap that exists in the terrain on which this chapter focuses. The assessment model that was validated from theory into practice is covered in the third section. This is followed by a discussion of the methodology that was applied in the study, including data collection and its validity. Analysis and findings from the validation are presented in the fifth section. The implication of practice is discussed in the sixth section, and thereafter, a conclusion is drawn.

11.2 Review of Related Works

Enterprise Business Architecture (EBA) is a domain of enterprise architecture (EA), which focuses on business design, processes, artefacts, and requirements (Iyamu, 2021; Tao et al., 2017). It is believed that organisations that deploy EA have a competitive edge through the consolidation of artefacts and processes to reduce cost and increase marketing time (Banaeianjahromi, 2018), improve business environment agility (Ross et al., 2006), and foster IT–business alignment (Shaanika & Iyamu, 2018). These premises have contributed to increasing interest in EBA over the years.

EBA is known to be a foundational domain that directs, guides, and integrates all the architectures of the enterprise (Whittle & Myrick, 2016). According to Al-Ghamdi and Saleem (2016), EBA is the central domain from which other architectural domains are derived and to which they can be traced back. Significantly, this means that EBA provides measurement value and benchmark for other domains. Lee and Yung (2010) suggest that EBA is a strategic system that is responsible for product and service development and business competition.

In corroboration, EBA enacts processes and other architectural elements (Iyamu et al., 2016), and it integrates disparate concepts of an organisation. Thus, EBA holistically covers an organisation's business processes, activities, and events (Gonzales-Lopez & Bustos, 2019).

Despite the importance of EBA, the practice of the concept continues to be challenging for many organisations (Zondani & Iyamu, 2021). Some organisations encounter challenges across the different stages, such as design, development, implementation, and post-implementation (Seppanen et al., 2018; Iyamu, 2015) Also, the challenges encountered are not purely technical; they include non-technical factors such as culture, administration, and process (Shaanika & Iyamu, 2018). A study by Banaeianjahromi (2018) presents 18 EA development obstacles, many of which affect EBA. The deployment of EBA is challenging due to the limitations of frameworks that are specific to EBA, and they are difficult to customise to an environment. Thus, the practice of EBA by organisations remains slow. These challenges manifest from a lack of assessment of organisations' readiness (Zondani & Iyamu, 2021).

Readiness is critical before embarking on the implementation of EBA (Hussein et al., 2019). Readiness assessment determines the implementation success factors, the appropriateness of requirements and environmental attributes which influence practices (Hussein et al., 2020). Akunyumu et al. (2021) suggest the assessment readiness to ascertain the possibility of implementing innovation in an environment. Although Yusif et al. (2017) argue that readiness assessment is about taking stock of relevant factors that can potentially influence implementation, Pirola et al. (2020) explain the criticality of readiness assessment in identifying and resolving potential barriers in implementation. The main challenges are that these factors are not empirically known, other than theorising them (Zondani & Iyamu, 2021).

Currently, in the literature, it is hard to find EBA (or EA) RAMs. in the last two decades, such a model did not seem to exist (Iyamu, 2022; Versteeg & Bouwman, 2006). However, EA models have found their way into the literature. This includes Hussein et al. (2020) and Zondani and Iyamu (2021). This chapter adopts the EBA-RAM by Zondani and Iyamu (2021). The EBA-RAM, presented in Table 11.1, is selected due to its complexity and sophistication in guiding the EBA readiness assessment process. Also, the model is recently published and thus demonstrates applicability to modern computing environments. However, the assessment model has not been tested (validated); thus, it remains a theory.

The validation of the EBA-RAM is purposely to test its efficacy in solving practical problems based on organisational requirements (Rakgoale & Mentz, 2015). Along the same line of argument, Hidayat and Mahardiko (2020) explain that models are validated to test their accuracy in describing and addressing real-world cases. An understanding of the test result might pose another type of challenge because of its subjective nature. Thus, translation from the perspective of actor–network theory (ANT) is applied as a lens.

Table 11.1 EBA Readiness Assessment Model (Zondani & Iyamu, 2021)

Factor / Weight	1	2	3	4	5
Requirements	There are no templates or processes for collecting and formulating requirements	There are processes, but no existing templates for collecting requirements	Different templates and processes are used to collect or formulate requirements	There are approved templates and processes for collecting requirements	Templates and processes are regularly reviewed for organisational purposes
Documentation	There is no documentation for most processes and events	There is no uniformity in documenting processes and events	Some processes and activities are documented; documentations are stored sparsely	All processes and activities are documented and stored in a central repository	Documentations are regularly reviewed for improvement purposes
Business/IT alignment	Desperate silos of processes and events	Change in the organisation is slow	Uniform processes, activities, and events	Unified teams meld skills and resources	Transformation is stable and ongoing.
Ownership	Identify key performance indicators (KPI)	Define responsibilities for KPI tasks, processes, and activities	Define and assign accountability for each responsibility	Define a role map for each responsibility and accountability	Executive control over processes, activities, and events

Factor \ Weight	1	2	3	4	5
Governance	Rules and regulations are not transparent.	Define authorities over rules and regulations	Define resources, processes, and value	Standards, principles, and policies are defined	Regular review of standards, principles, and policies
Risk	Potential factors of derailment are not completely identified	Identify and understand the different types of hindering factors	An operational plan to mitigate against potential factors of derailment	Strategic plan to mitigate against potential factors of derailment	Regular review of operational and strategic plans
Skillset	Personnel is trained; basic knowledge acquired	Qualified personnel are per the job description	Defined growth paths for the available qualified personnel	Highly skilled personnel in all areas of responsibility	Implement a strategy for skill retention
Funding	Resources and rationale have yet to be identified	Identify and understand the resources and benefits	Able to quantify and identify benefits and value	Able to compare the cost of IT services to the next best alternatives	Able to associate value with the identified benefits

11.3 Actor–Network Theory: Translation

ANT is a sociotechnical theory that focuses on constantly shifting negotiation between actors and within networks (Callon, 1986). In ANT, human and non-human factors are referred to as actors (Callon, 1986), and they together form a network of allied interests (Iyamu & Mgudlwa, 2018). The idea of allying is seen as a solution to a problem, such as embracing innovation in an environment (Iyamu, 2021). Based on its multiplicity, Best and Walters (2013) describe ANT as an influencer of science and technology, within which the theory is used to embrace devices and other non-human entities. One of the strengths of ANT is translation (Law, 1992).

ANT is used to underpin this phenomenon primarily for three reasons. First, because of its network's distinctive approach (Birke & Knierim, 2020). In organisations, humans (actors) are divided into groups or units in the deployment and practice of EBA. The units often think differently from each other as they carry out their respective tasks. Second, shifting negotiation entails in-depth interactions between actors (Iyamu, 2021). As humans interact, new knowledge is gained and positions are affirmed or shifted, and actions are executed. Third, translation happens at different stages or moments (Law & Callon, 1997). In the deployment of and practice of EBA, consciously or unconsciously, every interaction is translated to associate meanings to it. These make the rationale fundamental in validating the readiness model in organisations.

Translation builds and changes networks (Callon, 1986). It involves the process of reinterpreting interests (goals, problems, solutions) for other actors to align to ally (Law, 1992). During this process, the focal actor assigns roles and mobilises others to enrol in the network (Vickers et al., 2018). This was critical for this study because of the exotic identities of entities and the differentiation of cultures across organisations.

In the scheme of things, translation improves the understanding of the original text. It is within this context that Felski (2016) refers to translation as a vital mechanism in the creation of transnational networks of influence for enablers of texts. Devi and Kumar (2018) explain how innovations are the outcome of negotiations as actors attempt to extend their networks while maintaining the complex relationship that exists during the process of translation. Thus, some enablers employ translation as a source of power in their practices to explain texts for implementation purposes. This helps to contact heads of departments (units) to assist in translating the model to their team members for evaluation and validation purposes.

ANT is being employed as a way of making sense of complex paths and gaining established scientific knowledge (Best & Walters, 2013). From the standpoint of ANT, we employ the concept of translation as a lens in this study. Thus, translation is a key metaphor in ways of thinking and making sense of the application of the readiness model in an organisation. This is where the negotiation begins to shift until the evaluation and validation of the model are complete.

11.4 Research Methodology

Models can be validated through quantitative and qualitative approaches (Lin et al., 2011). The qualitative method was employed in the study because of its focus on quality rather than quantity (Conboy et al., 2012). Thus, the method was most appropriate because the aim of testing the EBA-RAM was beyond a 'yes' or 'no'; 'true' or 'false' type of event. The method is well documented and rationalised, and it is increasingly being used in information systems (IS) research. It therefore does not necessarily need an introduction or explanation in the IS context (see Markus and Lee, 1999; Sarker et al., 2012; Gehman et al., 2018). The qualitative method is applied in this study primarily because the objective deters insights into the rationalities of the participants.

Given the aim of this study to validate (test) the theoretical model by Zondani and Iyamu (2021), the case study approach is suitable. A total of five South Africa–based organisations partook in the testing of the EBA-RAM. A preliminary question ("Can the EBA-RAM be applied in your organisation?") was used in selecting organisations for the study if the answer was affirmative. This question was accompanied by an abstract and a synopsis of the EBA-RAM. The organisations were selected according to a set of empirical criteria thought to be most useful to the objective of the study (Yin, 2017). These are: (i) 13 organisations were invited, and eight agreed to partake; and (ii) of the eight, five have successfully implemented the business architecture. The five organisations were assigned pseudo names because the organisations (except the government administration) strongly opposed identity disclosure. As a result, we could not provide details more than what is contained in Table 11.2; otherwise, it would be easy to identify the organisations owing to the nature of the South African environment.

Four factors were employed in testing (validating) the model in the organisations. The factors were abstractions from literature in conjunction with the objective of the model being validated: (i) the usefulness of the model for the organisation's purposes; (ii) the application of the model for business goals and objectives; (iii) friendliness of the model to the users in the organisation; and (iv) the value the model can purportedly add to the organisation. A key observation from the validation exercise is that there are four key functional areas where the business architect adds unique value in practice (Hendrickx et al., 2011). To validate the model, a theoretical construct and determinant factors were abstracted. According to Molla et al. (2009), such factors are convergent to successful implementation. Peppard and Ward (2004) suggest that business values are derived through changes and innovations.

The organisations spent an average of three weeks applying the EBA-RAM in their environments. Written feedback from each of the organisations was received. Follow-up interviews were conducted with the lead participants to clarify and

Table 11. 2   Participating Organisations

#	Pseudo Name	Description	Number of participants	Org. Size
1	South Bank South Africa (SBSA)	SBSA is one of the largest banks in the country. It has about 600 people in its IT department. Within the IT department, it has a unit (team) that focuses on enterprise architecture, which includes the business architecture domain.	5 Lead: IT architecture manager	30,000+
2	Ocean Bank South Africa (OBSA)	A medium-sized banking institution in the South African context. It has about 180 IT specialists in the organisation, and nine were business architects. The architects report to a senior business analyst.	4 Lead: senior business analyst	20,000+
3	Green Insurance South Africa (GISA)	GISA is classified as a large company in the South African context. The company has been in existence for more than 45 years. There were over 200 employees in the IT department. The company had about 23 architects spread across the domains of EA, headed by the CTO. It was classified as a large company.	4 CTO	24,000+
4	Government Administration (GASA)	The GASA is a government administration which focuses on service delivery to the citizens. As of the time of this study, the administration had about 150 employees including contract workers in the IT department. The administration had about 11 business architects situated in both the IT and non-IT units.	5 Senior manager: IT	8,000+

#	Pseudo Name	Description	Number of participants	Org. Size
5	Essentials Retailing (ARSA)	The retail company had over 92 branches across the country. There were about 230 IT personnel in the company spread into units and teams. Like SBSA, ARSA had a dedicated EA unit, which consisted of three domains: information, business, and technology.	4 Head: IT architecture and governance	12,000+

confirm responses. Boudreau et al. (2001) argue that the confirmatory approach heightens the reliability and validity of the content. The transcript of the interviews and the written feedback were combined and sent back to each of the organisations through the lead participants, for verification and confirmation purposes. Zondani and Iyamu (2021) provided the procedure for applying the EBA-RAM.

The data were analysed with hermeneutics following the interpretivist approach. The concept of translation from the ANT perspective guided the analysis, as shown in Table 11.3. This allowed a two-phase approach. In Phase 1, the written feedback was repeatedly read in conjunction with the interview transcripts to comprehend how the EBA-RAM was applied; according to Eisenhardt (1989), this is crucial in qualitative data analysis. In Phase 2, the sets of data from each of the organisations were also repeatedly read with the EBA-RAM to understand the conclusions that were reached in the application (testing) of the model. ANT is used in the analysis of the result from the testing.

ANT has been embraced and critiqued over the years (Walsham, 1997), yet it remains a useful lens for inquiry (Iyamu, 2015). We relied on the concept of translation from three main standpoints, which are expanded in Table 11.3: (i) it broadens the logic of the EBA-RAM to the understanding of employees in the organisations; (ii) its translation is a means through which relationships between actors are established and understandings are connected with actions; and (iii) it helps actions to be coordinated, and meanings are used to transform the organisation's initiatives (Felski, 2016). In addition, as a lens, we chose to employ ANT primarily because it provides a framework that enables the analysis of social construct, including the interaction and relationship of actors in a dynamic fashion (Burga & Rezania, 2017).

Table 11.3   Translation of Events

#	Translation	Description
1	What can be translated?	Identify the material for the translation of activities involved in the EBA-RAM. This includes the factors that influence the activities, as well as the outcome of the deployment of EBA, to explain how the translation of an individual's interest manifests into material form (Callon, 1991).
2	Who translates the activities?	Identify human actors (managers and employees) and understand their roles in the process of evaluating the EBA-RAM. Translation allows for the investigation of the proliferation of related groups through systemic tactics by examining their roles and activities (Kinder et al., 2019).
3	Why was the translation carried out?	This encapsulates the various activities and interests involved in evaluating the EBA-RAM. The translation concept from the ANT perspective encourages an analysis of agency, whereby humans and non-humans are involved, and to understand how stakeholders work to strengthen their positions (Shiga, 2007).
4	How did the translation happen?	Through translation: (i) interpret the interests of the group; (ii) on behalf of himself/herself or the organisation, impose the significance of EBA-RAM on members of the group; and (iii) inscribe the EBA-RAM as a use case for practices in the organisation. Through translation, employees in a team (or group) become aligned with an interest defined for them by the focal actor (Islam et al., 2019).
5	Where was the translation carried out?	The EBA-RAM was conducted within the business units of organisations, but resulting in different types of outcomes in the process. Translation exposes how ideas move and change in activity within networks (Heeks & Stanforth, 2015).
6	When was the translation carried out?	Although the period or time factor does not influence the evaluation of the EBA-RAM, it was necessary to understand interpretation happened at a certain period in the process. The translation is an ongoing process (Callon, 1986) which allows for interpreting individual and group experiences (Green et al., 2019).

11.5 Translation of the Data

The key factors or areas are usefulness, value, design and automation, and ease of use. The factors require translation in ascribing them into actors for implementation purposes. Translation exposes how the interests of actors change in the implementation of technology or processes (Heeks & Stanforth, 2015).

11.5.1 What Was Translated and Who Was Involved?

Thus, it is the primary role of a business architect to have a holistic understanding of the business direction, context, and strategies when developing EBA. Iyamu et al. (2016) discussed the role of a business architect, which is to design and develop business process models and define the scope and boundaries among organisational activities. There were multiple levels of translation in the process of testing the model in the organisations. In the first level, the components of the model were translated to the participants. This was to help them decide on their participation and provide a useful response. At the second level, the participants translated the components in the context of their organisations to ensure relevance and fit. Some organisations view business architecture as interlinked with organisational goals and objectives towards value creation and competitiveness (Roelens et al., 2019). Consequently, one of the participants concluded as follows: "The model clearly presents the factors of readiness and also outlines the weight associated with these factors" (GASA_02).

Business model design and product design differ in several theoretically meaningful ways; hence, translating the components was critical. According to one participant (OBSA_02),

> the main value is that it helps to improve the capabilities to achieve the goals and objectives of business architecture. Also, it helps with design, to capture and address all elements related to customer service such as digitisation of its services.

Unswervingly, the managers (lead participants) established themselves as obligatory passage points by directly enforcing the testing of the model. Such action ensures a common understanding among participating employees, which helps with the corroboration of responses from the employees. In addition, some of the managers used the study as an opportunity to test employees' theoretical know-how about the concept of business architecture which they have inscribed in them as the organisation embarked on the route to developing the business. From the responses and actions, some of the managers translated employees' buy-in into indispensable interest.

11.5.2 Why and How Did Translation Happen?

The readiness assessment helps an organisation to understand the capacity of its resources towards improving the mandatory requirements for the successful implementation of EBA. Hussein et al. (2020) consider readiness assessment as the first step for adoption, as it can be useful in identifying gaps and risks. In successfully implementing business architecture, a method that detects and traces means and ends at the domain's level was needed. One of the participants briefly explains: "The value stream allows an organisation to document its processes and procedures, and create and improve business objectives" (OBSA_05). Business architecture involves the conceptualisation of organisational boundaries and defines the design flows of processes (Amit & Zott, 2015). Through translation, the assessment model is understood as "useful because it helps the organisation to deliver end-to-end business value to its customer" (ARSA_03).

Organisations must be able to assimilate change for purposes of value addition and realisation. "The model is useful in that it helps in the overall assessment of the enterprise-wide business architecture model, more so in identifying key areas when gathering requirements" (SBSA_03). The factors used for testing make the model suitable for the assessment of an environment toward readiness for EBA. The factors are fundamental for both the present and future, including potential changes. Peppard and Ward (2004) argue that the environment evolves to a point where change emerges, which therefore requires mechanisms for assessment. The position of the participants was that the assessment helps a great deal as a guiding plan when building the matrix to assess EBA maturity level (GISA_01).

11.5.3 Where and When Did Translation Occur?

During the test, translation occurred at stages that further allow us to analyse the proliferation of related networks (groups within organisations), to fathom explicitly why and how the EBA-RAM was evaluated and accepted as a readiness assessment mechanism in organisations: "the EBA model is designed to help organisations build a better visual representation of their business environment" (SBSA_02); "The model is useful because it helps an organisation capture and futuristically assess how business activities fit together to serve the end-to-end stakeholders' needs" (ARSA_02).

The readiness assessment helps an organisation to identify various factors that can impede the successful operationalisation of the business architecture. The factors are technical and non-technical, and they can be unique for each organisation. "The model is well constructed, and it is easy to interpret and use" (GASA_04). As a result, "it further helped in establishing the gaps in the current departmental enterprise architecture effort" (OBSA_02). Pirola et al. (2020) argue that by conducting an EBA readiness assessment, organisations not only identify the risks and potential challenges but also opportunities that might arise when EBA is implemented.

Fundamentally, translation reduces cognitive biases and strengthens the proposition to understand how the model can improve the stability, usefulness, and value of business architecture. "In my view, the model is useful because it provides a better business definition for every area of business architecture deployment which can lead to effective and efficient business processes and technology solutions within the environment" (SBSA_01). Assessment requires reconciling means with ends through translation in which change is ascribed to the actors within the environment. Consequently, actors prepare for the known and unpredictable changes that relate to both the ends and the means. "The model allows organisations to build business capability which can add value to the development and implementation of the business architecture" (OBSA_03).

11.6 EBA-RAM: Discussion of the Test Result

The EBA has been better theorised in literature rather than practice (Kotusev, 2019). This study provides an empirically validated model for organisational practice. Testing of the model provides practicable evidence for implementing EBA in organisations. The test focused on four fundamental factors, as shown in Table 11.4: usefulness, value addition, design and automation, and ease of use. Typically, these factors are indicators for IT and business improvement, risk mitigation (Amit & Zott, 2015), and alignment (or coexistence) with existing IT

Table 11.4 Test Result of the EBA-RAM

#	Organisation	Factor	Weight				
			1	2	3	4	5
1	SBSA	Usefulness					X
		Value addition					X
		Design and automation					X
		Ease of use				X	
2	OBSA	Usefulness					X
		Value addition				X	
		Design and automation				X	
		Ease of use				X	
3	GISA	Usefulness				X	
		Value addition				X	
		Design and automation					X
		Ease of use					X
4	GASA	Usefulness			X		
		Value addition			X		
		Design and automation		X			
		Ease of use				X	
5	ARSA	Usefulness					X
		Value addition				X	
		Design and automation				X	
		Ease of use					X

solutions (Őri, 2014). The factors enact structures, operations, governance, and alignment of the EBA with the current environment. The EBA-RAM implies the realistic construction of structures and operationalisation of alignment and translation of strategies toward EBA implementation in an organisation. The factors are discussed later in this section, and they should be read in conjunction with Table 11.4 to gain a better understanding of their criticality.

These notions of usefulness, value, design and automation, and ease of use were prevalent in the conversation and written responses from the participants. These were because of the translation of the business architecture goal and objectives. "The model also allows the measurement and monitoring of the key performance indicators within the environment" (SBSA_02).

11.6.1 The Usefulness of the Assessment Model

An object or system is deemed useful when it enhances the performance of activities towards achieving defined goals. Tsai et al. (2019) explain that individuals accept and use systems to the extent that they are better at addressing their needs. The EBA-RAM was considered useful by enforcing practicality in assessing organisations' readiness for business architecture implementation. Also, it helps to fortify implicit decisions in business processes towards achieving goals and objectives. Thus, determining areas of an organisation for the EBA focuses on improving performance. The absence of this type of model has made it difficult for many organisations to understand the extent of complexity and the readiness nature of their environments. In addition, the usefulness of the model also comes from its generalisation because it is not designed for a specific organisation. It is flexible and can be applied by different organisations wishing to implement the concept of business architecture.

The model is useful in guiding business and technology managers in assessing the environment to detect factors of influence in the deployment of EBA. Roelens et al. (2019) argue that the realisation of strategic fit within the business architecture is an important challenge for many organisations which has not been actualised. The test conducted in the five organisations proceed the model from a theoretical antecedent into practice. Significantly, the model illustrates how to carry out the assessment process. Through the weight associated with each cell, the model provides a valid reflection of the current business environment, enabling the identification of the existing gaps and the analysis of the efforts towards each factor. Also, it detects potential risks in business architecture's multifaceted view of the organisation's key components. The test validates the gap between an organisation's blueprint and the real-world readiness and capabilities required to deliver EBA.

11.6.2 Value Addition to EBA Development

A lack of understanding of factors that influence the deployment contributes to the inability to assess the value of business architecture in organisations (Zondani & Iyamu, 2021). Significantly, this is one of the contributions of the EBA-RAM to organisations in their pursuit of developing and implementing business architecture. The EBA-RAM brings a fresh perspective to organisations that enable management and employees to scrutinise their environments for readiness before committing to architecture activities. Thus, business architecture is considered the genesis domain of enterprise architecture because it is pivotal to value addition. Also, the EBA-RAM can be viewed as a communication tool through which the alignment of the various components necessary for the successful operation of EA is achieved. This addresses the concern that demonstrating the business value of architecture has proven elusive, as many of the benefits are intangible (Shanks et al., 2018).

The result from the test clearly shows that the EBA-RAM is resilient and adaptive to business architecture in organisations. Hendrickx et al. (2011) explain how business architecture resolves historical challenges in organisations and translates objectives into strategies, thereby aligning technology and operations. This can hardly be achieved without an assessment, a significant value that the EBA-RAM presents. From a value aspect, the EBA-RAM addresses the gap in processes, designs, and communication within business units which can be used to promote the quality of business functionalities and supports. The value is fortified through its provision of a managerial approach to reveal the reality of the current state and guide processes toward performance improvement. Consequently, the approach removes the incessant going in virtual circles without valuable contributions.

11.6.3 Design and Automation of EBA Processes

The implementation of EBA-RAM is influenced by various factors that are of technical and non-technical nature, which manifest from characteristics and categorisations. There are challenges of characteristics, constraints, and categorisation of resources which often hinder the implementation or practice of business architecture in organisations (Jayakrishnan et al., 2020). Without an initial assessment, it is difficult to detect some of these factors because of their uniqueness. The uniqueness of the factors requires a deep view to better understand their impacts on the successful development and implementation of the business architecture. This is critical, as it shapes the business process network and automation. Also, it enables management to develop a holistic view of an organisation's resources necessary for the design and development of business goals and objectives.

In theory, business architecture defines fundamental components such as transformation and strategy (Hendrickx et al., 2011). Through its design, workflow, and logical artefacts, it enables alignment and an integrated bridge between business units and IT (Kotusev, 2019). Therefore, its assessment should not be taken for granted in actualising the objectives. Also, the increasing complexity of business processes and operations requires fixing and manageability to promote cohesion and business–IT alignment. The factors that influence these aspects can be detected at the readiness stage to ensure stability and increase the chance of fulfilling the objectives for value purposes.

11.6.4 Ease of Use of the Assessment Model

In addition to other valuable components, the EBA-RAM is considered ease-of-use–focused when assessing an environment. Davis (1989) argues that when a system is perceived as having ease of use, there is a high possibility that the users will continue to use the system. This is important for the EBA-RAM in assessing the readiness of an environment and enhancing the model as technology and business evolve. The EBA-RAM's ease of use is attributed to its making a complex environment look simple, and easy to understand design. This simplicity was associated with the rows and columns of the model (Table 11.1). The comprehensive description of each cell in the model enhances employees' understanding of factors.

Organisations in all industries operate in dynamic environments. Constantly changing environments affect the business and IT structures, making some environments complex. Rakgoale and Mentz (2015) explained that IT landscapes continue to be a challenge due to constantly changing requirements and globalisation. These add to the complex environment. Numerous research conducted in the areas of business architecture does not aim to assess implementation gaps (Gromoff et al., 2017; Iacob et al., 2014). EBA implementation has been slow primarily because many organisations do not have a clear understanding of how to transform from it being a concept to practice. Also, it is difficult to demonstrate and quantify the value of EBA changes without being able to detect the risks and the bridging mechanism. The EBA-RAM is an easy-to-use approach that supports business model–driven migration from a baseline to the deployment of EBA.

11.7 Implications for Enterprise Business Architecture Practice

It is not sufficient to test a model; we need to be aware of the implications for practice. Significantly, there are implications for business managers, IT managers, and architects. For the EBA-RAM to add value to an organisation, the constantly changing nature of both business and IT requirements must be thoroughly understood. This requires effective service capability that must be developed and retained. In addition, the EBA-RAM should be enforced through governance which consists of policies, standards, and principles. This is to ensure that benefits are achieved beyond the implementation of the model.

Also, an organisation that intends to apply the EBA-RAM needs to develop two different requirements, one for the assessment model and the other for EBA. The two sets of requirements must complement each other to ensure the corroboration of capabilities and identification of opportunities for business process change. Applying the EBA-RAM creates a project that benefits the future of the organisation.

11.8 Summary

The business model concept has rich theoretical roots. The theoretical contribution of the chapter is the validation of the model, which connects findings from earlier literature and identifies new insights. From the practice front, the core stakeholders (architects, information technology [IT] managers, business managers, and project sponsors) now have a pragmatic tool for decreasing uncertainty before and during the implementation of the enterprise business architecture (EBA) in their organisations. Through the translation concept of actor–network theory (ANT), we provide the analysis of the outcome from the evaluation of an assessment model for EBA by examining the alliances in the process. The concept of translation helps to reveal relationship and rationality, based on which we propose a construct that extends previous research on how EBA can be deployed for value purposes. Applying ANT in the study, therefore, contributes to the evolving nature of the theory.

It is well documented that the deployment and practice of business architecture have been slow. The rationale for the slow pace seems to remain a mystery, despite the many studies conducted concerning the subject. This is the main significance of this chapter: empirically revealing the factors that can influence the business architecture readiness in an enterprise. The findings are so important that they have bearing and influence from both academic and enterprise (business/organisation) perspectives. On the one hand, the chapter demonstrates the criticality of readiness and assessment in the deployment and practice of business architecture. On the other hand, it creates awareness for the stakeholders of the concept in both academic and business domains.

From the academic front, the chapter theoretically positions the factors for further examination in the deployment and practice of business architecture.

Also, the chapter adds to existing academic resources, towards developing capacity and business architecture artefacts. Another significant aspect of the chapter is that it provides additional material for information systems (IS) and information management scholars or researchers that focus on the topic of business architecture. In practice, the chapter reveals factors of readiness and assessment which can be used as guidelines for practitioners, including business managers, information technology specialists, and enterprise and business architects in their quest to deploy and practice business architecture. The empirical nature of the findings gives the stakeholders the confidence to use the factors in formulating policies, standards, and principles for business architecture. Thus, the factors contribute to bridging the gap that makes business architecture lag in organisations.

References

Aji, A. S., & Widodo, T. (2019). Measuring enterprise architecture readiness at higher education institutions. *International Journal of Applied Business and Information Systems*, *3*(1), 14–20.

Akunyumu, S., Fugar, F., Adinyira, E., & Danku, J. (2021). A review of models for assessing readiness of construction organisations to innovate. *Construction Innovation*, *21*(2), 279–299.

Al-Ghamdi, A.-M. (2017). A proposed model to measure the impact of business architecture. *Cogent Business and Management*, *4*(1), 1405493.

Al-Ghamdi, A.-M., & Saleem, F. (2016). The impact of ICT applications in the development of business architecture Enterprises. *International Journal of Managerial Studies and Research*, *4*(4), 22–28.

Amit, R., & Zott, C. (2015). Crafting business architecture: The antecedents of business model design. *Strategic Entrepreneurship Journal*, *9*(4), 331–350.

Bakar, N., Harihodin, S., & Kama, N. (2016). Assessment of enterprise architecture implementation capability and priority in public sector agency. *Procedia Computer Science*, *100*(1), 198–206.

Banaeianjahromi, N. (2018, May 29–31). Where enterprise architecture development fails: A multiple case study of governmental organizations. In *The proceedings of the 12th international conference on research challenges in information science (RCIS)* (pp. 1–9). IEEE.

Best, J., & Walters, W. (2013). "Actor-network theory" and international relationality: Lost (and found) in translation: Introduction. *International Political Sociology*, *7*(3), 332–334.

Birke, F. M., & Knierim, A. (2020). ICT for agriculture extension: Actor-network theory for understanding the establishment of agricultural knowledge centers in South Wollo, Ethiopia. *Information Technology for Development*, *26*(3), 591–606.

Boudreau, M. C., Gefen, D., & Straub, D. W. (2001). Validation in information systems research: A state-of-the-art assessment. *MIS Quarterly*, *25*(1),1–16.

Burga, R., & Rezania, D. (2017). Project accountability: An exploratory case study using actor—network theory. *International Journal of Project Management, 35*(6), 1024–1036.

Callon, M. (1986). Some elements of a sociology of translation: Domestication of the scallops and the fishermen of St Brieuc Bay. In J. Law (Ed.), *Power, action & belief: A new sociology of knowledge?* (pp. 196–229). Routledge.

Callon, M. (1991). Techno-economic networks and irreversibility. In J. Law (Ed.), *A sociology of monsters. Essays on power, technology and domination* (pp. 132–161). Routledge.

Conboy, K., Fitzgerald, G., & Mathiassen, L. (2012). Qualitative methods research in information systems: Motivations, themes, and contributions. *European Journal of Information Systems, 21*(2), 113–118.

Davis, F. D. (1989). Perceived usefulness, perceived ease of use, and user acceptance of information technology. *Management Information Systems (MIS) Quarterly, 13*(3), 319–340.

Devi, W. P., & Kumar, H. (2018). Frugal innovations and actor—network theory: A case of bamboo shoots processing in Manipur, India. *The European Journal of Development Research, 30*(1), 66–83.

Eisenhardt, K. M. (1989). Building theories from case study research. *Academy of Management Review, 14*(4), 532–550.

Felski, R. (2016). Comparison and translation: A perspective from actor-network theory. *Comparative Literature Studies, 53*(4), 747–765.

Gehman, J., Glaser, V. L., Eisenhardt, K. M., Gioia, D., Langley, A., & Corley, K. G. (2018). Finding theory—method fit: A comparison of three qualitative approaches to theory building. *Journal of Management Inquiry, 27*(3), 284–300.

Gonzalez-Lopez, F., & Bustos, G. (2019). Integration of business process architectures within enterprise architecture approaches: A literature review. *Engineering Management Journal, 31*(2), 127–140.

Green, A. M., Brand, B. R., & Glasson, G. E. (2019). Applying actor—network theory to identify factors contributing to no persistence of African American students in STEM majors. *Science Education, 103*(2), 241–263.

Gromoff, A., Bilinkis, Y., & Kazantsev, N. (2017). Business architecture flexibility as a result of knowledge-intensive process management. *Global Journal of Flexible Systems Management, 18*(1), 73–86.

Hadaya, P., & Gagnon, B. (2017). *Business architecture: The missing link in strategy formulation, implementation and execution.* ASATE Publishing.

Heeks, R., & Stanforth, C. (2015). Technological change in developing countries: Opening the black box of process using actor—network theory. *Development Studies Research, 2*(1), 33–50.

Hendrickx, H. H., Daley, S. K., Mahakena, M., & von Rosing, M. (2011, September 5–7). Defining the business architecture profession. In *2011 IEEE 13th conference on commerce and enterprise computing* (pp. 325–332). IEEE.

Hidayat, T., & Mahardiko, R. (2020, December 10). Validation of information technology value model for petroleum industry. In *The proceedings of the 3rd international seminar on research of information technology and intelligent systems (ISRITI)* (pp. 1–6). IEEE.

Hussein, S., Mahrin, M., Maarop, N., & Bakar, A. (2019). Content validation of an Enterprise Architecture (EA) readiness assessment instrument. *Journal of Physics: Conference Series, 1196*(1), 1–9.

Hussein, S., Mahrin, M., Maarop, N., & Bakar, N. (2020). Development and validation of Enterprise Architecture (EA) readiness assessment model. *International Journal on Advance Science Engineering Information Technology*, 157–163.

Iacob, M. E., Meertens, L. O., Jonkers, H., Quartel, D. A., Nieuwenhuis, L. J., & Van Sinderen, M. J. (2014). From enterprise architecture to business models and back. *Software & Systems Modelling, 13*(3), 1059–1083.

Islam, A. N., Mäntymäki, M., & Turunen, M. (2019). Why do blockchains split? An actor-network perspective on Bitcoin splits. *Technological Forecasting and Social Change, 148*, 119743.

Iyamu, T. (2015). *Application of underpinning theories in information systems*. Heidelberg Press.

Iyamu, T. (2018). What are the implications of theorizing the enterprise architecture? *Journal of Enterprise Transformation, 8*(3–4), 143–164.

Iyamu, T. (2021). *Applying theories for information systems research*. Routledge.

Iyamu, T. (2022). *Enterprise architecture for strategic management of modern IT solutions*. Routledge, CRC Press.

Iyamu, T., & Mgudlwa, S. (2018). Transformation of healthcare big data through the lens of actor network theory. *International Journal of Healthcare Management, 11*(3), 182–192.

Iyamu, T., Nehemia-Maletzky, M., & Shaanika, I. (2016). The overlapping nature of business analysis and business architecture: What we need to know. *The Electronic Journal Information Systems Evaluation, 19*(3), 169–179.

Jahani, B., Javadein, S., & Jafari, H. (2010). Measurement of enterprise architecture readiness within organizations. *Business Strategies Series, 11*(3), 177–191.

Javanbakht, M., Pourkamali, M., & Derakhshi, M. (2009, August 23–29). A new method for enterprise architecture assessment and decision-making about improvement or redesign. In *The proceedings of the 4th international multi-conference on computing in the global information technology* (pp. 69–76). IEEE.

Jayakrishnan, M., Mohamad, A. K., & Yusof, M. M. (2020). Business architecture model in strategic information system management for effective railway supply chain perspective. *International Journal of Engineering Research and Technology, 13*(11), 3927–3933.

Kim, C., Kim, K., Lee, J., Kang, D., & Ryu, K. (2013). Ontology-based process model for business architecture of a virtual enterprise. *International Journal of Computer Integrated Manufacturing, 26*(7), 583–595.

Kinder, E., Jarrahi, M. H., & Sutherland, W. (2019, October 1–4). Gig platforms, tensions, alliances and ecosystems: An actor-network perspective. In *The proceedings of the ACM on human-computer interaction (CSCW)*. ACM Press.

Kitsios, F., & Kamariotou, M. (2019). Business strategy modelling based on enterprise architecture: A state-of-the-art review. *Business Process Management Journal, 25*(4), 606–624.

Kotusev, S. (2019). Enterprise architecture and enterprise architecture artifacts: Questioning the old concept in light of new findings. *Journal of Information Technology, 34*(2), 102–128.

Law, J. (1992). Notes on the theory of the actor-network: Ordering, strategy, and heterogeneity. *Systems Practice, 5*(4), 379–393.

Law, J., & Callon, M. (1997). The life and death of an aircraft: a network analysis of technical change. In W. E. Bijker & J. Law (Eds.), *Shaping technology/building society: Studies in sociotechnical change* (pp. 21–52). MIT Press.

Lee, H.-W., & Yung, I.-S. (2010). A comparative study on business architecture and business strategy. *Journal of Statistics & Management Systems, 13*(3), 617–625.

Lin, F., Fofanah, S. S., & Liang, D. (2011). Assessing citizen adoption of e-Government initiatives in Gambia: A validation of the technology acceptance model in information systems success. *Government Information Quarterly, 28*(2), 271–279.

Markus, M. L., & Lee, A. S. (1999). *Special issue on intensive research in information systems: Using qualitative, interpretive, and case methods to study Information technology: Forward.* Management Information Systems (MIS) Quarterly, 35–38.

Molla, A., Cooper, V. A., & Pittayachawan, S. (2009, December 15–18). IT and eco-sustainability: Developing and validating a green IT readiness model. In *International conference on information systems (ICIS)*. Association of Information Systems Press.

Őri, D. (2014). Misalignment symptom analysis based on enterprise architecture model assessment. *IADIS International Journal on Computer Science & Information Systems, 9*(2), 146–158.

Peppard, J., & Ward, J. (2004). Beyond strategic information systems: Towards an IS capability. *The Journal of Strategic Information Systems, 13*(2), 167–194.

Pirola, F., Cimini, C., & Pinto, R. (2020). Digital readiness assessment of Italian SMEs: A case-study research. *Journal of Manufacturing Technology Management, 31*(5), 1045–1083.

Rakgoale, M., & Mentz, J. (2015, October 14–15). Proposing a measurement model to determine enterprise architecture success as a feasible mechanism to align business and IT. In *The proceedings of the international conference on enterprise systems* (pp. 214–224). IEEE.

Roelens, B., Steenacker, W., & Poels, G. (2019). Realizing strategic fit within the business architecture: The design of a Process-Goal Alignment modelling and analysis technique. *Software & Systems Modelling, 18*(1), 631–662.

Ross, J., Weill, P., & Robertson, D. (2006). *Enterprise architecture as strategy: Creating a foundation for business execution.* Harvard Business Press.

Sarker, S., Xiao, X., & Beaulieu, T. (2012, December 16–19). Towards an anatomy of "successful" qualitative research manuscripts in IS: A critical review and some recommendations. In *The proceedings of the 33rd international conference on information systems (ICIS)*. Association of Information Systems (AIS) Press.

Seppanen, V., Penttinen, K., & Pulkkinen, M. (2018). Key issues in enterprise architecture adoption in the public sector. *Electronic Journal of E-Government, 16*(1), 46–58.

Shaanika, I., & Iyamu, T. (2018). Developing the enterprise architecture for the Namibian. *The Electronic Journal of Information Systems in Developing Countries, 84*(3), 1–13.

Shanks, G., Gloet, M., Someh, I., Frampton, K., & Tamm, T. (2018). Achieving benefits with enterprise architecture. *Journal of Strategic Information Systems, 27*(2), 139–156.

Shiga, J. (2007). Translations: Artifacts from an actor-network perspective. *Artefact: Journal of Design Practice, 1*(1), 40–55.

Tao, Z., Luo, Y., Chen, C., & Wang, M. (2017). Enterprise application architecture development based on DoDAF and TOGAF. *Enterprise Information Systems, 11*(5), 627–651.

Tsai, J. M., Cheng, M. J., Tsai, H. H., Hung, S. W., & Chen, Y. L. (2019). Acceptance and resistance of telehealth: The perspective of dual-factor concepts in technology adoption. *International Journal of Information Management, 49*, 34–44.

Versteeg, G., & Bouwman, H. (2006). Business architecture: A new paradigm to relate business strategy to ICT. *Information Systems Frontiers, 8*(2), 91–102.

Vickers, D. A., Moore, A., & Vickers, L. (2018). Performative narrative and actor-network theory—a study of a hotel in administration. *International Journal of Organizational Analysis, 26*(5), 972–983.

Walsham, G. (1997). Actor-network theory and IS research: Current status and future prospects. In *Information systems and qualitative research*. Springer.

Whittle, R., & Myrick, C. (2016). *Enterprise business architecture: The formal link between strategy and results*. CRC Press.

Yin, R. K. (2017). *Case study research and applications: Design and methods* (6th ed.). SAGE Publications.

Yusif, S., Hafeez-Baig, A., & Soar, J. (2017). e-Health readiness assessment factors and measuring tools: A systematic review. *International Journal of Medical Informatics, 107*, 56–64.

Zondani, T., & Iyamu, T. (2021). Towards an enterprise business architecture readiness assessment model. In *Empowering businesses with collaborative enterprise architecture frameworks* (pp. 90–109). IGI Global.

Chapter 12

Institutionalisation of Enterprise Architecture

12.1 Introduction

This chapter focuses on the institutionalisation of the concept of enterprise architecture (EA). Therefore, it is only logical to begin by clarifying the meaning of institutionalisation in the context of this book. In this chapter and book, institutionalisation is defined as the process whereby practice is assimilated into the norm. It is not easily disassociated, dismantled, or redesigned. Callon (1991) refers to institutionalisation as the degree of irreversibility, which depends on: (i) the extent to which it is subsequently impossible to go back to a point where that translation was only one amongst others; and (ii) the extent to which it shapes and determines subsequent translations. Institutionalisation is a social construct that exists not in objective reality but because of human interaction. Also, it exists because humans agree that it exists.

In the last decade, reliance on information technology (IT) solutions has increased tremendously, simplistically put, because of its amplified usefulness and relevance. Subsequently, there have been efforts to improve IT operations. The most critical aspect is the relationship between IT and the business community. This includes its role in the vision and strategy of organisations (Abouzahra & Ghasemaghaei, 2022; Radeke, 2010). This has led to improvements in the processes and activities in many organisations' computing environments. The business processes, too, have increased in complexity (Rahmanian et al., 2022). Despite the efforts, many organisations continue to struggle with business design and processes, while some still find it difficult to realise return on investment (ROI) on their IT solutions.

Thus, many organisations employ EA, as detailed in previous Chapters 3–11 of this book. Due to its significance, EA has been employed to guide, support, manage, and govern the business design, information artefacts, and IT solutions across industries, including the health (Masuda et al., 2018; McDermott, 2016), financial (Kotusev et al., 2020), and education (Williamson, 2018) sectors in public and private institutions. EA is a technical mechanism which defines the role of the business, information, and technical and application architectures that best support and enable the business needs of an enterprise, and it provides the migration plan which moves the enterprise from the current to the future architectural direction. This definition is provided to guide the study. This definition is buttressed by many studies such as Harmon (2005) who argues that architecture is becoming the prime representation of the enterprise. It is being used more and more as the basis for determining enhancement requirements and rationalising investments in capability development.

EA helps to improve quality and leverage existing efforts by constructing and applying multi-use and reuse of assets such as business patterns and IT solutions. Through the model, some studies suggest constructs to guide the conceptualisation, construction, and refinement of EA in organisations (Vallerand et al., 2017) without visible consideration for practice and institutionalisation. Consequently, demonstrating the business value and ROI of EA has proven elusive and challenging (Shanks et al., 2018). According to Dang and Pekkola (2020), in contrast to the benefits presented by EA, challenges exist and are highly likely to increase, which will often lead to implementation failure of EA.

Consequently, many organisations are increasingly relying on EA primarily to avoid business process disenfranchisement (Srinivas et al., 2021; Gonzalez-Lopez & Bustos, 2019), information fragmentation (Fahim et al., 2021), and conflicts of IT solutions (Ahlemann et al., 2021; Spijkman et al., 2021). Any of these consequential factors can lead to the refactoring of governance and management, which is a catalyst for the derailment of process and regression of competitiveness. Thus, Shaanika and Iyamu (2018) explain how the deployment of EA has implications in practice for both human and non-human actors, which includes IT architects, business users and managers, technology vendors, and IT solutions. Constantinides et al. (2018) claim that there is evidence to show that value-creating interactions between the actors renew opportunities for dynamically changing both organisational structures and the EA.

Chronically, although it seems clear, there is in practice confusion about EA deployment, from business architecture and information architecture to technical enterprise architecture perspectives. This confusion has continued for many years to this day, and it affects how EA is implemented, practised, and institutionalised in organisations. The institutionalisation of EA entails the inscription of the norm about the concept into individuals and groups in an organisation. It starts with successful deployment (development and implementation); next, the practice and the iterative process must be stable. This requires the routinisation of governance (policies, principles, and standards). Al-Kharusi et al. (2021) reveal standardisation, development scope, principles, and management capability as some of the factors influencing EA implementation and practice in organisations. Also, limited empirical research that examines or focuses on EA in the context of routinisation exists (Sukur & Lind, 2022).

The general expectation is that EA is a promising means of aligning business with IT units, governing information flow, and leveraging IT solutions with business initiatives to enhance competitiveness and improve the sustainability of an organisation (Iyamu, 2022). Thus, unsurprisingly, EA has increasingly become a popular topic of debate and discussion in recent years, primarily in the IT industry but also elsewhere (Kotusev et al., 2023; Ross et al., 2006). Despite the interest, it is very difficult to find an organisation that has successfully implemented and institutionalised EA. In some organisations, EA has been implemented to a certain extent (Ajer et al., 2021; Armour et al., 2007), while other organisations experience challenges in their attempt to institutionalise it. In a similar study, Zachman (1987, p. 281) points out that: "Many organisations face complex and unwieldy challenges in assessing and articulating the components required in the implementation of EA in their organisations". The institutionalisation of EA has not been a smooth or easy process. This could be attributed to the importance attached to the subject.

EA is fundamental to processes and activities in the computing environment, including the selection of IT solutions and the modelling of business patterns (Sari et al., 2021). As such, the problematisation, development, and implementation of EA are critical to the success or failure of its institutionalisation. The non-technical factors such as people and policies are critical in the development, implementation, and practice of EA in organisations. The enrolment of employees in the implementation of EA primarily dictates its competitive advantage, particularly in large organisations. However, as established in previous chapters, there exist human- and technology-related, including process-related, challenges. Some of the challenges in the development and implementation of EA include skillsets, processes, and manageability. According to Burke (2007), not everyone is an architect, but many technologists are unfortunately appointed as architects in some organisations. Other challenges include the lack of alignment between IT and business.

This chapter aims to help gain a deeper understanding of the sociotechnical factors that can affect and influence the institutionalisation of EA in an organisation. In achieving this aim, the objectives are streamlined threefold. The first aspect focuses on the relationship between technical and non-technical factors in the development, implementation, and practice of EA. The second part covers the roles of actors in the development, implementation, and practice of EA in an organisation. Attention is drawn to the non-technical factors such as people and processes in the last part, to better appreciate how certain factors influence the practice of EA in an organisation. Investigating the success factors of EA implementation and institutionalisation is essential to increasing its success rate (Bakar & Hussien, 2018). Essentially, Saint-Louis and Lapalme (2018) demonstrate how EA is not only an IT issue but also a strategic and organisational challenge. One of the main challenges of the existing studies is their abstract or contradictory nature (Niemi & Pekkola, 2020).

The chapter is structured into five main sections. Logically, it begins with the introductory section. Next, a literature review is conducted on the institutionalisation of the EA concept. The institutionalisation of EA is examined in the section that follows. Based on this, the factors that determine the implementation of EA are established and discussed in the next section. The following section covers the factors that influence the institutionalisation of EA in an organisation. Finally, a conclusion is drawn and the contribution of the chapter is highlighted.

12.2 Institutionalisation of Enterprise Architecture

EA is an approach for the integration of business and IT units, including the design and management of their processes and artefacts. Martin et al. (2010) argue that EA addresses the strategic and operational needs and shapes the heterogeneity, isolated, or distributed processes and artefacts across units and channels within an organisation. According to Gong and Janssen (2019), the concept of EA is broad and it is therefore interpreted and applied in many different ways. EA can be employed as a strategic tool for achieving IT solutions needs and challenges (Niemi & Pekkola, 2020). Kotusev et al. (2022) argue that EA is a comprehensive blueprint, which covers the core facets, such as business processes, information flow, and IT solutions of an organisation. EA has many claimed benefits, including the enterprise-wide capability for governance and management of the business and IT needs and challenges, making it increasingly attractive to practitioners and continuing to draw academic interest (Tamm et al., 2022).

Thus, EA's cruciality makes it necessary to institutionalise it beyond implementation. Simplistically, institutionalisation can be defined as the process of legitimately establishing a practice as a norm (Weiss et al., 2013). Pishdad and Haider (2013) describe institutionalisation as when the usage of an approach becomes stable, routinised, and embedded within the organisation's work processes and value chain. Seppänen et al. (2018) argue that institutionalisation is key to a legitimate practice of EA. A new arrangement or approach is considered institutionalised if it is widely accepted and practised (Ajer et al., 2021).

One of the factors of EA's increasing popularity is its support of efficiency and effectiveness from the perspectives of both business and IT units. According to Iyamu and Hamunyela (2013), the growing interest in the concept is not a determinant of its institutionalisation in organisations. There are other influencing factors and challenges, which are technical and non-technical, internal and external in nature. Faller and De Kinderen (2014) identified cultural differences among the stakeholders as one of the factors that hamper the institutionalisation of EA in organisations.

The institutionalisation of EA has many challenges, many of which have not been addressed. Hence, it is difficult to find organisations that have institutionalised the concept. As a contributing factor to the challenges, there are very few studies that have explored the factors that influence EA institutionalisation (Dang & Pekkola, 2016) or examined barriers to its institutionalisation (Dang, 2019).

The criticality of EA institutionalisation has since been identified, without contrast. Boh and Yellin (2006) emphasised the importance of institutionalising the concept to smoothly facilitate its activities in organisations. Typically, organisations will continue to struggle with EA without institutionalising the concept (Tamm et al., 2011a). For various reasons, the institutionalisation of EA remains a challenge in many organisations (Weiss et al., 2013). The success or failure of EA in an organisation depends on the support and understanding of many IT architects of the criticality of management and buy-in of other stakeholders (Niemi & Pekkola, 2020). Ilin et al. (2021a) suggest that EA harmonises the operationalisation of IT and business strategies. Thus, EA institutionalisation in an organisation is crucial. Institutionalisation is considered useful and critical in that it embeds the practice of EA in an organisation (Ajer et al., 2021).

Institutionalisation stabilises change in an environment. Weiss et al. (2013) argue that the effectiveness and ROI of EA implementation lie in its institutionalisation. Pishdad and Haider (2013) suggest that one of the benefits of institutionalisation is that it propels the 'generative' influence of IT solutions. Also, institutionalisation helps to streamline the process of defining individual roles and responsibilities (Iyamu & Mphahlele, 2014).

Different factors influence the process of institutionalisation (Mignerat & Rivard, 2009), from technical and non-technical standpoints. Iyamu (2009) reveals some of the factors that influence the institutionalisation of EA as non-technical, including organisational structure. According to Iyamu and Mphahlele (2014), organisational policies must be structured to institutionalise EA deployment and practice. Relatively, the importance of institutionalisation and its influencing factors vary in organisations and periodically (Dang & Pekkola, 2016). Furthermore, Weiss (2017) explains the necessity of institutionalising EA to anchor the coordination of its activities and processes. Seppänen et al. (2018) advocate the use of prerequisites in assessing and determining the institutionalisation of EA in organisations. This makes it an organisational responsibility rather than an IT duty. Dang (2019) argues that literature suggests factors influencing EA institutionalisation include legitimacy and alignment. EA plans and values are realised when business processes and IT solutions are implemented and remain stable for competitiveness (Niemi & Pekkola, 2020).

Thus, Iyamu and Hamunyela (2013) argue that the challenges of institutionalisation of EA make its strategic use difficult, which negatively affects the value contribution to an organisation. EA brings benefits and challenges by implementing and institutionalising it in an organisation (Van Zijl & Van Belle, 2014). Ajer et al. (2021) explain that there is a challenge in proving the value of EA, which is a critical obstacle to its institutionalisation process. Some of these challenges arise from limited empirical evidence. From empirical study, Dang and Pekkola (2016) show how rules, norms, and values change and influence the institutionalisation of EA in an organisation. However, only a few studies have been conducted on the institutionalisation of EA in organisations (Dang, 2019). Of the few studies, institutionalisation does not reach a plateau after implementation but contains downfalls and complexities (Ajer et al., 2021).

12.3 Institutionalisation of Enterprise Architecture in Organisations

To recap, the focus of this chapter is on better understanding of the factors which influence the institutionalisation of EA in organisations. Thus, the concentration is primarily on the non-technical issues in the implementation and practice of EA in an organisation. The institutionalisation of EA begins with a sequence of phases, from business visioning (extracted from business strategy), which defines and refines the respective domains, enterprise business architecture (EBA), enterprise information architecture (EIA), enterprise technical architecture (ETA), and enterprise application architecture (EAA). This is conveyed in a logical sequence of development based on interconnectedness and dependencies of the domains' phases, rather than a linear sequence of events. Though inter-related, each domain has a unique focus which enacts the EA as the union of an enterprise. Thus, the EA must be defined through a pragmatic need: the need to design and redesign, as it is intended to improve the functioning of the organisation.

Based on the focus of the chapter, it is necessary that EA is initiated by the chief technology officer (CTO) or chief information officer (CIO), depending on the structure of the organisation. IT architects, IT managers, project managers, business managers, and business users are the other actors or stakeholders usually involved in the implementation of EA in many organisations. Briefly, the IT architects are responsible for the development, while the IT managers, project managers, and business managers are typically tasked with the implementation of EA. The rationale for identifying the involved actors is to associate their roles with contributions towards the institutionalisation of the EA concept in an organisation.

Characteristically, IT managers and business managers dominate or remain the focal actors in the areas of technology and business aspects of architecture, respectively. The project managers facilitate the processes for both the IT manager and business managers. Within the rules and regulations set out in many organisations' policies, managers have the power to allocate tasks to individuals and groups, and to approve and terminate processes. Other stakeholders include business and IT analysts, software programmers, technology infrastructure specialists, and network administrators. Each of these stakeholders is tasked with secondary and detailed activities in the implementation of EA in organisations.

Typically, EA is developed and implemented with the intention of significant benefits and value at the level of strategic IT solutions' implementation and business engineering. Also, in practice, organisations expect EA to support and enable rapid change in the design, processes, management, and other activities of an organisation. According to Niemi and Pekkola (2020), EA can be employed as a strategic tool for achieving needs and challenges of business and IT solutions. The deliverables of EA are executed through its domains: EBA, EIA, ETA, and EAA. The intentions must be well articulated to enable a competitive advantage. Some of the key deliverables include the selection, deployment, and management of IT solutions, from software and databases to sever infrastructure, business processes, and information flow.

In assessing the deliverables, critical success factors (CSFs) should be formulated in the context of an organisation. Some of the common CSFs are cost reduction, rationalisation of IT solutions, enabling and optimisation of business processes, information value network optimisation, and organised application development and implementation. The CSFs are defined by the organisational vision and EA requirements, which are key for sustainability and competitive advantage (Iyamu, 2022). The CSFs influence and are influenced by the practitioners, stakeholders, and sponsors, either in the development or implementation phases. Thus, CSFs are used as a measurement and justification of the investment in EA. Due to the importance associated with EA in an organisation, processes and activities in the development and implementation are often highly politicised and are sometimes grossly overhyped. Usually, organisational politics are not a catalyst for stability. Therefore, politics can have an impact on the institutionalisation of EA in an organisation.

Organisational politics involve those activities undertaken within organisations to acquire, develop, and use power and other resources to obtain one's preferred outcomes in a situation in which there is uncertainty, lack of clarity, or lack of consensus about choices. Chaung and Lobberenberg (2010) argue that politics are a critical element to consider in the implementation and practice of EA. From the EA implementation perspective, Iyamu and Mphahlele (2014) explain how the different interests of stakeholders are often pursued through organisational politics, and therefore should not be taken for granted. Politics are evident and cannot be undermined. An organisational structure is a key component of organisational politics and power is the focal point of organisational structure. Pichault (1995) opines that the system of power distribution is characterised by relative stability: it is part of the organisational structure and may not be modified by a simple managerial intervention since it relates to other variables such as the task environment of the operators and the coordination mechanisms.

Each EA domain provides a unique view of an enterprise, which leads to its capabilities. It begins with the EBA's intention to provide the tools, models, and techniques for participants to manage the impact which change has on business activities and processes, including their partners. This practice is supported and enabled by EIA to enable the management of change in information flow and exchange, the ETA to enable the management of change in technology infrastructure, and the EAA to enable the development and the portfolio management of software applications. Tamm et al. (2022) suggest that EA assists in improving service delivery through enhanced coordination, contextual awareness, and accelerated guiding standards.

Specialised skills are needed in the development, implementation, and practice of EA. Not all IT specialists can be architects without the opportunity to learn and practice the tools and techniques required. This is covered in Chapter 13 of this book. A lack of appropriate skills implies and exposes the inability to perform competently and to recognise and articulate EA deliverables in an organisation. Thus, even when the process is understood, there are possibilities that the potential and objectives of EA would not be realised, which threatens ROI and challenges competitive advantage. It thus appears that the technical know-how and experiences of architects and their managers assume significance in applying the CFSs and achieving EA objectives in an organisation. Thus, according to Niemi and Pekkola (2020), IT architects should understand the criticality of their roles and the support of their managers and other stakeholders. Such understanding enables accessing organisational resources in addressing challenges during EA implementation and post-implementation (institutionalisation) in a holistic manner. (Georgiadis & Poels, 2021).

When it comes to EA implementation, there are feeble relationships between the IT and business units in many organisations. Usually, this results from the hierarchical structure of the organisations. Some employees employ such inimical situations to protect their domains from the EA team. Consequently, it becomes difficult to receive sufficient input from the business unit during the development and implementation of EA. As a result, some organisations had rather focus more on the EAA and ETA domains, which hamper EA deliverables. Ismagilova et al. (2022) therefore cautioned against inherent complexity and methods of interaction and proposed an inclusive and corroborative response.

Consequently, simply defining the concept of EA has three fundamental consequences. First, it exposes gaps in the business processes and strategy. Second, it reveals the challenges in IT solutions' governance and deployment strategies. Third, it helps to uncover the nature of the relationship that exists between the business and IT units of the organisation. Hence, there are continued efforts and emphasis on how and why EA facilitates the integration, collaboration, standardisation, deduplication, and re-engineering of business processes and IT solutions (Kotusev & Kurnia, 2021; Chitsa & Iyamu, 2020). This reminds the IT architects and their managers of their obligations to confront difficult questions and make decisions they had previously managed to avoid, such as applying policies and principles rather than employing subjectivism in the selection of IT solutions. This helps to make the institutionalisation of EA easy and possible in an organisation.

An organisation formulates a policy to guide the development and implementation of EA into institutionalisation. The policy is to ensure a successful design, development, implementation, and maintenance of EA through fundamental principles. As detailed in previous chapters, the principles are basic philosophies intended to guide the processes, from the problematisation of EA to its institutionalisation stages. In achieving the deliverables of EA, the principles are conjunctly applied to the domains in the development, implementation, and practice of EA. The principles provide guidelines and rationales for the constant examination and re-evaluation of technology and systems plans (Fischer et al., 2010). The principles are generally derived from an intensive discussion with senior IT and business management, and then validated by organisational needs. Non-technical factors such as financial budgets, personal or group interests, and the capability of the organisation are influenced by the formulation of the principles.

Some of the primary objects of EA institutionalisation are methods, processes, disciplines, and organisational structures to create, manage, govern, and organise change to business and IT environments in a stable manner, consistently and uniformly, and to use models for managing the impact of change in the organisations. The research found in both case studies that organisations typically did not take a holistic view and that the practice of EA was deficient when measured against the organisations' strategy and requirements. This has been acknowledged and was attributed to a manifestation of a lack of cooperation and understanding between the business and IT departments of the organisations.

Habitually, the principles should be used as validation points or checkpoints in the implementation of EA towards its institutionalisation. Also, in this process, the use of principles helps to detect how some employees, including managers, fear that architects could become too powerful if given the necessary support. Other stakeholders seldom envision that the institutionalisation of EA could render them redundant. This thought or behaviour is often associated with business units' employees who do not have a good understanding of the EA concept. These actions contribute to hindering the institutionalisation of the concept. This is because when the business unit is dynamic; and when unavoidable change is forced upon the organisation, an inability to link the exploitation of IT investments with changes to strategic business goals leads to greater difficulties.

12.4 Enterprise Architecture Implementation Determinant Factor

From the analysis presented in this chapter, the factors that determine the implementation of EA towards institutionalisation are extracted. The factors manifest themselves to influence the nationalisation of EA in organisations, which is covered in the section that follows. The factors, as determinants, have an impact on the institutionalisation of EA in many organisations. As revealed from the analysis, there are four key elements in the development, implementation, and practice of EA. The four elements are considered key elements because they appear more

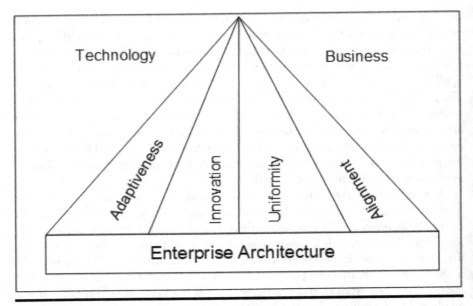

Figure 12.1   Factors of EA Institutionalisation.

important by their prevalence and are interconnected. As depicted in Figure 12.1, the factors are adaptation, innovation, uniformity, and alignment.

12.4.1 Adaptiveness

EA is adaptive, which enables it to be used to support business goals and objectives effectively and efficiently. Adaptability is a practice-based task executed through different channels of the EA domains. According to Gampfer et al. (2018), adaptive architecture enables an enterprise to be more sustainable and increases competitive advantage because it adapts to changing conditions rather than requiring a replacement. It is more beneficial when it is applied uniquely to the specific needs of the organisation, depending on its business strategies, architectural maturity, priorities, organisational culture, and political environment. Korhonen et al. (2016) argue that adaptiveness fortifies decision-making and helps to reduce environmental turbulence. Explicitly, IT solutions are to be adaptive to ensure ROI. Through adaptiveness, some consolidation and reuse could be achieved.

12.4.2 Innovation

EA engineers some innovations through its processes and activities in the organisations. Each EA domain has distinctive deliverables that can be associated with innovations. Ilin et al. (2021a) suggest that institutionalisation enables a stable innovative process, which is an essential capability for the competitiveness of an organisation. The primary aim of continuous innovations is to enhance the competitive advantage of an organisation's businesses, processes, and activities. proactively, innovation is used to promote and support the initiative of the organisation to achieve its CFSs. From Batmetan's (2022) empirical evidence, firmly, EA compels the planning and development of old and new business and IT solutions within its domain.

12.4.3 Uniformity

EA provides a uniform process and procedure for selecting IT solutions, documenting the current and future business, and detailing the gap between the current and future business. This is important, and it applies to the autonomous business units of organisations. It begins with project initiation and problematisation, ending at the implementation stages. Uniformity enables consistency of activities and ease of interaction towards achieving organisational goals and objectives (Shaanika & Iyamu, 2015). Thus, uniformity is instrumental to focusing on skill auditing, development, and assessment in alignment with organisational needs in the implementation of EA in an organisation.

12.4.4 Alignment

It is well documented that alignment is critical to EA's success or failure. This means that it is highly likely that EA will not work if there is no understanding between the business and IT management. In the circumstance that there is a lack of cooperation between the two management teams, events manifest themselves into rivalry on many issues, such as business-preferred processes and methods or criteria for the selection of IT solutions, business process standards, governance approach, and assessment criteria. This has a vital influence and impact on stability, that is, on the institutionalisation of EA in the organisation. According to Tamm et al. (2022), EA services help an organisation to improve its alignment between business and IT units, to increase business needs, resource utilisation, and resource complementarity.

Only when these identified key elements (adaptation, innovation, uniformity, and alignment) become routinised norms can EA implementation and institutionalisation become feasible. However, the process of institutionalisation does not stop at one point; it is a stable iterative approach. Other factors can influence and have an impact on these key elements in the success or failure of EA. The inter-relationships between the key elements and critical factors are illustrated in Figure 12.2. If not well managed, the manifestations of these factors could derail the institutionalisation of EA in an organisation that deploys it.

12.5 Factors Influencing the Institutionalisation of EA

The factors previously presented and discussed are now interpreted with a focus on how they can influence the institutionalisation of EA in an organisation. Objectivism is employed in the interpretation based on EA institutionalisation. From the interpretation, six factors are found to be most influential in the attempt to institutionalise EA in organisations. The factors are organisational structure, economic investment, administration, organisational politics, technical capability, and buy-in. As depicted in Figure 12.2, the factors are grouped into three categories: process, leadership and technology. These categories are reached based on the analysis in which they were relatively prevalent.

The advantage of the model in Figure 12.1 is that it enables a better understanding of how the institutionalisation of EA can be influenced and affected in an organisation that deploys the concept. While the factors could enhance institutionalisation, using this model can assist in counteracting with appropriate measures.

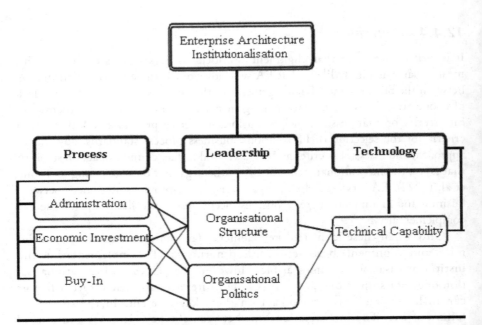

Figure 12.2 Factor Influencing Institutionalisation of EA.

12.5.1 *Organisational Structure*

Organisational structure plays a critical role in the implementation and practice of EA. The concept of EA is problematised through the structure of an organisation. This includes the development and implementation of EA, and how the architects including the business and IT managers perform their individual and group tasks. Zarvić and Wieringa (2014) suggest that organisational structure is one of the vital factors for the success or failure of EA in any organisation. Without structure, it is difficult or nearly impossible to develop and implement EA in organisations. this could be attributed to the fact that structure is embedded with roles, responsibilities, and power to execute the mandate of the organisation. As such, the organisational structure affects how alignments between units and departments within the organisation are shaped and adapted. How the organisation adapts and aligns its goals, in turn, manifests and influences innovation and uniformity across its business units.

The implementation and practice of EA require a deep understanding of the technical needs and business vision and requirements. As business processes change, projects are initiated, and technology grows, it becomes hard to structure an organisation to provide effective feedback loops which run between these constituencies. Although EA is intended to address this very area, if the organisation is predisposed to managing the activities in a challenging circumstance, then EA will not be an effective solution and it is highly likely to fail. According to Banaeianjahromi and Smolander (2019), an organisational structure is responsible for re-engineering business and IT processes and activities. Employees and other stakeholders legitimately employ their power to manoeuvre activities and processes within the organisational structure. In such circumstances, power is often exercised to protect individual and group interests rather than the interests of the organisation in the practice of EA.

12.5.2 *Economic Investment*

Funding for the implementation and practice of EA is critical in many organisations. Other important factors are the roles and responsibilities of the stakeholders because they determine the sponsorship and ownership of EA in an organisation. This depends on and is influenced by the structure of the organisation. In some organisations, the chief architect is in the IT department or unit, which is different from other organisations where the head of architecture is situated in the business unit. The investment in EA is influenced by where EA is situated—whether in the business or IT department. IT investment decisions appear to be important; hence, ownership is crucial (Van den Berg et al., 2019). The investment in EA determines how it is aligned with the IT and business goals and objectives, and it shapes its innovation capability and its uniformity across the organisation.

Supporting the concept of EA requires an economic investment, particularly if EA operates as a cost centre. Many organisations find it difficult to institute appropriate measures to fund their cost centre because the benefits are only indirectly evident and rarely are evident as simple financial benefits. Unfortunately, many architects are not able to articulate, translate, and quantify their work into monetary values. This could be attributed to the non-immediate realisation of their contributions. According to Ilin et al. (2021b), it is difficult to align EA investments with the strategic goals of the organisation, which affects the practice of the concept. As a result, its value is hotly contested by the business stakeholders in many organisations.

12.5.3 Administration

The administration of EA is often performed within the organisational structure as mandated by the policy, rules, and regulations of the organisation. This is primarily to ensure its manageability, which covers both technical and non-technical factors during the development, implementation, and practice of EA in the organisation. Administrative strategy or reform affects the functions that influence EA institutionalisation in an organisation (Ask & Hedström, 2011). Thus, the management focuses on how to gain uniformity across the units of the organisation. Otherwise, processes and activities would be duplicated and become exorbitant in the attempt to achieve organisational goals and objectives.

However, the administrative process depends on the participation of employees, particularly the stakeholders associated with the implementation and practice of EA. The administrative process of EA could be employed to promote adaptation, innovation, and alignment across the organisation. For example, the administrative process provides a channel through which innovation is embarked upon, including those who legitimately get involved and who lead the team. Due to administrative functions, many contemporary organisations regularly encounter challenges in achieving their business and IT needs (Saint-Louis & Lapalme, 2018), which subsequently derails efforts to institutionalise EA.

EA as something process-oriented makes it inevitable to align with the administrative process and the structure of the organisation. However, it is difficult to catalogue, archive and retrieve the 'as-is' (or silo) architectures across multiple business units within large organisations. Although it is common to scavenge small classes or functions opportunistically from existing programmes, architects often find it hard to consolidate suitable architecture outside their immediate area. This could be achieved through the effective and efficient administration of processes and activities.

12.5.4 Organisational Politics

Employees in the IT and business units often view architects with suspicion. This is because they resent the fact that they may no longer be empowered to make key technology and related decisions. They also perceive a threat to their job security and resource control. There is also rivalry between architects and other IT specialists over domination and ownership of tasks. Iyamu and Mphahlele (2014) emphasise that the diverse interests of stakeholders lead to the practice of organisational politics, which has the power to derail routines of EA tasks geared towards institutionalisation.

The factors of rivalry, struggle for ownership, resource control, and domination manifest themselves in acts of organisational politics, which result in a lack of trust and cooperation. These factors harm the relationship between the business and IT departments on the one hand, and on the other hand, between the IT specialists and architects. Tamm et al. (2011b) firmly stated that EA implementation is highly likely to be hampered by organisational politics.

12.5.5 Technical Capability

Capabilities can be engineered to focus on improving efficiency and reducing costs to transform key business processes and practices (Kasemsap, 2018), which contribute to the institutionalisation of the concept. Despite this historical awareness in some organisations, EA efforts frequently fail because some architects lack appropriate skills and the enterprise at large lacks the competencies necessary to develop, implement, and practice EA. This is a consequence of many architects being appointed based on their seniority in the organisation rather than skill. For instance, some architects lack knowledge and experience of the fundamental design patterns in the domain tasks they are assigned to undertake. Gong and Janssen (2021) revealed that EA-based benefit realisation is a more complex process than theoretically expressed and it is influenced by EA capability. Therefore, efforts should not be compromised.

Thus, Kasemsap (2018) suggests that EA capabilities functionally integrate the value chain and eliminate the non–value-added processes of an enterprise. However, many architects lack the abilities, knowledge, or skills required to effectively develop and implement EA. This is attributed to a lack of awareness or narrowness in vision, leading to very different interpretations and definitions of EA. Capability is the ability to achieve a goal, which prevents associated or available resources from being inconsequential to the operationalisation of strategic intents (Kitsios & Kamariotou, 2019). Also, this leads to incompatible views about the full range of required EA processes and phases, and it deprives the participants of the possibility of achieving best practices through a failure to take a holistic view of what must be done. This makes it hard for the stakeholders to understand how to implement and practice the EA frameworks and components effectively.

12.5.6 Business Buy-In

The strategy used for communicating with the business unit is critical. Poor communication leads to a general view amongst the business units that the architecture is inconsequential. If the concept of EA is not understood, the business unit finds it difficult to accept or 'buy-in' into the concept. Getting senior management buy-in is a challenge in many organisations because of the difficulty in showing or demonstrating the tangible value of EA (Khateeb, 2016). It is increasingly challenging in many organisations (Olsen, 2017). Lack of buy-in will always fail EA to achieve its aims and objectives.

An emphasis on the technical or application architecture domain of EA increases a lack of interest and understanding of EA by the business units. Arising from these factors is new pressure on IT units to improve the value for financial investment or provide ROI. However, many stakeholders argue that the IT unit has no means to achieve it because of the gulf between it and the business units. EA addresses this gap, but if it is not supported or sponsored by the business unit, failure is bound to happen and resultantly the problems remain. According to Olsen (2017), EA is an instrumental approach for aligning IT and business strategies. In practice, organisations rely on EA capabilities for their strategies (Gong & Janssen, 2021); hence, inclusiveness and buy-in are critical.

Many organisations face complex and unwieldy challenges in assessing and articulating the necessary changes in their environments. This includes the factors which influence and affect the practice of EA across an organisation. If an organisation is to be successful in bridging the context gap between the development and implementation of EA, including institutionalisation, a mechanism must be deployed to articulate the impact of the influencing factors on the enterprise. The institutionalisation of EA increases ROI and the quality of IT investment decisions (Van den Berg et al., 2019). Kitsios and Kamariotou (2019) insist on a matrix that can be used to measure the EA value and capabilities within an organisation.

12.6 Summary

The contribution of this chapter arises from implications for the key stakeholders, sponsors, and architects responsible for the development, implementation, and practice of enterprise architecture (EA) in an organisation. These stakeholders need to gain a deeper understanding of the factors that affect the institutionalisation of EA, in which they wholly play parts, and more importantly, how to mitigate the risks posed by these factors.

Another contribution of the chapter is its significance for decision-makers, including information technology (IT) managers, business managers, and architects within an organisation. This is because the influencing factors discussed in the chapters can guide EA-related decision-making. Also, it is expected that the key contribution will arise from the understanding of the fundamental elements through which EA impacts change. Through this will a better understanding of the contribution of non-technical factors in the development, implementation, and practice of EA be gained.

References

Abouzahra, M., & Ghasemaghaei, M. (2022). Effective use of information technologies by seniors: The case of wearable device use. *European Journal of Information Systems*, *31*(2), 241–255.

Ahlemann, F., Legner, C., & Lux, J. (2021). A resource-based perspective of value generation through enterprise architecture management. *Information & Management*, *58*(1), 103266.

Ajer, A. K., Hustad, E., Vassilakopoulou, P., & Olsen, D. H. (2021, June 14–16). Strengthening the use of enterprise architecture: An institutional work perspective. In *The proceedings of the 29th 29th European conference on information systems (ECIS)*. Association of Information Systems (AIS) Press.

Al-Kharusi, H., Miskon, S., & Bahari, M. (2021). Enterprise architects and stakeholders alignment framework in enterprise architecture development. *Information Systems and e-Business Management*, *19*(1), 137–181.

Armour, F., Kaisler, S., & Bitner, J. (2007, January 3–6). Enterprise architecture: Challenges and implementations. In *The proceedings of the 40th international conference on system sciences (HICSS)*. IEEE.

Ask, A., & Hedström, K. (2011). Taking initial steps towards enterprise architecture in local government. In *Electronic government and the information systems perspective: Second international conference (EGOVIS), Toulouse, France, August 29–September 2. Proceedings 2* (pp. 26–40). Springer.

Bakar, N. A. A., & Hussien, S. S. (2018). Association of people factors with successful enterprise architecture implementation. *International Journal of Engineering & Technology*, *7*(4.31), 52–57.

Banaeijahromi, N., & Smolander, K. (2019). Lack of communication and collaboration in enterprise architecture development. *Information Systems Frontiers*, *21*, 877–908.

Batmetan, J. R. (2022). Model enterprise architecture for information technology services in universities. *International Journal of Information Technology and Education*, *1*(4), 18–34.

Boh, W. F., & Yellin, D. (2006). Using enterprise architecture standards in managing information technology. *Journal of Management Information Systems*, *23*(3), 163–207.

Burke, B. (2007). *The role of enterprise architecture in technology research*. Gartner Inc. Retrieved April 14, 2010, from http://gartner.com/technology/research.jsp

Callon, M. (1991). Techno-economic networks and irreversibility. In J. Law (Ed.), *A sociology of monsters. Essays on power, technology and domination*. Routledge.

Chaung, C. J., & Lobberenberg, J. (2010, January 5–8). Challenges facing enterprise architects: A South African perspective. In *Proceeding of the 43rd Hawaii international conference on system sciences (HICSS)*. IEEE.

Chitsa, F., & Iyamu, T. (2020). Towards enterprise technical architecture for the implementation of the South African NHIA. *Advances in Science, Technology and Engineering Systems Journal*, *5*(2), 724–728.

Constantinides, P., Henfridsson, O., & Parker, G. G. (2018). Introduction—platforms and infrastructures in the digital age. *Information Systems Research*, *29*(2), 381–400.

Dang, D. D. (2019). Institutional logics and their influence on enterprise architecture adoption. *Journal of Computer Information Systems*, *61*(1), 42–52.

Dang, D. D., & Pekkola, S. (2016, June 12–15). Institutionalising enterprise architecture in the public sector in Vietnam. In *24th European conference on information systems (ECIS)*. Association of Information Systems (AIS) Press.

Dang, D. D., & Pekkola, S. (2020). Institutional perspectives on the process of enterprise architecture adoption. *Information Systems Frontiers*, *22*(6), 1433–1445.

Fahim, P. B., An, R., Rezaei, J., Pang, Y., Montreuil, B., & Tavasszy, L. (2021). An information architecture to enable track-and-trace capability in Physical Internet ports. *Computers in Industry*, *129*, 103443.

Faller, H., & De Kinderen, S. (2014, September 3–5). The impact of cultural differences on enterprise architecture effectiveness: A case study. In *The proceedings of the 8th mediterranean conference on information systems (MCIS)*. IEEE.

Fischer, C., Winter, R., & Aier, S. (2010). What is an enterprise architecture principle? Towards a consolidated definition. *Computer and Information Science*, *2010*, 193–205.

Gampfer, F., Jürgens, A., Müller, M., & Buchkremer, R. (2018). Past, current and future trends in enterprise architecture—A view beyond the horizon. *Computers in Industry*, *100*, 70–84.

Georgiadis, G., & Poels, G. (2021). Enterprise architecture management as a solution for addressing general data protection regulation requirements in a big data context: A systematic mapping study. *Information Systems and e-Business Management*, *19*(1), 313–362.

Gong, Y., & Janssen, M. (2019). The value of and myths about enterprise architecture. *International Journal of Information Management*, *46*, 1–9.

Gong, Y., & Janssen, M. (2021). Roles and capabilities of enterprise architecture in big data analytics technology adoption and implementation. *Journal of Theoretical and Applied Electronic Commerce Research*, *16*(1), 37–51.

Gonzalez-Lopez, F., & Bustos, G. (2019). Integration of business process architectures within enterprise architecture approaches: A literature review. *Engineering Management Journal*, *31*(2), 127–140.

Harmon, K. (2005, October 10–12). The "systems" nature of enterprise architecture. In *The proceedings of IEEE international conference on systems, man and cybernetics*. IEEE.

Ilin, I. V., Levina, A. I., Dubgorn, A. S., & Abran, A. (2021a). Investment models for enterprise architecture (Ea) and it architecture projects within the open innovation concept. *Journal of Open Innovation: Technology, Market, and Complexity*, *7*(1), 1–18.

Ilin, I. V., Maydanova, S., Levina, A., Jahn, C., Weigell, J., & Jensen, M. B. (2021b). Smart containers technology evaluation in an enterprise architecture context (business case for container liner shipping industry). In *Technological transformation: A new role for human, machines and management: TT-2020* (pp. 57–66). Springer International Publishing.

Ismagilova, E., Hughes, L., Rana, N. P., & Dwivedi, Y. K. (2022). Security, privacy and risks within smart cities: Literature review and development of a smart city interaction framework. *Information Systems Frontiers*, *24*(2), 393–414.

Iyamu, T. (2009). The factors affecting institutionalisation of enterprise architecture in the organisation. In *The proceedings of the 11th IEEE conference on commerce and enterprise computing* (pp. 221–225). IEEE Computer Society.

Iyamu, T. (2022). *Enterprise architecture for strategic management of modern IT solutions*. Routledge CRC Press.

Iyamu, T., & Hamunyela, S. (2013). Enterprise architecture strategic framework. *Issues in Information Systems, 14*(2), 60–70.

Iyamu, T., & Mphahlele, L. (2014). The impact of organisational structure on enterprise architecture deployment. *Journal of Systems and Information Technology, 16*(1), 2–19.

Kasemsap, K. (2018). The role of information system within enterprise architecture and their impact on business performance. In *Global business expansion: Concepts, methodologies, tools, and applications* (pp. 1078–1102). IGI Global.

Khateeb, Y. A. (2016, May 26–28). Enterprise architecture management (EAM) practice implementation success factors. In *The proceedings of universal technology management conference (UTMC)* (p. 27). The Society of Digital Information and Wireless Communications (SDIWC).

Kitsios, F., & Kamariotou, M. (2019). Business strategy modelling based on enterprise architecture: A state of the art review. *Business Process Management Journal, 25*(4), 606–624.

Korhonen, J. J., Lapalme, J., McDavid, D., & Gill, A. Q. (2016, August 29–September 1). Adaptive enterprise architecture for the future: Towards a reconceptualization of EA. In *2016 IEEE 18th conference on business informatics (CBI)* (Vol. 1, pp. 272–281). IEEE.

Kotusev, S., & Kurnia, S. (2021). The theoretical basis of enterprise architecture: A critical review and taxonomy of relevant theories. *Journal of Information Technology, 36*(3), 275–315.

Kotusev, S., Kurnia, S., & Dilnutt, R. (2022). The practical roles of enterprise architecture artifacts: A classification and relationship. *Information and Software Technology, 147,* 106897.

Kotusev, S., Kurnia, S., & Dilnutt, R. (2023). Enterprise architecture artifacts as boundary objects: An empirical analysis. *Information and Software Technology, 155,* 107108.

Kotusev, S., Kurnia, S., Taylor, P., & Dilnutt, R. (2020, January 7–10). Can enterprise architecture be based on the business strategy? In *The proceedings of the 53rd Hawaii international conference on system sciences (HICSS)*. Association of Information Systems (AIS) Press.

Martin, A., Dmitriev, D., & Akeroyd, J. (2010). A resurgence of interest in information architecture. *International Journal of Information Management, 30*(1), 6–12.

Masuda, Y., Shirasaka, S., Yamamoto, S., & Hardjono, T. (2018). Architecture board practices in adaptive enterprise architecture with digital platform: A case of global healthcare enterprise. *International Journal of Enterprise Information Systems (IJEIS), 14*(1), 1–20.

McDermott, K. (2016). Achieving data liquidity across health care requires a technical architecture. *Bulletin of the Association for Information Science and Technology, 43*(1), 19–22.

Mignerat, M., & Rivard, S. (2009). Positioning the institutional perspective in information systems research. *Journal of Information Technology, 24*(4), 369–391.

Niemi, E., & Pekkola, S. (2020). The benefits of enterprise architecture in organizational transformation. *Business & Information Systems Engineering, 62,* 585–597.

Olsen, D. H. (2017). Enterprise architecture management challenges in the Norwegian health sector. *Procedia Computer Science, 121,* 637–645.

Pichault, F. (1995). The management of politics in technico-organisational change. *Organisation Studies, 16*(3), 449–476.

Pishdad, A., & Haider, A. (2013). Institutionalisation of enterprise systems through organisational isomorphism. In *ACIS 2013: Information systems: Transforming the future: Proceedings of the 24th Australasian conference on information systems* (pp. 1–10). RMIT University.

Radeke, F. (2010, August 12–15). Awaiting explanation in the field of enterprise architecture management. In *The proceedings of Americas conference on information systems (AMCIS)*. Association of Information Systems (AIS) Press.

Rahmanian, M., Nassiri, R., Mohsenzadeh, M., & Ravanmehr, R. (2022). Test case generation for enterprise business services based on enterprise architecture design. *The Journal of Supercomputing*, 1–31.

Ross, J., Weill, P., & Robertson, D. (2006). *Enterprise architecture as strategy: Creating a foundation for business execution*. Harvard Business Press.

Saint-Louis, P., & Lapalme, J. (2018). An exploration of the many ways to approach the discipline of enterprise architecture. *International Journal of Engineering Business Management, 10*, 1847979018807383.

Sari, N. A., Hidayanto, A. N., Sandhyaduhita, P. I., Munajat, Q., & Phusavat, K. (2021). Impact of enterprise architecture management on business benefits through information technology benefits in companies in Indonesia. *International Journal of Business Information Systems, 36*(1), 71–97.

Seppänen, V., Penttinen, K., & Pulkkinen, M. (2018). Key issues in enterprise architecture adoption in the public sector. *Electronic Journal of E-Government, 16*(1), 46–58.

Shaanika, I., & Iyamu, T. (2015). Deployment of enterprise architecture in the Namibian government: The use of activity theory to examine the influencing factors. *The Electronic Journal of Information Systems in Developing Countries, 71*(1), 1–21.

Shaanika, I., & Iyamu, T. (2018). Developing the enterprise architecture for the Namibian government. *The Electronic Journal of Information Systems in Developing Countries, 84*(3), e12028.

Shanks, G., Gloet, M., Someh, I. A., Frampton, K., & Tamm, T. (2018). Achieving benefits with enterprise architecture. *The Journal of Strategic Information Systems, 27*(2), 139–156.

Spijkman, T., Molenaar, S., Dalpiaz, F., & Brinkkemper, S. (2021). Alignment and granularity of requirements and architecture in agile development: A functional perspective. *Information and Software Technology, 133*, 106535.

Srinivas, S., Gill, A. Q., & Roach, T. (2021). Can business architecture modeling be adaptive? *IT Professional, 23*(2), 81–88.

Sukur, A., & Lind, M. L. (2022). Enterprise architecture to achieve information technology flexibility and enterprise agility. *International Journal of Information Systems and Social Change (IJISSC), 13*(2), 1–20.

Tamm, T., Seddon, P. B., & Shanks, G. (2022). How enterprise architecture leads to organisational benefits. *International Journal of Information Management, 67*, 102554.

Tamm, T., Seddon, P. B., Shanks, G., & Reynolds, P. (2011a). Delivering business value through enterprise architecture. *Journal of Enterprise Architecture, 7*(2), 17–30.

Tamm, T., Seddon, P. B., Shanks, G., & Reynolds, P. (2011b). How does enterprise architecture add value to organisations? *Communications of the Association for Information Systems, 28*(1), 141–168.

Vallerand, J., Lapalme, J., & Moïse, A. (2017). Analysing enterprise architecture maturity models: A learning perspective. *Enterprise Information Systems, 11*(6), 859–883.

Van den Berg, M., Slot, R., van Steenbergen, M., Faasse, P., & van Vliet, H. (2019). How enterprise architecture improves the quality of IT investment decisions. *Journal of Systems and Software, 152*, 134–150.

Van Zijl, C., & Van Belle, J. P. (2014). Organisational impact of enterprise architecture and business process capability in South African organisations. *International Journal of Trade, Economics and Finance, 5*(5), 405–413.

Weiss, S. (2017). Institutionalisation of ACET: Needs and foundations. *Architectural Coordination of Enterprise Transformation*, 123–136.

Weiss, S., Aier, S., & Winter, R. (2013, December 15–18). Institutionalization and the effectiveness of enterprise architecture management. Association for information systems. In *Thirty fourth international conference on information systems*. Association of Information Systems (AIS) Press.

Williamson, B. (2018). The hidden architecture of higher education: Building a big data infrastructure for the 'smarter university'. *International Journal of Educational Technology in Higher Education, 15*(1), 1–26.

Zachman, J. A. (1987). A framework for information systems. *IBM Systems Journal, 26*(3), 276–283.

Zarvić, N., & Wieringa, R. (2014). An integrated enterprise architecture framework for business-IT alignment. *Designing Enterprise Architecture Frameworks: Integrating Business Processes with IT Infrastructure, 63*(9), 1–9.

Chapter 13

The Impact of Training and Skillsets on Enterprise Architecture Implementation

13.1 Introduction

Often, organisations are confronted with challenges that manifest from business processes and information technology (IT) solutions (software, hardware, database, and networks). Also, some of the challenges are caused by change due to the driving factors of globalisation, technology erosion, and rapid growth of organisational structure (Cekerekil et al., 2013). In an attempt to address the challenges, some organisations employ approaches such as enterprise architecture (EA) to guide and manage their business and IT challenges. Over the years, EA has increasingly become an important discipline for the management and governance of both business and IT processes and activities (Kotusev et al., 2023; Osterlind et al., 2013). Many organisations consider the EA approach to be of importance to their processes and activities. This is because the approach is often used to translate business vision and strategy into business and technical requirements (Kaisler et al., 2005). However, the use of EA depends on how it is understood, defined, and scoped (Schekkerman, 2009).

Individuals, including organisations, view and define the concept of EA differently. The definition is informed and guided by their understanding and objectives. The definition is critical because it shapes how EA is developed and implemented.

 DOI: 10.1201/9781003390879-13

Also, the number of enterprise architects is increasing, but there is no commonly accepted baseline of knowledge or standards to ensure consistent service performed by the architects (Walrad et al., 2013). Ahlemann et al. (2021) emphasise that the success or failure of EA depends on the enterprise skills and capabilities of enterprise architects. However, EA is often entwined with the IT field. Ylinen and Pekkola (2020) argue that the skills of enterprise architects are not sufficiently differentiated from other IT professionals in many organisations. According to Leidig and Salmela (2022), there are increasing calls from the industry that information systems (IS) graduates need more technical skills such as those of EA. Robl and Bork (2022) reveal that curricula of IT-related courses are currently designed to have only one or a few units on EA.

EA is applied for operational and strategic purposes to holistically address the gap between the business and IT units in an organisation (Hiekkanen et al., 2013). Despite their essentiality, uniqueness, and specialised nature, EA skills are scarce to be found (Walrad et al., 2014) The architect is an intermediator between IT and business units (van der Torre & Van Zee, 2017). The skills assist in organising the technical and non-technical functions of EA (Gong & Janssen, 2022). Vazirigohar and Khaleghi Rad (2022) explain that a major and critical skill of an architect is to identify existing and emerging IT solutions that are likely to enable and support the goals and objectives of the business and enhance the competitiveness of the organisation. Iyamu (2022) provides skill and competence guidelines specific for training and developing capacity and skillsets for architects. Yet, the challenges of scarcity of EA specialists persist. According to Robl and Bork (2022), EA is scantly part of a few courses such as IT management and IT strategy, and only at postgraduate levels.

Many organisations have not been able to develop or implement EA primarily because they do not have skilled personnel. What is even more challenging is the availability of training facilities. Very few institutions of higher learning around the world offer EA as a course. Primarily, skills and capacity are developed through training offered by professional bodies such as The Open Group Architecture Framework (TOGAF), and Gartner Inc. As a result, many organisations and researchers are unimpressed by how and where such skills can be developed (Walrad et al., 2014; Gøtze, 2013; Wagter et al., 2012). This has made some organisations consider developing their skills internally. Erosa and Arroyo (2009) argued that some technical skills could be best developed through experience, but others are best acquired during professional studies.

EA functions require more than a basic understanding of the approach. It is therefore vital to have highly skilled personnel. Empirically, Iyamu (2009) reveals that there is a lack of sufficient EA-related skills, which results in insufficient performance in the development and implementation of EA. Yang and Qixial (2012) therefore suggest that institutions of higher learning, as the cradles of learning, theorising, and research could be used as platforms for developing EA skills. That does not seem to be happening speedily enough to respond to business needs. Walrad et al. (2013) expand the argument by explaining that skill is about having the know-how and ability to perform tasks and to produce appropriate or desired results. Thus, EA skills are not only about extensive comprehension of technical knowledge or third-party collaboration (Besker et al., 2015). Ylinen and Pekkola (2020) argue that the roles and tasks of enterprise architects vary from one organisation to another.

Owing to the limited skills, many organisations are continually challenged with the development and implementation of EA. Also, some organisations find it difficult to articulate the requirement and qualities that an enterprise architect should possess. Furthermore, some organisations that are knowledgeable about the requirements and qualities of enterprise architects struggle to develop the capacity because lack of knowledge is a hindrance. EA skillsets extend beyond expertise in technical knowledge (Besker et al., 2015). It is argued that EA benefits depend on the quality of EA service provision (Tamm et al., 2022), which contributes to the criticality of the skills. Gong and Janssen (2022) revealed the root factor and suggest enhancing EA knowledge of high-level managers and ensuring that the communication and leadership skills of enterprise architects are the starting point to avoid EA failure.

An architect requires an in-depth knowledge and understanding of business or IT artefacts or both. van der Torre and Van Zee (2017) suggest that an architect should be skilled to be able to explain complex technical issues in a way that non-technical people understand and can translate business requirements into IT solutions. Currently, the development of architects' skills and capabilities is a concern and challenge in many organisations (Mirsalari & Ranjbarfard, 2020). Vazirigohar and Khaleghi Rad (2022) explain that skills are the ability and capacity to perform processes using knowledge to achieve results.

Thus, the focus of this chapter is on the factors that influence EA skills development. This helps to gain an insight into the factors that hinder the development of the capacity for the purposes of organisations. The chapter is organised into five main sections. The first section is the introduction. The two chapters that follow present a review of literature, which focuses on EA and training, respectively. The next section covers the factors that can enable the development of EA skills and capacity. Finally, a conclusion is drawn.

13.2 Enterprise Architecture

The concept of EA is covered extensively and comprehensively in Chapters 3–12 of this book. Despite this comprehensive coverage, it is necessary to revisit the concept with a particular focus on skills. EA is defined as "the organising logic for business process and IT infrastructure, reflecting the integration and standardisation requirements of the company's operating model" (Ross et al., 2006, p. 9). The purpose of an EA is to guide business processes and enable IT toward achieving the organisation's goals and objectives (Cekerekil et al., 2013).

In many organisations, the business strategy and IT strategy are often misaligned (Rahmanian et al., 2023). Gøtze (2013) argues that the lack of alignment results in faulty IT planning. Consequently, some organisations identify the need to employ EA as a bridging tool between business strategy and IT strategy (Jin et al., 2010). According to Iacob et al. (2012), closing the gap between business and IT maximises alignment, thus reducing duplications and inconsistencies among business processes and IT solutions. Niemi and Pekkola (2020) emphasise that EA is strategic for the planning of business and IT activities to enhance the integration of processes. However, EA is often confronted with derailing factors due to organisational and technical complexities (Ajer et al., 2021).

Relevance and context are associated with rapid changes in organisations. Change in business environments causes businesses to change their processes, services, and products for competitiveness (Abouzahra & Ghasemaghaei, 2022; Williams et al., 2022). Also, changes influence IT solutions deployed in an organisation, as new solutions are introduced, developed, or reused to refocus on new competitiveness. Business and IT continue to change, and EA is used as a supporting tool (Tallon et al., 2019). Thus, Iyamu (2022) asserts that EA is an agent of change in the quest for competitiveness. It formalises the organisation and its IT solutions to manage potential risks related to changes (Lakhrouit & Baïna, 2013). Qadri et al. (2020) argue that EA is used as a tool for the integration of IT solutions within an environment.

EA promotes the belief that an enterprise—as a complex system—can be designed and managed in an orderly manner to improve performance (Rosasco & Dehlinger, 2001). Such performances shape an organisation's competitiveness and sustainability. Additionally, Alonso et al. (2010) point out that EA helps in communicating key elements that explain the operations and strategic intents of an organisation. Therefore, the implementation of EA helps organisations to innovate and engineer change through stability and flexibility (Rouhani et al., 2013). However, the development and implementation of EA continue to be challenging in many organisations. Iyamu (2010) suggests that EA experiences technical and non-technical challenges. Kaisler et al. (2005) identified that the challenges are rarely technical but they arise from factors such as politics and other organisational issues. However, the mechanisms underpinning EA benefit realisation are not fully understood and have only relatively recently begun to receive research attention, according to Tamm et al. (2022).

The development and deployment of EA are conducted through its domains, which are enterprise business architecture (EBA), enterprise information architecture (EIA), enterprise application architecture (EAA), and enterprise technical architecture (ETA), and are guided by the organisation's goals and objectives (Iyamu, 2022; Alonso et al., 2010). The development and implementation through the enterprise domain approach can be horizontal (across the organisation) or vertical (within a unit or division). According to Iyamu (2013), the development and implementation of EA are based on how the organisation defines and understands the concept; hence, skillset is crucial. Also, the definition and understanding can be influenced by the EA framework that is adopted in an organisation. Antunes et al. (2011) argued that highly skilled personnel are required due to the different approaches applied by EA, including their tailoring and adaptation to specific domains.

EA provides an overview of how IT solutions are employed to enable and support the different business logic, processes, and operating model selected to facilitate organisational activities (Erosa & Arroyo, 2009). Across the organisation, a common understanding is required between IT and business operating models. Enterprise architects provide such an understanding by translating and transforming knowledge across an organisation's boundary. This includes the boundaries between an organisation and vendors, business units, and IT units (Gøtze, 2013). Hence, architects have crucial roles in finding the relevant varieties for the different contexts, often in the form of principles, standards, patterns, and policies. Wagter et al. (2012) describe EA architects as professionals with competencies that are responsible for the creation of organisational strategies.

13.3 Enterprise Architecture Skills and Training

EA is a specialised discipline and requires highly skilled and competent personnel to perform its tasks. The competencies are required to develop synergy between the stakeholders in the development and implementation of EA in an organisation (Bradley et al., 2012). As a result, not everyone is qualified to undertake the responsibility to perform the task of an architect. Vatankhah Barenji et al. (2015) state that architect competency refers to knowledge and capability that describes the skills and abilities for EA development, implementation, and practice. Syynimaa (2017) suggests that architects' proficiency levels should be assessed using the maturity model. This is to find a balance and get to a detailed level of specialisation. Usually, one of the challenges is to balance the different skills and competence levels of each EA architect (Al-Kharusi et al., 2021).

The roles of architects are critical in the deployment (development and implementation) of EA in organisations. According to van der Torre and Van Zee (2017), an enterprise architect should be equipped with in-depth skills, from technical to non-technical artefacts, comprehensively covering the knowledge of hardware, software, applications, systems engineering, business, and communication. Due to its broad nature, the typical skills of an architect should be categorised to enhance the quality of the competency assessment that is conducted (Syynimaa, 2017). In some organisations, the skillsets are not mapped with the tasks of the enterprise architects, which vary from very technical to very business-related tasks and activities (Ylinen & Pekkola, 2020). This brings about one of the challenges of many architects confining themselves to technical spaces, leaving a gap in non-technical aspects (Musukutwa, 2022).

Often, enterprise architects attend business meetings geared towards providing IT solutions to the organisation (van der Torre & Van Zee, 2017). Also, measurement, evaluation, and management capabilities and skills are essential for the development, implementation, and practice of EA (Mirsalari & Ranjbarfard, 2020). However, according to Ylinen and Pekkola (2020), EA skills and competencies are increasingly difficult to define by many organisations. Consequently, skills capability is prohibitive because inadequate decisions can induce significant adverse effects in the implementation of EA (Ahlemann et al., 2021). Musukutwa (2022) recommends that the future enterprise architect must have enterprise-wide skills, from technical to non-technical competence levels. Such clarion suggestions and the growing importance of IT solutions for organisations' purposes challenge higher institutions to offer formal education that can equip students with analysis and management skills and capabilities (Robl & Bork, 2022).

Based on requirements, enterprise architects develop business models and IT (van der Torre & Van Zee, 2017). Critically, many architects do not necessarily have the appropriate skills to develop or implement EA, including the reuse of its models or framework (Niemi & Pekkola, 2017). This is attributable to the lack of a model or framework for the classification and assessment of EA skills in many organisations. According to Bui (2017), a capability framework should be used to define the structures, processes, roles, responsibilities, and skills for the development, implementation, and practice of EA. This is a challenge in many organisations. The enterprise architects' skills and capabilities are critical to the successful delivery of EA (Ylinen & Pekkola, 2020). Architects are technical leaders and therefore should be highly skilled when it comes to communication and other business and technology-related issues (Gong & Janssen, 2022), which are fundamental to bridging the gap between business and IT units.

From an organisational standpoint, Wagter et al. (2012) describe EA architects as professionals with competencies that are responsible for the creation of organisational strategies. According to Wagter et al. (2012), competencies represent a dynamic combination of knowledge, expertise, attitudes, and responsibilities. An enterprise architect develops an IT strategy and enables decisions for designing and developing and deploying IT to support the business process (Armour et al., 2012). Steghuis and Proper (2008) differentiated between EA architects and domain architects, stating that EA architects cover the breadth of business and IT, while domain architects focus on the specific aspect of the enterprise, such as business, information, applications, and the technical aspects. Gøtze (2013) categorised enterprise architects into core, implicit, and applied. The artefacts form an enterprise architecture team that is capable of conducting gap and business requirement analysis at various levels of the enterprise (Wagter et al., 2012).

Enterprise architects therefore need to know how the organisation's businesses operate and how decisions are made for modelling purposes (Walrad et al., 2014). Modelling is essential to describing and understanding EA (Kaisler et al., 2005).

Lakhrouit and Baïna (2013) elaborated that knowing how an enterprise works is important for architects to be able to identify the strengths and weaknesses of the organisation and lead to recognition of gaps.

13.4 Enterprise Architecture Skills

EA skilled personnel hold the positions of architects, named or referred to as enterprise architect or domain architect, such as business architect or information architect. The roles and responsibilities of architects differ but are not entirely independent of each other. Also, organisations sometimes differ in the job descriptions or the tasks assigned to the architects. Van der Torre and Van Zee (2017) suggest that many responsibilities and skills are increasingly associated with an enterprise architect. This allows and enables architects to cover a wide area and utilise different resources effectively within an organisation. Many organisations expect architects to carry out various functions in the development and implementation of EA, primarily because they are thought to be highly specialised. Owing to the depth of knowledge and domain specialisation, architects bring a high level of focus and concentration into the development and implementation of EA in an organisation.

As depicted in Figure 13.1, enterprise architects focus on the entire organisational needs while domain architects concentrate on the areas of their specialisation. The architects are required to guide IT solutions activities such as selection, implementation, and post-implementation, and to ensure that the IT solutions are aligned with the business goals and objectives of the organisation. Similar to the role of technical architects, business architects are responsible for the strategic modelling of processes and activities. In many organisations, the responsibility of the business architects includes defining the structure of process flow in the organisation and building performance measurement models. Mulder (2023) argues that the primary role of EA is to connect IT with the business unit and to leverage goals and objectives with solutions.

The architectural process is holistic, meaning that it is required across the entire units of an organisation that deploys EA. This could be attributed to the wide scope, which ranges from software development and implementation, business and systems analysis, business applications, and project management to networking and operating systems. The need often focuses on unique and critical areas of both the business and IT units of an organisation. In some organisations, areas of critical need are creating maturity models and risk analysis. Due to the well-documented significance of EA to organisations, it is critical to have knowledgeable personnel in the field, thus, creating a knowledge hub. However, the development of EA capabilities and skills is currently a major concern for many organisations (Mirsalari & Ranjbarfard, 2020). Thus, more institutions of higher learning should focus on the development of enterprise and domain architects (Robl & Bork, 2022).

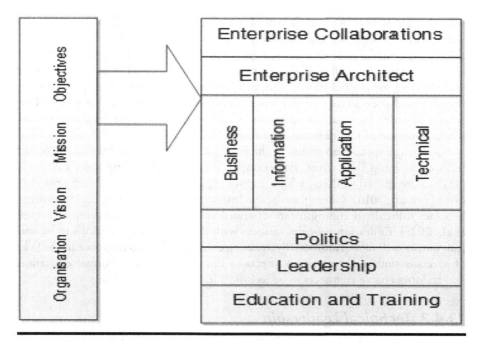

Figure 13.1 EA Skill Development.

Increasingly, many organisations are confronted with stiffer competition, making a more justifiable case for approaches such as EA, which enhances competitiveness. However, it requires developing and leveraging EA skills appropriately. EA skills provide an organisation with deeper comprehension and cohesion of how the business strategy should be supported and enabled using IT solutions. Such understanding is fundamental in defining the relationship between business and IT units, and how their alignment can enhance business sustainability and competitiveness (Iyamu, 2022). Despite the relevance and fathoming of EA for many years, the challenges of skillset persist. As subjectively dissected from experience and literature, some of which reflect in the preceding sections, the most prevalent and fundamental factors hindering EA skills and capacity development in organisations are: (i) lack of formal education and training; (ii) lack of technical leadership; and (iii) lack of political will (Kaisler et al., 2005). The factors, as shown in Figure 13.1, are discussed in the rest of this section. The discussion should be read with the figure to gain a better understanding.

13.4.1 Formal Education and Training

The shortage of skills is often attributed to a lack of formal education or training, or both. Skills cannot be developed based on experience alone. Some professional bodies, such as TOGAF and Gartner Inc., offer training and should increase the momentum. Also, more institutions of higher learning should offer courses on EA. Complementary to the theorised nature of the course and practical, hands-on exercises offered by professional bodies, it will grow the development of EA skills and capacity for organisations. This will help reduce or eradicate, among other things, the challenges that are deepening as organisations introduce new sets of IT solutions, which increases the spectrum of skills required for the development and implementation of EA for business purposes (Ahlemann et al., 2021).

Due to the specialised nature of the field, architects need formal education and training to equip themselves. For example, creating and reading most EA products require special skillsets, which are not typically common in many organisations (Trionfi, 2016). Consequently, the information contained in EA documents becomes difficult to communicate or translate within an organisation (Kotusev et al., 2023). Education provides trainees with the knowledge and skills to be and function as architects. Additionally, training enhances their competence in the field of specialisation as enterprise architects or domain architects. Formal education and training enable architects to be technical leaders in organisations.

13.4.2 Technical Leadership

Based on the high skill levels and specialisation of enterprise and domain architects, they are supposedly relied upon in organisations. As such, architects are expected to provide leadership to guide, motivate, and mobilise colleagues and other stakeholders in an organisation. According to Mirsalari and Ranjbarfard (2020), capabilities and skills are seen as essential technical and leadership responsibilities for developing and implementing EA in organisations. Also, through their leadership roles, the architects are expected to create the vision and architecture culture in the organisation. Through leadership, it would be easier and more flexible to govern and manage people and complexity, and to document processes and activities within the organisation.

One of the challenges is that, in many organisations, architects are sometimes assigned new responsibilities (Ylinen & Pekkola, 2020) such as leadership, often considered a soft skill from a people management perspective. According to Mulder (2023), soft skills are getting more important in the role of architects in the development and implementation of EA in organisations. It is sometimes difficult to disassociate leadership from political interplay. Therefore, some leadership components can be attributed to political will. This is due to the role of a leader to drive and lead in the network where the actor finds themselves. An IT specialist cannot be an architect if they cannot lead the people towards achieving the organisation's objectives. Thus, van der Torre and Van Zee (2017) suggest that the role and responsibility of architects should be split into technical and management, as engineer and facilitator, respectively. In this context, an engineer develops business and IT models and mediates between the business and IT units.

13.4.3 Political Will

Empirically, from the study, another reason why the EA approach is not considered or employed in some organisations is due to a lack of political will to do so. EA depends for success on factors, such as efficiency and effectiveness, that often manifest from political will. These factors are driven by motivation, mobilisation, and resources, which manifest from politics and political will. According to Iyamu (2019), politics are sometimes employed to enrich the power to influence processes and activities during the development and implementation of EA, which sometimes makes the concept complex. Where more than one person is involved, politics is involved consciously or unconsciously, or what Giddens refers to as practical unconsciousness. Giddens (1984, p. 375) defines practical unconsciousness as "What actors know (belief) about social conditions, including especially the conditions of their action but cannot express discursively without repression but which, however, protects practical consciousness as is the case with the unconscious".

The deployment and exercise of EA processes and activities can be political. This is primarily because of the roles and responsibilities associated with its development and implementation. To some extent, architects are powerful and take away some functions from certain individuals and groups in the organisation. Institutions of higher learning need to begin to introduce EA as a course at both undergraduate and postgraduate levels. As revealed in this study, the curriculum of the course should encompass components such as technical leadership and political know-how.

13.5 Summary

The growing interest in enterprise architecture (EA) does not complement the limited skills and capacity. This is the motivation for this chapter. The chapter emphasises the implications of EA skills and capacity, and it reveals three fundamental influencing factors. Thus, it helps organisations to better understand the root of the challenges. Also, the chapter is intended to guide business and information technology (IT) managers to learn some critical factors, thoughts, and beliefs about the gaps created by limited skills in the development and implementation of EA in many organisations. It thereby contributes to the knowledge of the stakeholders on the quality required of and by architects in developing and implementing EA in an organisation.

Because EA is considered to be a field that requires highly skilled and competent personnel, it is essential to focus on developing capacity in the organisations. Commonly, EA is intended to bridge the gap between the business and IT units, as well as drive the strategies of an organisation from both business and IT standpoints. The roles of EA require the personnel to be highly skilled through formal education, training, and experience. As revealed in the study, EA skills are not easily accessible or available. The skill is beyond technical know-how, which includes non-technical factors such as leadership and politics. As such, the developers of the EA curriculum need to take non-technical factors (soft skills) into account.

References

Abouzahra, M., & Ghasemaghaei, M. (2022). Effective use of information technologies by seniors: The case of wearable device use. *European Journal of Information Systems, 31*(2), 241–255.

Ahlemann, F., Legner, C., & Lux, J. (2021). A resource-based perspective of value generation through enterprise architecture management. *Information & Management, 58*(1), 103266.

Ajer, A. K., Hustad, E., Vassilakopoulou, P., & Olsen, D. H. (2021). Strengthening the use of enterprise architecture: An institutional work perspective. In *ECIS*. Association for Information Systems (AIS) Press.

Al-Kharusi, H., Miskon, S., & Bahari, M. (2021). Enterprise architects and stakeholders alignment framework in enterprise architecture development. *Information Systems and e-Business Management, 19*, 137–181.

Alonso, I., Verdún, J., & Caro, E. (2010). The IT implicated within the enterprise architecture model. *Analysis of Architecture Models and Focus IT Architecture Domain*, 1–5.

Antunes, G., Barateiro, J., Becker, C., Borbinha, J., & Vieira, R. (2011). Modeling contextual concerns in enterprise architecture. In *The proceedings of the 15th IEEE international enterprise distributed object computing conference workshops* (pp. 3–10). IEEE.

Armour, F., Kaisler, S., & Huizinga, E. (2012). Business and enterprise architecture: Processes, approaches and challenges. In *The proceedings of the 45th Hawaii international conference on system sciences (HICSS)* (p. 4229). IEEE.

Besker, T., Olsson, R., & Pessi, K. (2015, September 21–21). The enterprise architect profession: An empirical study. In *The proceedings of the 9th European conference on IS management and evaluation (ECIME)* (Vol. 2015, p. 29). Academic Conferences and Publishing International Limited.

Bradley, R. V., Pratt, R. M., Byrd, T. A., Outlay, C. N., & Wynn, Jr D. E. (2012). Enterprise architecture, IT effectiveness and the mediating role of IT alignment in US hospitals. *Information Systems Journal, 22*(2), 97–127.

Bui, Q. (2017). Evaluating enterprise architecture frameworks using essential elements. *Communications of the Association for Information Systems, 41*(1), 129–140.

Cekerekil, S., Mticahit, G., & Emin, B. (2013). *An agile approach for converting enterprise Architectures*. IEEE.

Erosa, V., & Arroyo, P. (2009). Technology management competences supporting the business strategy. In *PICMET 2009 proceedings* (pp. 2190–2199). PICMET.

Giddens, A. (1984). *The constitution of society: Outline of the theory of structuration*. Polity Press.

Gong, Y., & Janssen, M. (2022). Why organizations fail in implementing enterprise architecture initiatives? *Information Systems Frontiers*, 1–19.

Gøtze, J. (2013). The changing role of the enterprise architect. In *The proceedings of the 17th IEEE international enterprise distributed object computing conference workshops* (pp. 319–326). IEEE.

Hiekkanen, K., Mykkänen, J., & Korhonen, J. J. (2013, July 15–18). Architects' perceptions on EA use: An empirical study. In *The proceedings of the 15th IEEE conference on business informatics (CBI)*. IEEE.

Iacob, M.-E., Jonkers, H., & Quartel, D. (2012). Capturing business strategy and value in enterprise architecture to support portfolio valuation. In *The proceedings of the 16th international enterprise distributed object computing conference* (pp. 11–19). IEEE.

Iyamu, T. (2009, July 20–23). The factors affecting institutionalisation of enterprise architecture in the organisation. In *The proceedings of the international conference on commerce and enterprise computing* (pp. 221–225). IEEE.

Iyamu, T. (2010). Theoretical analysis strategic implementation of enterprise architecture. *International Journal of Actor-Network Theory and Technological Innovation, 2*(3), 17–32.

Iyamu, T. (2013). *Enterprise architecture: From concept to Practise*. Heidelberg Press.

Iyamu, T. (2019). Understanding the complexities of enterprise architecture through structuration theory. *Journal of Computer Information Systems, 59*(3), 287–295.

Iyamu, T. (2022). *Enterprise architecture for strategic management of modern IT solutions*. Routledge, CRC Press.

Jin, M., Peng, W., & Kung, D. (2010). Research of information system technology architecture. In *The proceedings of the 2nd international conference on industrial and information systems* (pp. 293–296). IEEE.

Kaisler, S., Armour, F., & Valivullah, M. (2005). Enterprise architecting: Critical problems. In *The proceedings of the 38th Hawaii international conference on system sciences (HICSS)*. IEEE.

Kotusev, S., Kurnia, S., & Dilnutt, R. (2023). Enterprise architecture artefacts as boundary objects: An empirical analysis. *Information and Software Technology, 155*, 107108.

Lakhrouit, J., & Baïna, K. (2013). *State of the art of the maturity models to an evaluation of the enterprise architecture*. IEEE.

Leidig, P. M., & Salmela, H. (2022). The ACM/AIS IS2020 competency model for undergraduate programs in information systems: A joint ACM/AIS task force report. *Communications of the Association for Information Systems, 50*(1), 25.

Mirsalari, S. R., & Ranjbarfard, M. (2020). A model for evaluation of enterprise architecture quality. *Evaluation and Program Planning, 83*, 101853.

Mulder, J. (2023). The changing role of the enterprise architect. In *Modern enterprise architecture: Using devsecops and cloud-native in large enterprises* (pp. 173–194). Apress.

Musukutwa, S. C. (2022). The future of enterprise architecture. In *SAP enterprise architecture: A blueprint for executing digital transformation* (pp. 187–202). Apress.

Niemi, E., & Pekkola, S. (2017). Using enterprise architecture artefacts in an organisation. *Enterprise Information Systems, 11*(3), 313–338.

Niemi, E., & Pekkola, S. (2020). The benefits of enterprise architecture in organizational transformation. *Business & Information Systems Engineering, 62*(6), 585–597.

Osterlind, M., Johnson, P., Karnati, K., Lagerstro, R., & Välja, M. (2013). Enterprise architecture evaluation using utility theory. In *The proceedings of the 17th IEEE international enterprise distributed object computing conference workshops* (pp. 347–351). IEEE.

Qadri, Y. A., Nauman, A., Zikria, Y. B., Vasilakos, A. V., & Kim, S. W. (2020). The future of healthcare internet of things: A survey of emerging technologies. *IEEE Communications Surveys & Tutorials, 22*(2), 1121–1167.

Rahmanian, M., Nassiri, R., Mohsenzadeh, M., & Ravanmehr, R. (2023). Test case generation for enterprise business services based on enterprise architecture design. *The Journal of Supercomputing, 79*(2), 1877–1907.

Robl, M., & Bork, D. (2022). Enterprise architecture management education in Academia: An international comparative analysis. *Complex Systems Informatics and Modeling Quarterly, 31*, 29–50.

Rosasco, N., & Dehlinger, J. (2001). Business architecture elicitation for enterprise architecture: VMOST versus conventional strategy capture. In *The proceedings of the 9th international conference on software engineering research, management and applications* (pp. 153–157). Baltimore.

Ross, J., Weill, P., & Robertson, D. (2006). *Enterprise architecture as a strategy: Creating a foundation for business execution.* Harvard Business Press.

Rouhani, B., Mahrin, M., Nikpay, F., & Nikfard, P. (2013). A comparison enterprise architecture implementation methodologies. In *The proceedings of the international conference on informatics and creative multimedia* (pp. 1–5). IEEE.

Schekkerman, J. (2009). *How to survive in the jungle of enterprise architecture frameworks.* Trafford Publishing.

Steghuis, C., & Proper, E. (2008). Competencies and responsibilities of enterprise architects. In *Advances in enterprise engineering I* (pp. 93–107). Springer Press.

Syynimaa, N. (2017). Method and practical guidelines for overcoming enterprise architecture adoption challenges. In *Enterprise information systems: 18th international conference, ICEIS 2016, Rome, Italy, April 25–28, 2016* (pp. 488–514). Springer International Publishing.

Tallon, P. P., Queiroz, M., Coltman, T., & Sharma, R. (2019). Information technology and the search for organizational agility: A systematic review with future research possibilities. *The Journal of Strategic Information Systems, 28*(2), 218–237.

Tamm, T., Seddon, P. B., & Shanks, G. (2022). How enterprise architecture leads to organisational benefits. *International Journal of Information Management, 67*, 102554.

Trionfi, A. (2016). Guiding principles to support organization-level enterprise architectures. *Journal of Enterprise Architecture, 12*(3), 40–45.

van der Torre, L., & Van Zee, M. (2017). Rational enterprise architecture. In *Advances in artificial intelligence: From theory to practice: 30th international conference on industrial engineering and other applications of applied intelligent systems, IEA/AIE 2017, Arras, France, June 27–30, 2017, Proceedings, Part I 30* (pp. 9–18). Springer International Publishing.

Vatankhah Barenji, R., Hashemipour, M., & Guerra-Zubiaga, D. A. (2015). A framework for modelling enterprise competencies: From theory to practice in enterprise architecture. *International Journal of Computer Integrated Manufacturing, 28*(8), 791–810.

Vazirigohar, H., & Khaleghi Rad, M. (2022). Technical benefits of Enterprise architecture over organizational performance by mediated of business process. *Journal of Strategic Management Studies, 13*(49), 97–121.

Wagter, R., Proper, H., & Witte, D. (2012). Enterprise architecture: A strategic specialisma. In *The proceedings of the 14th international conference on commerce and enterprise computing* (pp. 1–8). IEEE.

Walrad, C. C., Lane, M., Jeffrey, W., & Hirst, D. V. (2013). Architecting a profession. *IT Professional, 16*(1), 42–49.

Walrad, C. C., Lane, M., Wallk, J., & Hirst, D. (2014). Architecting a profession. *IT Pro*, 42–49.

Williams, J. A., Torres, H. G., & Carte, T. (2022). A review of IS strategy literature: Current trends and future opportunities. *Journal of Computer Information Systems, 62*(1), 1–11.

Yang, Z., & Qixial, L. (2012). Innovation pattern analysis of the industry-university-research cooperation. In *The proceedings of the international symposium on information technology in medicine and education* (pp. 274–277). IEEE.

Ylinen, M., & Pekkola, S. (2020). Jack-of-all-trades torn apart: Skills and competencies of an enterprise architect. In *The proceedings of the 28th European conference on information systems (ECIS)*. Association for Information Systems.

Index

Note: Locators in *italics* represent figures and **bold** indicate tables in the text.

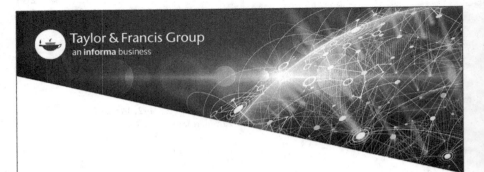

Printed in the United States
by Baker & Taylor Publisher Services